DRAMACONTEMPORARY

CZECHOSLOVAKIA

DRAMACONTEMPORARY

CZECHOSLOVAKIA

plays by

Milan Kundera
Václav Havel
Pavel Kohout
Milan Uhde
Pavel Landovský
Ivan Klíma

Edited, with an Introduction, by
Marketa Goetz-Stankiewicz

Performing Arts Journal Publications
New York

04 03 02 01 00 99 98 97 96 95   6 5 4 3 2

Distributed by The Johns Hopkins University Press
2715 North Charles Street
Baltimore, Maryland 21218-4319
The Johns Hopkins Press Ltd., London

Library of Congress Cataloging in Publication Data
DramaContemporary: Czechoslovakia
CONTENTS: *Jacques and His Master, Protest, Fire in the Basement, The Detour, A Blue Angel, Games.*
Library of Congress Catalog Card No.: 84-61622
ISBN: 0-933826-75-3 (cloth)
ISBN: 0-933826-76-1 (paper)

A catalog record for this book is available from the British Library.

Graphic Design: Gautam Dasgupta
Printed in the United States of America

Publication of this book has been made possible in part by grants received from the National Endowment for the Arts, Washington, D.C., a federal agency, and the New York State Council on the Arts.

General Editors of the DramaContemporary series:
   Bonnie Marranca and Gautam Dasgupta

for Ivan Havel

THE DRAMACONTEMPORARY SERIES

DramaContemporary is a series specializing in the publication of new foreign plays in translation, organized by country or region. The series developed in response to the increasing internationalism of our age that now links world societies more closely, not only economically, but culturally as well. The last twenty years, in particular, is characterized by cross-cultural references in writing and performance, East and West and throughout the Americas. The new drama series is designed to partake of this movement in world patterns of culture, specifically in the area of our specialty, theatre.

Each volume of DramaContemporary features a selection of recent plays that reflects current social, cultural, and artistic values in individual countries. Plays are chosen for their significance in the larger perspective of a culture, as a measure of the concerns of its artists and public. At times, these plays may find their way into the American theatrical repertoire; in other instances, this may not be possible. Nevertheless, at all times the American public can have the opportunity to learn about other cultures—the speech, gestures, rhythms and attitudes that shape a society—in the dramatic life of their plays.

The Publishers

Contents

Introduction

Marketa Goetz-Stankiewicz

I. THE ABSURD SITUATION

This anthology is the first of its kind. It presents examples of the remarkably lively Czech theatre of the 1970s. Yet such are the artistic and political ironies of Central Europe that any generalization about the contemporary Czech theatre becomes, the moment one has said it, a suspect half-truth, distorting the real situation as much as it reflects it. For the fact is that what I have called "the remarkably lively Czech theatre" does not exist in Czechoslovakia itself.

To understand this apparent paradox, one must imagine oneself as a visitor to Prague, where more than thirty theatres play nightly to full houses. The city's stage offerings are so varied and thoroughly international that one might easily (and naively) imagine oneself to be in a major capital of dramatic culture. On any given evening an extremely varied selection of theatre fare is available, including such plays as *The Captain from Köpenick* (Carl Zuckmayer's comedy on Wilhelminian Germany revived some years ago by the renowned Thalia Theatre of Hamburg), the Austrian dramatist Ödön von Horvath's *Tales from the Vienna Woods* (recently made into a West German film), Peter Shaffer's popular *Amadeus,* and many other plays of international significance.

For all this choice, however, the visitor to Prague will look in vain for performances of works by the best contemporary Czech playwrights. Though he might already have seen a Havel play in London or Stockholm, a Kohout play in Brussels or New York, a Klíma play in Vancouver, or heard one of Uhde's dramas on Swiss or Austrian radio, he will not find them in Czech or Slovak theatres. A search for such plays in the libraries or bookstores of Prague (or any other Czech city) will prove equally fruitless. Even the telephone book will reveal no trace of these writers' names. They and their work have become publicly invisible in their own country.

In fact they lead a strange double life. Though absent from libraries and theatres, the same plays are clandestinely circulated throughout Czechoslovakia and read in the form of typescripts, referred to as numbers of underground editions, the most famous of which is *edice petlice* (Padlock Edition). While officially banned in their own country, they can be found a short distance from the Czechoslovakian border—in Munich, say, or Vienna—where they are regularly produced on stage and television, reviewed in the press and discussed on the radio. Within the range of a hundred miles, they are simultaneously secret and famous, condemned and celebrated. There is perhaps no better proof of the absurdity of the Czech theatrical situation than the fact that a simple statement about its remarkable vitality should require so much explanation. Yet this is the kind of ironic stuff of which the plays themselves are made.

II. THE TRAGI-COMIC MASK

The works in this volume thus grow out of—and reflect—the paradoxical state of Czechoslovakia today. In reading them, one is immediately thrust into a situation that is both explosively comic and deeply tragic. It is comic because Czech life today is fundamentally a game—a game everyone knowingly plays yet pretends to regard as reality. As a result, the whole nation is, as it were, performing an inside-out version of "The Emperor's New Clothes." In the fable, the naked Emperor's robes are imaginary, becoming "visible" only in response to an official command. In contemporary Czechoslovakia a large number of outstanding writers and plays have been rendered "invisible" by a comparable order from on high. But as with the Emperor's nudity, everyone knows that they are there. The tragic aspect of this basically ludicrous state of affairs has a private and a public dimension. The private one is the price of pain, isolation and exile many of the writers have paid (and are still paying) in their lives as people and artists. The public tragedy is the conscious denial of reality in the nation's cultural life, along with the abandonment of any search for or expression of truth.

Given the situation in Czechoslovakia today that truth is bound to be dark, however skillfully the writers mask it in smiles and laughter. The recipient of the 1983 Nobel Peace Prize, Manès Sperber, a Jewish writer born in Poland, who lived in Paris and wrote in German (in short, a true Central European) offers an analysis of what happens to human beings when they live under a government that deprives them of their dignity. Referring to Hitler's Germany, he asks: "What fears, horrors and anxieties were dominating the conscious and unconscious life of a man during those times? What was his image of happiness? How did he conceive his ideal of personality? . . . The theme of happiness is quickly exhausted while fear, anxiety and terror remain inexhaustible themes, no matter whether one thinks of exploring the life of an individual or society." Though Sperber is talking about a system theoretically at the opposite end of the political spectrum from that of contemporary Czechoslovakia, his words apply in a deep sense to all the plays in this anthology. While there are flashes of intense love, laughter and hope in all of them, there are also fear and anxiety appearing in countless variations and shadings.

This is true of course of much modern dramatic writing, perhaps even of the literature of all ages. The dark passages and corners of life are often more interesting to dramatists than the lighter ones. Even the great creators of comedy invariably give their funniest characters dark and often fearful shadows. It is precisely this chiaroscuro of light and darkness which relates the contemporary Czech drama to the great dramatic works of the last century—those of Ibsen, Chekhov, Brecht, and, most of all, Beckett. Ibsen's *Wild Duck* is both funny and tragic (Shaw, for example, tells us how in watching a performance he both shook with laughter and shuddered with horror). Chekhov called three of his major three plays "comedies," yet their pain and pathos are inescapable. And as we laugh our way through a performance of *Waiting for Godot,* we are haunted by an uneasy sense of despair. In the same way several of the plays in this volume could be performed on stage for either comic or tragic effect, depending on the approach of the director and the perceptions of the spectator. In the final analysis, however, all of them are meant to arouse in an audience a mixture of gaiety and seriousness, a sense that laughter, even if not curing all ills, nevertheless helps to keep a sense of proportion as well as a sense of spiritual victory. This feeling is characteristically Czech. Yet another irony of these plays is that the audience most fully capable of understanding and responding to their tragi-comic equivocality is the audience not officially permitted to see or read them: the people of Czechoslovakia.

Though he has generally had a kinder history than his Czech counterpart, the Western reader can still perceive and experience this double effect—he must sharpen his sensibilities and draw on his deepest experiences. Doing so, he will find that as he enjoys the charades played in Klíma's *Games,* for example, he will simultaneously be disturbed by the anxious questions that lie beneath them: Do people recognize a symbol of freedom when they see it? Are false beliefs not more confining and injurious than handcuffs? Or when Kundera's servant Jacques makes his repeated and vain attempts to tell his master the story of his great love, these attempts, while extremely funny in themselves, will also remind us that the most important and essential stories of our own lives can never be told because reality—shot through with lies and illusion—constantly interrupts them. At the same time an opposite effect is felt when, in Uhde's *A Blue Angel,* the hapless heroine's suffering at being deprived of her meager but rightful inheritance is rendered simultaneously comic by the nature of the objects she covets, and by the catch-as-catch-can character of the plaintiff herself. In Landovský's *The Detour,* to give another example, the potentially tragic fact that the political prisoner Hevrle is unjustly imprisoned is never permitted to cast a shadow over the play's high spirits and slapstick situations. In this way the Czech plays, in fact Czech literature as a whole, are in Milan Kundera's words "a game with fire and demons . . . combining the lightest and the hardest, the most serious with the most light-hearted," an activity whose task begins "where simple truths cease and where the multi-levelled nature of the world and its questions begin."

III. POLITICAL ANGLES

We in the West frequently tend to assume that any drama from the "Eastern Bloc" (as we have come to call it since politics has won over geography as well as culture) is likely to be obviously, perhaps even heavy-handedly, political. But none of these plays is in fact what one would call a "political play." Though the writers live or used to live in a country where life is deeply affected by political factors, the tone of the plays is in no way plaintive or obviously satirical. The scenes of action, for example, are those of ordinary lives and everyday situations: a young couple's basement apartment (*Fire in the Basement*), a middle class living room (*Games*), a writer's study (*Protest*), a compartment on a train (*A Blue Angel*). The plays are political only in the widest, Greek sense of the term. They deal—mostly in a light, even off-hand way—with the basic issues that affect people living together in social groups: their individual rights and liberties; their fears of punishment; their anxieties about themselves; their attempts to understand what they are all about and make sense of what is going on in the world; their hopes to change things for the better. Engagingly and always theatrically, the plays raise questions about the nature of freedom—both freedom *from* and freedom *to*; reflect on the experience and meaning of hope with all its implications; examine how fear and anxiety affect human minds and behavior; ponder whether economic security really changes man's basic desires and aspirations; show how ready-made "strategic" arguments can appropriate a person's thinking and render him a replaceable commodity while the phrases he uses and the fossilized meaning behind them remain the constants. For all these fundamental social and individual concerns, however, the plays are never "political" in the narrow sense. There is hardly a single explicit reference to the violent political upheavals their small country of origin has undergone during the last four or five decades. Yet, in a concealed and oblique way, each of the plays shows the repercussions of these events, their profound effect on individual lives. Together, they provide a subtle and moving history-from-the-inside of the political period in which they were written.

IV. THE PLAYWRIGHTS

The playwrights included here do not by any means represent the full range of contemporary Czech dramatic writing. Many important names had to be omitted (most regrettably those of Josef Topol and Karol Sidon). The selection of writers and plays has at every stage entailed a disturbing awareness of how much good drama has had to be left out. This is the inevitable price, however, of presenting only a sample of so rich and varied a body of work.

As it happens, the writers in this collection belong more or less to the same generation. The oldest (Kohout) was born in 1928, the youngest (Havel, Landovský and Uhde) in 1936. During the 1960s, all of them were part of the cultural Renaissance of Czechoslovakia, during which an astonishing flood of first-rate writing poured forth, culminating in the famous Prague Spring of 1968 and finally cut short by the Soviet occupation in August of that year. For more than a decade and a half these playwrights and many others have been removed from the public scene by a process of "normalization," a euphemism for the suppression of nearly all writers, artists and intellectuals who did not toe the official line.

Three of the writers represented here are still living in Czechoslovakia (Havel, Klíma and Uhde), the other three either in Paris (Kundera) or in Vienna (Kohout and Landovský). Between them they are the recipients of numerous international literary prizes: in 1981 Havel was awarded the French prize Plaisir du théâtre; both Havel and Kohout received the prestigious Austrian Staatspreis for European Literature (in 1976 and 1978 respectively); Kundera was awarded the French Prix Medicis in 1973 and the Italian Premio Modello in 1976 for two of his novels and the George-Pitoeff Prize in 1982 for *Jacques and His Master*.

Works by all six writers have been translated, published and performed in many Western countries. Václav Havel's plays are especially well-known, having been staged in all major cities of Western Europe, and his three one-act plays *Interview, Private View* and *Protest* were seen at the Public Theater in New York during the 1983/84 season. Milan Kundera's prose works have been translated into more than twenty languages, and the American première of his *Jacques and His Master* premiered at Cambridge's American Repertory Theater in January 1985, in a production directed by Susan Sontag. Pavel Kohout's plays have been produced from Finland to Greece and Japan (his *Poor Murderer* was staged in New York in 1981); Ivan Klíma's plays have been produced in the United States and Canada; Milan Uhde and Pavel Landovský are well known to German and Austrian radio and television audiences.

V. THE PLAYS

The plays span most of the decade of the seventies. It is perhaps typical of the ironies of the Czech cultural situation that the most "literary" of them, Milan Kundera's *Jacques and His Master* which takes up a scintillating game with the eighteenth-century French writer Diderot's famed work *Jacques le fataliste* and plays with matters of fictional form and reality in story telling, is also the earliest. Its first version was written in 1971, when the artistic and intellectual hopes of the Prague Spring were not yet completely crushed and the whole extent of the subsequent "normalization" was not yet being fully realized. On the other hand, the most personal of the plays is the most recent: Milan Uhde's *A Blue Angel*, which probes the costs of the human psyche's surviving the pressures of one totalitarian system after another. The play could be seen as a kind of emotional inventory, recording the scars, calluses and injuries inflicted on the character of an average woman by her ride on the violent roller coaster of political change. We are shown the inevitable toll it has taken on her resilience of spirit, her common sense and her ethical values.

Rather than including the most well-known play by each author (which in the case of Havel would be *The Memorandum* and in the case of Kohout *August, August, August*) this anthology is intended to indicate some of the main qualities of modern Czech theatre in general. Three of these qualities are especially significant. First, this theatre is realistic, in the sense that it reflects the quality of individual life in Czechoslovakia with a vividness which can come only from close and knowing observation. Under a political dictatorship, for example, the most personal of places, the bed, can become the object of government scrutiny, the refuge it traditionally provides can be destroyed at any moment. In Kohout's *Fire in the Basement* a young couple's bedroom becomes the hunting ground for officially sanctioned brutality in the guise of aid in distress. Several interpreters have called the play a satirical allegory on the Soviet occupation of 1968, which intruded on a nation's newly found freedom. But the play has wider and deeper implications as well. The local realism of *Fire in the Basement*—which would be immediately recognizable to a Czech audience—can thus, beyond the borders of Czechoslovakia, emerge either as a statement on social structures in a farcical mode or as an ironic statement on the gullibility of those unexperienced in the ways of the world. In the case of Uhde's talkative train passenger dressed in blue, who insists on imparting to her fellow passenger the story of her life, the hapless woman might as well have been telling the story of a real life spent under the actual historical circumstances. On one level the story could be regarded as a documentary, realistic in every detail. On another level, however, the same story reveals a timeless pattern of human illusion and hope, joys and disappointments, efforts rewarded and denied, applicable to human life in general. Referring to his one-act plays, Václav Havel provides an explanation of this in-depth realism which permeates the Czech plays: having explored various dramatic methods in his earlier plays, he came to the realization that he, as he put it, "had to lean on what I knew, on my concrete living background, and that, only by means of this authenticity, I could—perhaps—provide a more general testimony of our times."

Second, the Czech theatre is never without humor. Whether it is the breezy good nature of slapstick, the subtle mood of multiple irony, or the grim smile of what we have come to call black humor—some kind or shade of comedy is always present. In Landovský's *Detour*, for example, a military truck gets stuck in a ditch with ludicrous consequences because its occupants have taken a shortcut through the woods on their way to what they hope to be a sexual rendezvous arranged to relieve the boredom of official business. In Kundera's *Jacques and His Master* an eminent classical character vents his anger to the audience that the modern playwright who rewrote Diderot's venerable eighteenth-century text has deprived him of his habitual transportation: "Tell me, where are our horses? . . . A Frenchman traveling through France on foot? Do you know who it is who dared to rewrite our story? . . . You know what I would do with all people who dare rewrite what is written? Burn them at the stake over a slow fire!" In Klíma's *Games*, a group of guests, knowing a murderer is in their midst, find an innocent scapegoat who will die (or will he?—the play is open-ended) for the sake of solidarity with the world's downtrodden and unfree. The audience, who has been roused to laughter in various ways throughout the action, is not permitted to wallow in gloomy, righteous sympathy with the victim: "He acts brilliantly!" comments a philosophic character in the play, raising his eyes from his book. "Finally he has found the part that's right for him." Though the remark may elicit one last laugh from the spectator, any such amusement is likely to be accompanied by an uneasy feeling that one may be laughing at the wrong joke.

Third, playful and funny as the texts may be, they insistently weigh questions of ethics and truthfulness, explore problems of illusion and reality in life and theatre, and deal with moral values in many dimensions. Each play, whatever its particular subject or style, represents an impassioned search for truth in its own terms. The most striking example is Havel's *Protest*. In a brilliant display of specious circular logic, a "normalized" writer, asked by a courageous dissident "colleague" to join in signing a letter of protest, responds with an ingenious, indeed irresistible, string of reasons why he would harm the cause of the dissidents if he did sign it. His arguments tread the tightrope between true and false logic with such agility that the ethical values of the audience themselves are put to a real test. This is Václav Havel at his best. However, the other plays also raise moral and philosophical questions of a wide range, from the possibly dangerous implications of idealism (Klíma), to the need for fictionalizing our lives (Kundera).

In its realism of character and situation, its varied humor and irony, its intellectual honesty and subtlety, the contemporary Czech theatre is firmly rooted in the finest traditions of Western drama. If this sounds too neat a statement, perhaps it is worth recalling that Prague's most famous twentieth-century writer, Franz Kafka, whose shadow moves through all these plays, has been defined at once as existential philosopher, absurd comedian and religious mystic. Yet in today's Czechoslovakia he can be seen as essentially a Realist.

VI. PROBLEMS OF TRANSLATION AND EXILE

It is a strange fate for a good dramatist to be born to a language spoken in only one small nation. Whom is he to address? His few countrymen? But what if his countrymen can never see his plays and are only allowed to read them clandestinely, if at all? To whom can he speak? And what, if for more than fifteen years he has hardly had the opportunity to venture outside the borders of his country, as is the case with Havel, Klíma and Uhde? And what about the writer who lives abroad in involuntary exile, as Kundera, Kohout and Landovský? As he writes, whom does the playwright imagine sitting in the audience? The citizens of Paris? The theatre-goers of Vienna? The vital interaction between playwright and audience, inextricably tied to the language the playwright uses, becomes frustrated and complicated beyond words. It has become a truism that Brecht's development as a dramatist was inhibited by fourteen years of exile from Germany.

The six Czech writers in this volume too are exiled: three beyond the borders of their country, the other three within their own country. All have been cut off from their natural audience. At the same time, they have been deprived of the chance to follow their work through to its completion in stage performance before a Czech-speaking audience. Kohout, for example, has seen his plays in numerous languages—English, German, Swedish, Greek, among others—but he has never seen *Fire in the Basement* in the original Czech. The same is true of Kundera (though he, as the latest best seller lists on the American and French markets show, is primarily a novelist), who has seen *Jac- and His Master* only in French, Italian, and English (to date). There are even more absurd examples of this frustrating dilemma: Havel, Klima and Uhde have never seen on stage the plays with which they are represented in this volume—nor indeed any of the plays they have written since 1968. (A notable exception is Havel's adaptation of John Gay's *The Beggar's Opera*, which was staged in 1975 in one single memorable performance by amateur actors in a village near Prague. The performance was a great event for the suppressed writers and artists of the country but it had disastrous consequences for those involved in the production.)

In such circumstances, the playwright becomes more than ever dependent not only on directors, actors and designers—as all dramatists are—but especially upon translators. For these playwrights, yet another collaborator is required before the playwright can speak to his audience.

The three writers in this selection who are still in Czechoslovakia must send their works abroad, launching them like bottles on the sea, never quite knowing which shores they will reach, how they will be received or understood. Despite their isolation, however, they all go on writing. Václav Havel, for example, writes as if his plays could be performed even in Czechoslovakia. As he himself puts it, he addresses "concrete countrymen in their concrete world," because "drama's success in transcending the limits of its age and country depends entirely on how far it succeeds in finding a way to its own place and time . . . If Shakespeare is played all over the world in the twentieth century it is not because in the seventeenth century he wrote plays for the twentieth century and for the whole world but because he wrote plays for seventeenth century England as best he could."

So much for the problems and loyalties of the author, who, though faced with great difficulties and complexities, still can find some kind of purpose and aim for his work. But what about his shadowy collaborator, the translator? In some ways, he has an even more complex set of relationships to deal with. Where should his loyalties lie? With the author? With his new reading or viewing public? Should he make the English-speaking reader aware of the foreignness of the text he is translating, hoping to expand the boundaries of his literary sensibilities? Or should he try to integrate the new work into English language literature, denying it its foreign quality? In each case he loses something, in each case he possibly gains something. But all his compromises are likely to be uneasy ones.

The translators represented in this volume have had these kinds of decisions to face. Will the play be better understood if the living room where Klíma's dangerous games are played is imagined in New York? In London? Or in some nebulous island, untinged by local customs and colloquialisms? Should the army types in Landovský's *Detour* be resettled in some Texas military camp? Wherever he may decide to place them, the translator also has to decide whether to call them "chaps," "fellows" or "guys," and their vehicle a "lorry" or a "truck." Should Kundera's Master speak in measures that echo the rhythms of eighteenth-century prose (after all, he and his servant Jacques replay scenes from Diderot's time-honored work)? Could Uhde's resolute and talkative heroine be travelling from Baltimore to Washington? Or from Norwich to London? No, she is unmistakably travelling to Prague. And the conversation in Havel's *Protest* between the writer who is "in favor" and the writer who is "out of favor" could not possibly take place in a North American city. It can only have its full meaning in a country where dissidence of any sort is a crime with real and serious consequences. The charades about freedom and violence in Klíma's text are played by characters well aware that to make people feel guity is a sure way to exercise control over them. Jacques's indestructible spirit dances over the heads of French intellectuals who know their Diderot and must remain suspended in a timeless omnipresent story even if he tells his stories to an Ohio audience. In a fundamental way, the plays, though uniquely Czech on one level, are about the world each one of us lives in.

VII. THE CONCEPT OF CENTRAL EUROPE

It may come as a surprise to someone who has had no previous acquaintance with Czech theatre and who has given no further thought to the area called Central Europe for centuries that these plays from behind the Iron Curtain (even Kohout's and Kundera's plays were written while their authors were still in Czechoslovakia) should deal with issues of immediate interest to an international audience. However, this is not surprising at all. In his essay "The Tragedy of Central Europe" (*New York Review of Books*, April 26, 1984) Milan Kundera eloquently argues how detrimental the "disappearance of the cultural home of Central Europe" is to Western civilization. Kundera shows how the great modern novels of Central Europe (by Broch, Musil, Hašek, Kafka) can be understood as prophetic meditations of enormous relevance to Western culture. As for the plays collected in this volume, it may be a sign of the spiritual resilience of the Central European writer that works written after decades of enforced alienation from the traditions of their culture are, in style and content, in meaning and implication, an integral part of contemporary world theatre. Havel's exploration of moral tightrope-walking by means of linguistic decoys are as close to Tom Stoppard (a Czech by birth) as they are to Beckett. Kohout's fiery farce, beginning in the world of Ayckbourn, becomes more and more Pinteresque in its display of language as an instrument of power by obfuscation. Klíma's combination of theatricality and philosophical speculation parallels Dürrenmatt at his best, while Kundera's elegant exploration of the reality-fiction conundrum lodges him in a strong literary tradition extending from Sterne to Borges. Uhde's low-key investigation of the human psyche under social pressure relates him in different ways to Ionesco, Edward Bond and Neil Simon. Landovský (an eminent Czech actor before he left Prague) has created a Švejkian prank linked to the traditions of both French and American farce.

Living at the pivot point of giant power struggles but powerless to influence them, this small Czech nation has given birth to writers who reflect and interpret modern man's confusion and fear, his resilience and humor, his determination to recognize and speak the truth. And although Kundera's wise Jacques is sceptical of the writer's activity because "everything that's ever happened here below has been rewritten hundreds of times . . . so often people don't know who they are any more," the characters created by these playwrights, though proving Jacques right in one way, prove him wrong in another because they achieve something important: they speak to the East as well as to the West and thus eradicate a political border.

Jacques and His Master

An Homage to Diderot in Three Acts

Milan Kundera

translated from the French by Michael Henry Heim

Richard Feldman

JACQUES AND HIS MASTER
[American Repertory Theatre, Cambridge, U.S.A.]
Directed by Susan Sontag

The play should be performed without intermission.

I imagine Jacques as a man of at least forty. His Master is the same age or somewhat younger. François Germond, who directed the excellent production in Geneva, had an interesting idea: When Jacques and his Master meet again at the beginning of Act Three, Scene 6, they are already old; years have passed since the preceding scene.

The stage remains the same throughout the play. It is divided in two: a downstage area, below, and a raised upstage area, in the form of a large platform. All action taking place in the present is performed downstage; episodes from the past are performed on the upstage platform.

As far upstage as possible (and therefore on the platform) is a staircase (or ladder) leading to an attic. Most of the time, the set (which should be utterly plain and abstract) is completely bare. For certain episodes, however, actors bring on chairs, a table, etc. The set must avoid all ornamental, illustrative, and symbolic elements. These are contrary to the spirit of the play, as is any exaggeration in the acting.

The action takes place in the eighteenth century, but in the eighteenth century as we dream of it today. Just as the language of the play does not aim to reproduce the language of the time, so the setting and costumes must not stress the period. The historicity of the characters (especially the two protagonists), though never in question, should be slightly muted.

CHARACTERS:

Jacques
Jacques's Master
Innkeeper
Chevalier de Saint-Ouen
Young Bigre
Old Bigre
Justine
Marquis
Mother
Daughter
Agathe
Agathe's Mother
Agathe's Father
Police Officer
Bailiff

ACT ONE

Scene 1

Enter Jacques and his Master. After they have taken a few steps, Jacques gazes at the audience. He stops short.

JACQUES: (*Discreetly.*) Sir . . . (*pointing out the audience to him*) why are they staring at us?

MASTER: (*A bit taken aback and adjusting his clothes as if afraid of calling attention to himself by a sartorial oversight.*) Pretend there's no one there.

JACQUES: (*To the audience.*) Wouldn't you rather look somewhere else? All right then, what do you want to know? Where we've come from? (*He stretches his right arm out behind him.*) Back there. Where we're going? (*Philosophically.*) Which of us knows where we're going? (*To the audience.*) Do you know where you're going?

MASTER: I'm afraid, Jacques, that *I* know where we're going.

JACQUES: Afraid?

MASTER: (*Sadly.*) Yes. But I have no intention of acquainting you with my painful obligations . . .

JACQUES: None of us knows where we're going, sir, believe me. But as my captain used to say, "It's all written on high . . . "

MASTER: And right he was . . .

JACQUES: Damn Justine and the vile attic where I lost my virginity!

MASTER: Why curse the woman, Jacques?

JACQUES: Because the day I lost my virginity, I went out and got drunk. My father, mad with rage, gave me a beating. A regiment was passing through,

I signed up, a battle broke out, a bullet hit me in the knee. And that was the start of a long string of adventures. Without that bullet, I don't think I'd ever have fallen in love.

MASTER: You mean you've been in love? You've never told me that before.

JACQUES: There are many things I haven't told you.

MASTER: But how did you fall in love? Tell me that!

JACQUES: Where was I? Oh, yes, the bullet in my knee. I was buried under a pile of dead and wounded bodies. Next day they found me and tossed me in a cart. The road to the hospital was bad, and I howled in pain at the slightest bump. Suddenly we stopped. I asked to be let down. We were at the edge of a village, and I'd noticed a young woman standing in the doorway of a hut. . . .

MASTER: Aha! Now I see. . . .

JACQUES: She went inside, came out with a bottle of wine, and held it to my lips. They tried to load me back in the cart, but I grabbed the woman's skirt. Then I passed out, and when I came to I was inside the hut, her husband and children crowding around me while she applied compresses.

MASTER: You scoundrel, you! I see how it ended!

JACQUES: You don't see a thing, sir.

MASTER: A man welcomes you into his house, and look how you repay him!

JACQUES: But are we the masters of our actions? As my captain used to say, "The good and evil we encounter here below are written first on high." Dear Master, do you know any way of erasing what has been written? Can I cease to be? Can I be someone else? And if I am myself, can I do anything other than what I do?

MASTER: There's something that's been bothering me: Are you a scoundrel because it's written on high? Or was it written on high because they knew you were a scoundrel? Which is the cause, which the effect?

JACQUES: I don't know, sir, but you mustn't call me a scoundrel . . .

MASTER: A man who cuckolds his benefactor . . .

JACQUES: . . . or that man my benefactor. You should have heard the names he called his wife for taking pity on me.

MASTER: And right he was . . . Tell me, Jacques, what was she like? Describe her to me.

JACQUES: The young woman?

MASTER: Yes.

JACQUES: (*After a moment of hesitation.*) Average height . . .

MASTER: (*Not too pleased.*) Hm . . .

JACQUES: Though actually on the tall side . . .

MASTER: (*Nodding his approval.*) On the tall side . . .

JACQUES: Yes.

MASTER: Just the way I like them.

JACQUES: (*Making graphic use of his hands.*) Beautiful breasts.

MASTER: Bigger in front or behind?

JACQUES: (*Hesitating.*) In front.

MASTER: (*Sadly.*) What a shame.

JACQUES: So you love big bottoms?

MASTER: Yes . . . Big ones like Agathe's . . . And her eyes? What were they like?

JACQUES: Her eyes? I don't remember. But she had black hair.

MASTER: Agathe was blond.

JACQUES: Is it my fault she didn't look like your Agathe? You'll have to take her as she is. But she did have beautiful long legs.

MASTER: (*Dreamily.*) Long legs. That makes me so happy!

JACQUES: And a majestic bottom.

MASTER: Majestic? Really?

JACQUES: (*Showing him.*) Like this . . .

MASTER: You scoundrel, you! The more you tell me about her, the wilder I get. . . . The wife of your benefactor, and you went and . . .

JACQUES: No, sir. Nothing ever happened between us.

MASTER: Then why bring her up? Why waste our time with her?

JACQUES: You keep interrupting me, sir. It's a very bad habit.

MASTER: And I already wanted her . . .

JACQUES: I tell you I'm in bed with a bullet in my knee, suffering agonies, and all you can think about is your lusts. And Agathe, whoever she is.

MASTER: Don't mention that name.

JACQUES: You mentioned it first.

MASTER: Have you ever wanted a woman desperately, only to be rejected by her? Again and again?

JACQUES: Yes. Justine.

MASTER: Justine? The girl you lost your virginity with?

JACQUES: The same.

MASTER: Tell me about her . . .

JACQUES: After you, sir.

Scene 2

Several characters have taken their places on the upstage platform. Young Bigre is sitting on the steps; Justine is standing next to him. On the opposite side of the stage, Agathe is sitting on a chair that the Chevalier de Saint-Ouen has brought out for her; the Chevalier is standing by her side.

SAINT-OUEN: (*Calling to the Master.*) Greetings, my friend!

JACQUES: (*Turning, together with the Master, and indicating Agathe with his head.*) Is she the one? (*The Master nods.*) And the man next to her? Who is he?

MASTER: A friend, the Chevalier de Saint-Ouen. He's the one who introduced me to her. (*He looks up at Justine.*) And the other one, is she yours?

JACQUES: Yes, but I like yours better.

MASTER: And I prefer yours. More flesh. How about swapping?

JACQUES: You should have thought of that earlier. It's too late now.

MASTER: (*With a sigh.*) Yes, too late. And who's the brawny fellow?

JACQUES: Bigre, an old pal. We both wanted her, that girl. But for some mysterious reason, he's the one who got her.

MASTER: My problem exactly.

SAINT-OUEN: (*Moving toward the Master, to the edge of the platform.*) You might be a bit more discreet, old boy. The parents are fearful of their daughter's reputation. . . .

MASTER: (*To Jacques, with indignation.*) The filthy shopkeepers! They were perfectly happy to let me shower her with gifts!

SAINT-OUEN: No, no, you don't understand! They have great respect for you. They simply want you to state your intentions. Otherwise you'll have to stop going there.

MASTER: (*To Jacques, with indignation.*) When I think that he's the one who introduced me to her! Who egged me on! Who promised me she'd be easy!

SAINT-OUEN: I'm merely passing on their message, my friend.

MASTER: (*To Saint-Ouen.*) Very well. (*He mounts the platform.*) Then please pass on my message to them: Don't count on dragging me to the altar just yet. As for Agathe, tell her she had best be more tender with me in the future if she doesn't wish to lose me. I have no intention of wasting my time and money on her when I can put them to better use elsewhere.

(*Saint-Ouen hears him out, bows, and returns to his place beside Agathe.*)

JACQUES: Bravo, sir! That's how I like you! Brave for a change.

MASTER: (*To Jacques, from the platform.*) I have my moments. I stopped seeing her.

SAINT-OUEN: (*Moving back to the Master along a semicircle.*) I've passed on your message word for word, but I can't help thinking you were a bit cruel.

JACQUES: My master? Cruel?

SAINT-OUEN: Hold your tongue, boy! (*To the Master.*) The whole family is horrified by your silence. And Agathe . . .

MASTER: Agathe?

SAINT-OUEN: Agathe weeps.

MASTER: She weeps.

SAINT-OUEN: She spends her days weeping.

MASTER: And so you feel that if I resumed my visits . . .

SAINT-OUEN: It would be a mistake! You can't retreat. You'd lose everything by going back to them now. You must teach those merchants some manners.

MASTER: But what if they never ask me back?

SAINT-OUEN: They will.

MASTER: And if it takes a long time?

SAINT-OUEN: Do you wish to be a master or slave?

MASTER: So she's weeping . . .

SAINT-OUEN: Better she than you.

MASTER: And if they never ask me back?

SAINT-OUEN: They will, I tell you. Now make the most of the situation. Agathe must be made to see that you're not ready to eat out of her hand and that she must make an effort . . . But tell me . . . We're friends, aren't we? Give me your word of honor. Have you and she . . .

MASTER: No.

SAINT-OUEN: Your discretion does you credit.

MASTER: Not in the least. It's the plain truth.

SAINT-OUEN: What? No one small moment of weakness?

MASTER: Not one.

SAINT-OUEN: I wonder if you haven't behaved too much like a virgin with her.

MASTER: And you, Chevalier? Have you never desired her?

SAINT-OUEN: Of course I have. But the moment you came along, I became invisible to Agathe. Oh, we're still good friends, but nothing more. My only consolation is that if my best friend sleeps with her, I'll feel just as if I myself were doing it. Take my word for it. I'll do my utmost to put you in her bed.

(At the end of the speech, he moves slowly back to the chair that Agathe is still sitting on.)

JACQUES: Have you noticed what a good listener I am, sir? I haven't interrupted you once. If only you'd follow my example.

MASTER: You boast about not interrupting me only to interrupt me.

JACQUES: I butt in because you've set a bad example.

MASTER: As master I have the right to interrupt my servant as often as I please. My servant has no right to interrupt his master.

JACQUES: I don't interrupt you, sir; I talk to you, the way you've always asked me to. And let me tell you: I don't like that friend of yours, and I'll bet it's his mistress he wants you to marry.

MASTER: Enough! I have no more to say! *(He steps down from the platform in a huff.)*

JACQUES: No, sir! Please! Go on!

MASTER: What's the use? Your insights are conceited and tasteless; you know everything in advance.

JACQUES: You're right, sir, but do go on. All I've guessed is the barest outline of the story. I can't begin to imagine all the charming details of your talks with Saint-Ouen and all the twists and turns of the plot.

MASTER: You've upset me. I refuse to say another word.

JACQUES: Please!

MASTER: If you wish to make peace, you must tell me *your* story. Then I can interrupt as often as I please. What I want to hear is how you lost your virginity, and you can be certain I'll interrupt you a few times during your first act of love.

Scene 3

JACQUES: As you wish, sir; as is your privilege. Look. (*He turns and points to the staircase that Justine and Young Bigre are climbing; Old Bigre is standing at its foot.*) This is the shop where my godfather, Old Bigre, sells the wheels he makes. The ladder goes to the attic, and my friend, Young Bigre, has his bed up there.

OLD BIGRE: (*Calling up to the attic.*) Bigre! Bigre, you damned do-nothing!

JACQUES: Old Bigre had his bed downstairs, in the shop. Every night after he was sound asleep, Young Bigre would softly open the door and sneak Justine up the ladder with him.

OLD BIGRE: The morning bells have rung, and you're still snoring away. Do you want me to go up there with a broom and sweep you out?

JACQUES: They'd had such a good time that night they overslept.

YOUNG BIGRE: (*From the attic.*) Calm down, Father!

OLD BIGRE: The farmer will be here soon for the axle. Get a move on.

YOUNG BIGRE: Coming! (*He runs down the stairs, buttoning his trousers.*)

MASTER: So she had no way out?

JACQUES: None. She was trapped.

MASTER: (*Laughing.*) And shaking in her shoes, I imagine.

OLD BIGRE: Ever since he fell for that little slut, he's been snoring half the day away. I wouldn't mind so much if she were worth the trouble. But *that* wench! If his poor mother could have seen them, she'd have long since given him a trouncing and scratched the slut's eyes out in front of the church after mass! But I put up with it, like an idiot. Well, it's time things changed around here! (*To Young Bigre.*) Take this axle, and go and deliver it to the farmer! (*Exit Young Bigre with the axle on his shoulder.*)

MASTER: And Justine heard every word up there?

JACQUES: Naturally!

OLD BIGRE: Damn it to hell, where's my pipe? I bet that good for nothing of mine took it! Let's see if it isn't up in the attic. (*He climbs the stairs.*)

MASTER: And Justine? Justine?

JACQUES: She slipped under the bed.

MASTER: And Young Bigre?

JACQUES: As soon as he'd delivered the axle, he ran over to my house. "Listen," I told him, "go and take a walk around the village. In the meantime, I'll find a way to keep your father busy so Justine can escape. Just be sure to give me enough time." (*He mounts the platform. The Master smiles.*) What are you smiling about?

MASTER: Oh, nothing.

OLD BIGRE: (*Who has come down from the loft.*) Godson Jacques! Good to see you! What brings you here so bright and early?

JACQUES: I'm on my way home.

OLD BIGRE: Well, well, Jacques, my boy. Getting to be quite the rake!

JACQUES: What can I say?

OLD BIGRE: You and my son both, I'm afraid. Out all night, eh?

JACQUES: What can I say?

OLD BIGRE: With a whore?

JACQUES: Yes. But with my father I can't even mention the subject!

OLD BIGRE: Which is perfectly understandable. He owes you the same sound beating I owe my son. But how about some breakfast? Wine gives good counsel.

JACQUES: Sorry, Godfather, I can't. I'm dead tired.

OLD BIGRE: Gave it your all, eh? I hope it was worth it. Look, I have an idea. My son is out. Why don't you go up to the attic and stretch out on his bed? (*Jacques climbs the stairs.*)

MASTER: (*Calling up to Jacques.*) Traitor! Scoundrel! I should have guessed.

OLD BIGRE: Oh, children! . . . Damned children! . . . (*Noises and muffled cries come from the attic.*) Poor boy, some dream he's having. . . . He must have had a rough night.

MASTER: Dream! Ha! He's not dreaming! He's terrorizing her! She tries hard to fight him off, but since she's afraid of being caught, she keeps her mouth shut. You scoundrel, you! You should be tried for rape!

JACQUES: (*Looking down from the attic.*) I don't know, sir, if I raped her or not. What I do know is that we had rather a good time, the two of us. All she asked me was to promise . . .

MASTER: What did you promise, you villain?

JACQUES: Never to breathe a word of it to Young Bigre.

MASTER: Which gave you the right to go at it again.

JACQUES: And again!

MASTER: How many times?

JACQUES: Many times, and each better than the last.

(*Enter Young Bigre.*)

OLD BIGRE: What took you so long? Here, take this rim and finish it outside.

YOUNG BIGRE: Outside? Why?

OLD BIGRE: So as not to wake up Jacques.

YOUNG BIGRE: Jacques?

OLD BIGRE: Yes, Jacques. He's up in the attic, taking a nap. Oh, a father's lot! You're all scoundrels, every last one of you. Well, what are you waiting for? Get a move on! (*Young Bigre tears over to the stairs and is about to start climbing.*) Where are you going? Let the poor fellow sleep!

YOUNG BIGRE: (*Loudly.*) Father! Father!

OLD BIGRE: He was dead tired!

YOUNG BIGRE: No, you're not! Do you like it when someone wakes you?

MASTER: And Justine heard all that?

JACQUES: (*Sitting at the head of the stairs.*) As clearly as you hear me now.

MASTER: Oh, that's wonderful! The perfect scoundrel! And what did you do?

JACQUES: I laughed.

MASTER: You gallows bird! And Justine?

JACQUES: Tore her hair, raised her eyes to heaven, wrung her hands.

MASTER: You're a brute, Jacques. A brute with a heart of stone.

JACQUES: (*Coming down the stairs, highly serious.*) No, sir, no. I am a man of great sensitivity. But I reserve it for the proper occasions. Those who squander their sensitivity have none left when there's a need for it.

OLD BIGRE: (*To Jacques.*) Ah, there you are! Had a good nap? You really needed one. (*To Young Bigre.*) He looks as fresh as a daisy now. Go get a bottle from the cellar. (*To Jacques.*) Now you feel like having some breakfast, don't you?

JACQUES: Do I!

(*Young Bigre comes back with a bottle, and Old Bigre fills three glasses.*)

YOUNG BIGRE: (*Pushing away his glass.*) I'm not thirsty this early in the morning.

OLD BIGRE: You don't want anything to drink?

YOUNG BIGRE: No.

OLD BIGRE: Ah! I know what it is. (*To Jacques.*) Justine's at the bottom of this. He was out a long time just now. He must have stopped off at her place and caught her with somebody else. (*To Young Bigre.*) Serves you right! I told you she was nothing but a whore! (*To Jacques.*) And now he wants to take it out on an innocent bottle!

JACQUES: You may just be right.

YOUNG BIGRE: This is no laughing matter, Jacques.

OLD BIGRE: Well, we can drink even if he won't. (*Raising his glass.*) Your health, Godson Jacques!

JACQUES: (*Raising his glass.*) Your health! (*To Young Bigre.*) And you, my friend, have a drink with us. Whatever it is that's bothering you can't be all that bad.

YOUNG BIGRE: I told you, I'm not drinking.

JACQUES: By the next time you see her, the whole thing will have blown over.

You have nothing to fear.

OLD BIGRE: Well, I hope she makes him suffer. . . . And now let me take you back to your father and ask him to forgive you your escapades. Damned children! You're all the same! You filthy beasts . . . Let's go. (*He takes Jacques by the arm and starts off with him. Young Bigre runs up the stairs to the attic. Jacques disengages himself after several steps and turns toward his Master. Exit Old Bigre, alone.*)

MASTER: An admirable story, Jacques! It teaches us to know our women better—and our friends.

(*Saint-Ouen appears on the platform, which he crosses slowly in the direction of the Master.*)

JACQUES: Did you really think a friend of yours would give up a chance at your mistress?

Scene 4

SAINT-OUEN: Friend! Dear friend! Come . . . (*He is at the edge of the platform, holding out his arms to the Master, who is at its foot. The Master mounts the platform, and there he joins Saint-Ouen, who takes him by the arm and promenades back and forth with him.*) Ah, how wonderful, dear friend, to have a friend for whom one feels true friendship. . . .

MASTER: I'm touched, Saint-Ouen.

SAINT-OUEN: Indeed, I have no friend who is a better friend than you, dear friend, while I . . .

MASTER: You? You, kind friend, are likewise the best of friends.

SAINT-OUEN: (*Shaking his head.*) I'm afraid you don't know me at all, my friend.

MASTER: I know you as I know myself.

SAINT-OUEN: If you knew me, you wouldn't want to know me.

MASTER: How can you say such a thing!

SAINT-OUEN: I'm despicable. Yes, that's the word, and I have no choice but to apply it to myself: I am a despicable man.

MASTER: I refuse to let you slander yourself in my presence.

SAINT-OUEN: Despicable!

MASTER: No!

SAINT-OUEN: Despicable!

MASTER: (*Kneeling before him.*) Hold your tongue, my friend. Your words are breaking my heart. Why torture yourself so? Why reproach yourself?

SAINT-OUEN: My past is tarnished. Merely a single stain, yes, but. . . .

MASTER: You see? What harm can there be in a single stain?

SAINT-OUEN: A single stain can sully an entire life.

MASTER: One swallow does not make a summer. A single stain is no stain at all.

SAINT-OUEN: Oh, no. Single, solitary stain though it be, it's odious. I—I, Saint-Ouen—have betrayed, yes, betrayed a friend!

MASTER: Come now! How did it happen?

SAINT-OUEN: The two of us were pursuing the same young woman. He was in love with her and she was in love with me. While he kept her, I took my pleasure. I never had the courage to admit it to him. But now I must. The next time I see him, I must tell him all, confess to him, unburden myself of the frightful secret. . . .

MASTER: Yes, you must, Saint-Ouen.

SAINT-OUEN: Is that what you advise?

MASTER: I do.

SAINT-OUEN: And how do you think my friend will respond?

MASTER: He'll be touched by your sincerity and remorse. He'll embrace you.

SAINT-OUEN: Do you think so?

MASTER: I do.

SAINT-OUEN: And that is how you yourself would respond?

MASTER: I? Certainly.

SAINT-OUEN: (*Opening his arms.*) Then embrace me, my friend!

MASTER: What do you mean?

SAINT-OUEN: Embrace me! The friend I've deceived is you!

MASTER: (*Devastated.*) Agathe?

SAINT-OUEN: Yes . . . Ah, your face has fallen! I give you back your word! Yes, yes! You may do with me as you see fit. You're right. What I did was unforgivable. Leave me! Abandon me! Despise me! Ah, if only you knew what that bitch has done to me, how I've suffered from the treacherous role she forced me into.

Scene 5

The two dialogues proceed simultaneously.

Young Bigre and Justine come down the stairs and sit side by side on the lowest step. They both seem devastated.

JUSTINE: But I swear to you! I swear by my father and mother both!

YOUNG BIGRE: I'll never believe you!

(*Justine bursts into tears.*)

MASTER: (*To Saint-Ouen.*) The bitch! And you, Saint-Ouen, how could you. . . .

SAINT-OUEN: Don't torture me, my friend!

JUSTINE: I swear he never touched me!
YOUNG BIGRE: Liar!
MASTER: How could you?
YOUNG BIGRE: With that swine!

(*Justine bursts into tears.*)

SAINT-OUEN: How could I? I'm the most despicable man under the sun! Here I have the best of men for a friend, and I betray him shamefully. And you ask me why? Because I'm a swine! Nothing but a swine!
JUSTINE: He's no swine! He's your friend!
YOUNG BIGRE: (*Angrily.*) My friend?
JUSTINE: Yes, friend! He never touched me!
YOUNG BIGRE: Shut up!
SAINT-OUEN: Yes, nothing but a swine!
MASTER: No. Stop spitting on yourself!
SAINT-OUEN: But I must spit on myself!
MASTER: No matter what's happened, you must not spit on yourself.
JUSTINE: He told me he was your friend and there could never be anything between us, even if we were alone on a desert island.
MASTER: Stop torturing yourself.
YOUNG BIGRE: He really said that?
JUSTINE: Yes!
SAINT-OUEN: I want to feel pain.
MASTER: We are both victims of the same beast, you and I! She seduced you! You've been so sincere, you've kept nothing from me. You're still my friend!
YOUNG BIGRE: Did he say: "Even on a desert island"?
JUSTINE: Yes!
SAINT-OUEN: I'm unworthy of your friendship.
MASTER: On the contrary. Your pain makes you worthy. You've earned it with the torture of your remorse!
YOUNG BIGRE: Did he really say he was my friend and wouldn't touch you even if you were alone on a desert island?
JUSTINE: Yes!
SAINT-OUEN: Ah, how generous you are!
MASTER: Embrace me! (*They embrace.*)
YOUNG BIGRE: Did he really say he wouldn't touch you even if you were alone on a desert island?
JUSTINE: Yes!
YOUNG BIGRE: On a desert island? Swear to it!
JUSTINE: I swear!
MASTER: Come, let's have a drink!

JACQUES: Oh, sir, I feel sorry for you!

MASTER: To our friendship, which no tart can destroy!

YOUNG BIGRE: On a desert island. I've been very unfair to him. He's a true friend.

JACQUES: Our adventures, Master, seem strangely similar.

MASTER: (*Leaving his role.*) What was that?

JACQUES: I said that our adventures were strangely similar.

YOUNG BIGRE: Jacques is a true friend.

JUSTINE: Your best friend.

SAINT-OUEN: All I can think of now is revenge! And since the bitch has abused the two of us, we must avenge ourselves together! You have only to give the command—tell me what I must do!

MASTER: (*More interested in Jacques and his story, to Saint-Ouen.*) Later. We'll finish this story later. . . .

SAINT-OUEN: No, no! Immediately! I'll do anything you ask! Tell me what you have in mind.

MASTER: Yes, yes, but later. Now I want to see how things turn out for Jacques. (*He steps down from the platform.*)

YOUNG BIGRE: Jacques! (*Jacques jumps up on the platform and goes over to Young Bigre.*) Thank you. You're my best friend. (*He embraces him.*) And now embrace Justine. (*Jacques holds back.*) Don't be shy. When I'm around, you have the right to embrace her! I order you to! (*Jacques embraces Justine.*) We'll be the best of friends, the three of us, friends for life. . . . On a desert island . . . You mean you really wouldn't touch her? Not even on a desert island?

JACQUES: If she belonged to a friend? Are you out of your mind?

YOUNG BIGRE: You're a true friend!

MASTER: The scoundrel! (*Jacques turns toward his Master.*) But *my* story is still far from over. . . .

JACQUES: So being cuckolded wasn't enough for you?

YOUNG BIGRE: (*Overjoyed.*) The truest of women! The truest of friends! I'm as happy as a king! (*During these lines, Young Bigre exits with Justine. Saint-Ouen remains for the first few lines of the following scene, then exits as well.*)

Scene 6

MASTER: My story ended badly. With the worst of endings a human story can have . . .

JACQUES: And what is the worst of endings of a human story?

MASTER: Think it over.

JACQUES: Let me think . . . What is the worst of endings of a human story . . . But my story isn't over yet either, sir. I lost my virginity, I found my best friend. I was so happy I went out and got drunk. My father gave me a beating. A regiment was passing through, I signed up, a battle broke out, a bullet hit me in the knee, I was loaded into a cart, the cart stopped in front of a hut, and a woman appeared on the threshold. . . .

MASTER: You've been through that before.

JACQUES: Butting in again, are you?

MASTER: Go on, go on!

JACQUES: I will not! I refuse to be constantly interrupted.

MASTER: (*Testily.*) All right, but let's keep going. We've still got a long way to go. . . . Wait a minute, damn it! Why is it we have no horses?

JACQUES: You forget that we're on stage. You can't have horses on stage!

MASTER: You mean I have to walk because of a ridiculous play? The master who invented us meant us to have horses!

JACQUES: That's a risk you take when you're invented by too many masters.

MASTER: You know, I've often wondered whether or not we're good inventions. What do you think, Jacques? Are we well invented?

JACQUES: By whom, sir? The one on high?

MASTER: It was written on high that someone here below would write our story, and I can't help wondering whether he did a good job. Was he at least talented?

JACQUES: If he weren't talented, he wouldn't write.

MASTER: What?

JACQUES: I said he wouldn't write if he weren't talented.

MASTER: (*Laughing heartily.*) That shows you are nothing but a servant. Do you think everyone who writes has talent? What about that young poet who once came to call on the master of us both?

JACQUES: I don't know any poet.

MASTER: Clearly you know nothing about our master. You are a most uneducated servant.

(*Enter the Innkeeper. She goes up to Jacques and his Master and bows to them.*)

INNKEEPER: Welcome, gentlemen.

MASTER: And just where are we welcome, Madame?

INNKEEPER: The Great Stag Inn.

MASTER: I don't believe I've heard the name.

INNKEEPER: Bring me a table! And some chairs! (*Two Waiters run in with a table and chairs and seat Jacques and his Master at them.*) It was written that you would stop at our inn, where you would eat, drink, sleep, and listen to the tales of the innkeeper, who is known far and wide for her exceptionally big mouth.

MASTER: As if my servant's wasn't big enough!

INNKEEPER: What can I do for you, gentlemen?

MASTER: (*Surveying the Innkeeper with a greedy eye.*) That's worth thinking about.

INNKEEPER: Don't bother. It was written that what you want is duckling, potatoes, and a bottle of wine. . . . (*She exits.*)

JACQUES: You were about to tell me something about a poet, sir.

MASTER: (*Still under the charm of the Innkeeper.*) Poet?

JACQUES: The young poet who once paid a visit to the master of us both . . .

MASTER: Oh, yes. Well, one day a young poet came to call on the master who invented us. He was constantly being pestered by poets. There's always a surplus of young poets. They increase at the rate of approximately four hundred thousand a year. In France alone. It's even worse in less cultivated countries!

JACQUES: What do people do with them? Drown them?

MASTER: They used to. In the good old days, in Sparta. Back then, poets were tossed from a high rock into the sea the moment they were born. But in our enlightened century we let all sorts live out their days.

(*The Innkeeper brings back a bottle of wine and fills their glasses.*)

INNKEEPER: How do you like it?

MASTER: (*Tasting it.*) Excellent! Leave the bottle. (*The Innkeeper exits.*) Now then, one day a young poet turned up at our master's with a sheet of paper. "What a surprise," said our master, "these are poems!" "Yes, Master, poems from my own pen," said the poet, "and I beg you to tell me the truth about them, nothing but the truth." "And are you not afraid of the truth," said our master. "No," the poet answered in a quavering voice. And our master said to him: "My friend, not only have you shown me that your poems are not worth their weight in shit; your work will never be any better!" "I'm sorry to hear that," said the young poet. "It means I shall have to write bad poetry all my life." To which our master replied, "Let me warn you, young man. Neither gods nor men nor signposts forgive mediocrity in a poet!" "I understand, master," said the poet, "but I can't help myself. It's a compulsion."

JACQUES: A what?

MASTER: A compulsion. "I have a tremendous compulsion to write bad verse." "Let me warn you again of the consequences!" our master exclaimed, but the young poet replied, "You are the great Diderot, I am a bad poet. But we bad poets are the most numerous; we'll always be in the majority! All of mankind consists of bad poets! And the public—its mind, its taste, its sensibility—is nothing but a crowd of bad poets! Why do you think that bad poets offend other bad poets? The bad poets who make up mankind are crazy about bad verse! Indeed, it is just because I write bad verse that I shall one day be in the pantheon of great poets!"

JACQUES: Is that what the young poet said to our master?

MASTER: His very words.

JACQUES: They're not without a certain truth.

MASTER: Certainly not. And that gives me a blasphemous thought.

JACQUES: I know what it is.

MASTER: You do?

JACQUES: I do.

MASTER: Out with it, then.

JACQUES: No, you had it first.

MASTER: We had it simultaneously. Don't lie, now.

JACQUES: I had it after you.

MASTER: All right then. What is it? Come now! Out with it!

JACQUES: You suddenly wondered whether *our* master wasn't a bad poet too.

MASTER: And who's to say he wasn't?

JACQUES: Do you think we'd be better if we'd been invented by somebody else?

MASTER: (*Thoughtfully.*) It depends. If we'd sprung from the pen of a truly great writer, a genius . . . certainly.

JACQUES: (*Sadly, after a pause.*) I judge the creator by his work.

MASTER: What's sad?

JACQUES: That you have such a low opinion of your creator.

MASTER: (*Looking at Jacques.*) I judge the creator by his work.

JACQUES: We should love the master who made us what we are. We'd be much happier if we loved him. More serene and self-confident. But you, you want a better creator. To be quite frank, Master, I call that blasphemy.

INNKEEPER: (*Entering with food on a tray.*) Your duckling, gentlemen . . . And when you're finished eating, I'll tell you the story of Madame de La Pommeraye.

JACQUES: (*Annoyed.*) When we're finished eating, *I'm* going to tell you about how I fell in love!

INNKEEPER: Your master will decide who speaks first.

MASTER: No, no! I refuse! It all depends on what is written on high!

INNKEEPER: What is written on high is that it's my turn to speak.

ACT TWO

Scene 1

The setting is the same: the stage is entirely empty except for the downstage table at which Jacques and his Master are sitting as they come to the end of their supper.

JACQUES: It all began with the loss of my virginity. I went out and got drunk, my father gave me a beating, a regiment was passing through . . .

INNKEEPER: (*Entering.*) Was it good?

MASTER: Delicious.

JACQUES: Excellent!

INNKEEPER: Another bottle?

MASTER: Why not?

INNKEEPER: (*Calling offstage.*) Another bottle . . . (*To Jacques and his Master.*) I promised to tell the gentlemen the story of Madame de La Pommeraye to round off their fine supper. . . .

JACQUES: Damn it all, Madame Innkeeper! I'm telling about how I fell in love!

INNKEEPER: Men are quick to fall in love and just as quick to throw you over. Nothing new about that. Now *I'm* going to tell you a story of how they get their comeuppance.

JACQUES: You have a big mouth, Madame Innkeeper, and eighteen thousand barrels of words in your gullet, and you're always on the lookout for an unfortunate ear to spill them in!

INNKEEPER: You have a perfect lout for a servant, Monsieur. He thinks he's a wit and dares to keep interrupting a lady.

MASTER: *(Reprovingly.)* Do stop putting yourself forward, Jacques. . . .

INNKEEPER: Now then, there once was a marquis by the name of Des Arcis. An odd bird and incorrigible skirt-chaser. In short, a fine fellow. Only he had no respect for women.

JACQUES: For good reason.

INNKEEPER: You're interrupting, Monsieur Jacques!

JACQUES: I'm not speaking to you, Madame Keeper of the Great Stag Inn.

INNKEEPER: In any case, the Marquis got wind of a certain Marquise de la Pommeraye, a widow of good manners and birth, of wealth and dignity. After duly taxing the Marquis's time and energy, she succumbed at last and bestowed her favors on him. In a few years, however, his interest began to wane. You know what I mean, gentlemen. First he suggested that they spend more time in society. Then that she entertain more. Soon he failed to appear at her receptions. He always had something urgent to attend to. When he did come to see her, he would scarcely speak, would stretch out in an armchair, pick up a book, toss it aside, play with her dog, and then fall asleep in her presence. But Madame de La Pommeraye still loved him, and suffered dreadfully, until one day, proud woman that she was, she flew into a rage and determined to put an end to it.

Scene 2

During the speech of the Innkeeper, the Marquis enters upstage on the platform, carrying a chair. He sets it down, then drops into it, lazily and with an air of bliss.

INNKEEPER: *(Turning to the Marquis.)* My dear friend . . .

OFFSTAGE VOICE: Madame Innkeeper!

INNKEEPER: *(Calling offstage.)* What is it?

OFFSTAGE VOICE: The key to the pantry!

INNKEEPER: It's hanging on the hook. . . . *(To the Marquis.)* You're dreaming, my friend. . . . *(She mounts the platform and walks over to the Marquis.)*

MARQUIS: As are you, Marquise.

INNKEEPER: True, and rather sad dreams at that.

MARQUIS: What's ailing you, Marquise?

INNKEEPER: Oh, nothing.

MARQUIS: *(Yawning.)* Not so! Come now, Marquise, do tell me. If nothing else, dispel our boredom.

INNKEEPER: So you're bored, are you?

MARQUIS: No, no! . . . It's just that there are days . . . when . . .

INNKEEPER: . . . when we are bored together.

MARQUIS: No! It's not that, my dear. . . . But there are days . . . Heaven only knows why . . .

INNKEEPER: There's something I've long been meaning to tell you, my friend.

I only fear it will grieve you.

MARQUIS: You? Grieve me?

INNKEEPER: Heaven only knows I'm not at fault in the matter.

OFFSTAGE VOICE: Madame Innkeeper!

INNKEEPER: (*Calling offstage.*) Haven't I told you to stop bothering me? Ask my husband!

OFFSTAGE VOICE: He's not here!

INNKEEPER: Well, what the hell is it this time?

OFFSTAGE VOICE: The straw merchant.

INNKEEPER: Pay him and chuck him out. . . . (*To the Marquis.*) Yes, Marquis, it happened before I was even aware of it, and I myself am devastated. Every night I ask myself, "Is the Marquis any less worthy of my love? Have I any reason to reproach him? Has he been unfaithful? No! Then why has my heart changed when his remains constant? I no longer feel alarmed when he's late nor sweetly moved when at last he appears."

MARQUIS: (*Joyfully.*) Really!

INNKEEPER: (*Covering her eyes with her hands.*) Oh, Marquis! Spare me your reproaches. . . . Or rather, no. Spare me not. I deserve them. . . . Should I have concealed my feelings? I'm the one who has changed, not you. That is why I respect you more than ever. I'll not lie to myself. Love has abandoned my heart. It is a terrible discovery, terrible but true.

MARQUIS: (*Falling at her feet with joy.*) You charming creature, you! You are the most charming woman on earth! How happy you have made me! Your sincerity puts me to shame. You tower above me! I am nothing next to you! For the tale your heart tells is word for word the tale my heart would tell, had I the courage to speak.

INNKEEPER: Is that true?

MARQUIS: Nothing could be truer. Now the only thing left for us to do is rejoice that we've both lost, at the very same time, the fragile and deceptive sentiment uniting us.

INNKEEPER: Quite. It is a great misfortune when one continues to love after the other no longer does.

MARQUIS: Never have you appeared more lovely to me than in this moment, and if experience had not made a more prudent man of me, I should go so far as to say that I love you more than ever.

INNKEEPER: But, Marquis, what do we do now?

MARQUIS: We have never deceived each other nor spoken falsely. You have a right to my deepest respect; I trust I have not entirely lost yours. We shall be the best of friends. We shall assist each other in our amorous intrigues! And who knows what may happen one day. . . .

JACQUES: Good God, who does know?

MARQUIS: Perhaps . . .

OFFSTAGE VOICE: Nothing!

INNKEEPER: (*To Jacques and his Master.*) It's enough to drive you crazy, gentlemen! Wouldn't you know he'd call me just when things seem to have settled down in this godforsaken hole, just when everyone's asleep. Now he's made me lose the thread, the clumsy oaf. . . . (*She steps down from the platform.*) Gentlemen, I am truly to be pitied. . . .

Scene 3

MASTER: And I am perfectly willing to pity you, Madame. (*He gives her a slap on the behind.*) But I must congratulate you as well, for you are an excellent storyteller. I've just had an odd thought. What if instead of the clumsy oaf, as you've just called your husband, you were married to Monsieur Jacques here? What I mean is, what would a husband who never stops jabbering do with a wife who never closes her mouth?

JACQUES: Exactly what my grandmother and grandfather did with me all the years I lived with them. They were very strict. They'd get up, get dressed, get to work; then eat and go back to work. In the evening, Grandmother did her sewing and Grandfather read the Bible. Nobody said a word all day.

MASTER: And you? What did you do?

JACQUES: I ran back and forth in the room with a gag in my mouth!

INNKEEPER: A gag?

JACQUES: Grandfather liked his quiet. So I spent the first twelve years of my life gagged. . . .

INNKEEPER: Jean!

OFFSTAGE VOICE: What is it?

INNKEEPER: Two more bottles! But not the ones we serve the customers. Way in the back, behind the firewood!

OFFSTAGE VOICE: Right!

INNKEEPER: Monsieur Jacques, I've changed my mind about you. You're actually quite a touching man. The moment I pictured you with that gag in your mouth, dying to talk, I felt a great love for you well up inside me. What do you say? . . . Let's make peace. (*They embrace.*)

(*A waiter enters and places two bottles on the table. He opens them and fills three glasses.*)

INNKEEPER: Gentlemen, you'll never drink a better wine!

JACQUES: You must have been a devilishly beautiful woman, Madame Innkeeper!

MASTER: You lout! She *is* a devilishly beautiful woman!

INNKEEPER: Oh, I'm not what I used to be. You should have seen me in my prime! But that's neither here nor there. . . . Back to Madame de La Pommeraye . . .

JACQUES: (*Raising his glass.*) But first, to every man whose head you've turned!
INNKEEPER: With pleasure. (*They clink glasses and drink.*) And now . . .
Madame de La Pommeraye.
JACQUES: But first, let's drink to Monsieur le Marquis. I'm worried about
him.
INNKEEPER: And well you might be.

(*They clink glasses and drink.*)

Scene 4

*During the last lines of the preceding scene, Mother and Daughter have entered and
mounted the platform upstage.*

INNKEEPER: Can you imagine her fury? Telling the Marquis she no longer
loves him and watching him jump for joy! Gentlemen, she had her pride!
(*She turns toward the Mother and Daughter.*) So she sought out these two
creatures. Women she had known long before. A mother and daughter.
They had come to Paris for a lawsuit, and having lost it, were ruined. The
mother was reduced to running a small casino.
MOTHER: (*From the platform.*) Necessity knows no law. I did everything possible to place my daughter at the Opera. Is it my fault the silly goose has a
rasp for a voice?
INNKEEPER: The gentlemen who frequented the casino came to gamble and
dine, but more often than not, one or two would stay on and spend the
night with mother or daughter. Which makes the two of them. . . .
JACQUES: Which makes the two of them . . . But let's drink their health all the
same. Like your wine, they go down nicely. (*Jacques raises his glass. All three
clink glasses and drink.*)
MOTHER: (*To the Innkeeper.*) I shall be frank, Madame la Marquise. Our profession is a delicate one and quite dangerous.
INNKEEPER: (*Mounting the platform and going up to the Mother and Daughter.*) I hope
you're not too well known in the profession.
MOTHER: Fortunately not. At least I don't believe so. Our . . . establishment
. . . is located in the Rue de Hambourg . . . on the outskirts of town. . . .
INNKEEPER: I presume you have no desire to persist in your profession and
would not be averse to bettering your lot if I saw fit to help you.
MOTHER: (*With gratitude.*) Oh, Madame la Marquise!
INNKEEPER: Then you must do everything I say.
MOTHER: You may count on us.
INNKEEPER: Very well, then. Return home. Sell all your furniture and any
clothes that are the least bit ostentatious.
JACQUES: (*Raising his glass.*) To the health of Mademoiselle! No doubt that

melancholy air of hers comes from changing masters every night.

INNKEEPER: (*To Jacques from the platform.*) Don't mock her, Monsieur. If only you knew how nauseating it can be! (*To the two women.*) I shall find you some rooms and have them furnished as soberly as possible. You are to leave them only to go to church. You are to walk with your eyes to the ground and never go off anywhere on your own. You are to speak only of God. I shall of course refrain from visiting you. I am unworthy . . . to associate with women as devout as you. . . . And now, do as I say! (*The two women exit.*)

MASTER: That woman gives me the shudders.

INNKEEPER: (*To Master from the platform.*) And you don't even know her yet.

Scene 5

The Marquis has entered from the other side of the stage. He goes up to the Innkeeper and touches her arm lightly. Surprised, she turns to face him.

INNKEEPER: Oh, Marquis! How glad I am to see you! What news do you bring of your intrigues? Of all your tender little girls?

(*The Marquis takes her by the arm and strolls back and forth along the platform with her, leaning over and whispering his response in her ear.*)

MASTER: Look at them, Jacques! He's telling her everything, the blind pig!

INNKEEPER: I do admire you! (*The Marquis whispers something else in her ear.*) Still the successful womanizer!

MARQUIS: Well, and have *you* nothing to confide? (*The Innkeeper shakes her head.*) What about that runt of a count, that dwarf who was always after you. . . ?

INNKEEPER: I no longer see him.

MARQUIS: Well, well! What made you give him up?

INNKEEPER: I didn't care for him.

MARQUIS: Didn't care for him? The most adorable of dwarfs? Or is it that you're still in love with me?

INNKEEPER: And if I am. . . ?

MARQUIS: So you're counting on my return and hoping to reap the benefits of your spotless conduct!

INNKEEPER: Does that frighten you?

MARQUIS: You're a dangerous woman!

(*Continuing their stroll, the Marquis and the Innkeeper notice two women coming from the opposite direction; they are the Mother and Daughter.*)

INNKEEPER: (*Feigning surprise.*) Goodness! Can it be? (*She lets go of the Marquis's arm and goes up to the two women.*) Is it you, Madame?

MOTHER: Yes, it is I.

INNKEEPER: How are you? What's become of you after all these years?

MOTHER: You know of our misfortunes. We lead a modest and secluded existence.

INNKEEPER: You do well to shun society, but why shun me? . . .

DAUGHTER: I have often spoken to Mother of you, Madame, but she always says, "Madame de la Pommeraye? Surely she has forgotten us."

INNKEEPER: How unjust! I'm delighted to see you. This is Monsieur le Marquis des Arcis. He's a friend of mine. You may speak freely in his presence. My, how Mademoiselle has grown!

(*All four continue their stroll together.*)

MASTER: You know, Jacques, I like that innkeeper. Mark my words, she wasn't born at any inn. She's of a higher station. I have a sense for such things.

INNKEEPER: Indeed! You've blossomed into a beauty.

MASTER: Say what you like. She's a noble female.

MARQUIS: (*To the two women.*) Stay awhile! Please! Don't go!

MOTHER: (*Timidly.*) No, no. We shall be late for vespers. . . . Come along, my dear. (*They bow and exit.*)

MARQUIS: Heavens, Marquise! Who are those women?

INNKEEPER: The happiest creatures I know. Did you notice how calm they were, how serene? There's much to be said for a life of seclusion.

MARQUIS: It would cause me great remorse, Marquise, to learn that our separation has led you to such lamentable extremes.

INNKEEPER: Would you rather I opened my door again to the count?

MARQUIS: The runt? Most certainly.

INNKEEPER: Is that what you advise me to do?

MARQUIS: Without the slightest hesitation.

INNKEEPER: (*Stepping down from the platform; to Jacques and his Master.*) Do you hear that? (*She picks up her glass from the table and takes a drink. Then she sits on the edge of the platform. The Marquis sits beside her.*) How old she makes me feel! When I first saw her, she hardly came up to my waist.

MARQUIS: You mean that woman's daughter?

INNKEEPER: Yes. I feel like a wilted rose next to one in bloom. Did you notice her?

MARQUIS: Obviously.

INNKEEPER: What do think of her?

MARQUIS: She's like a Raphael madonna.

INNKEEPER: Those eyes!

MARQUIS: That voice!

INNKEEPER: That skin!

MARQUIS: That walk!

INNKEEPER: That smile!

JACQUES: Good Lord! If you go on like this, Marquis, you're done for!

INNKEEPER: (*To Jacques.*) Right you are. He's done for. (*She stands, picks up her glass, and takes a drink.*)

MARQUIS: That body! (*With these words, he stands and exits, describing a semicircle on the platform as he goes.*)

INNKEEPER: (*To Jacques and his Master.*) He's swallowed the bait.

JACQUES: Madame Innkeeper, she's a monster, your Marquise.

INNKEEPER: And the Marquis? He shouldn't have fallen out of love with her!

JACQUES: I see, Madame, that you don't know the pretty little fable of the Knife and the Sheath.

MASTER: Nor do I. You've never told it to me!

Scene 6

The Marquis retraces his semicircle downstage in the direction of the Innkeeper and begins to speak to her in a supplicatory voice.

MARQUIS: Tell me, Marquise, have you met your friends lately?

INNKEEPER: (*To Jacques and his Master.*) You see? He's caught.

MARQUIS: It's not right of you! They're so poor, and you never invite them to dine.

INNKEEPER: Ah, I do. But in vain. And no wonder. If word got around that they were seeing me, people would say Madame de La Pommeraye was their patron and they would forfeit their charity.

MARQUIS: What! They live on charity?

INNKEEPER: Yes, charity from their parish.

MARQUIS: They're your friends, and they live on charity?

INNKEEPER: Ah, Marquis, we who move in society are ill-equipped to appreciate the sensitivity of such God-fearing souls. They won't accept aid indiscriminately. It must come from pure, unsullied hands.

MARQUIS: Do you know that I was tempted to visit them?

INNKEEPER: A visit from you could be their downfall. With that girl's charms, it wouldn't take long before tongues began to wag!

MARQUIS: (*With a sigh.*) How cruel . . .

INNKEEPER: (*Maliciously.*) Cruel is the word.

MARQUIS: You mock me, Marquise.

INNKEEPER: I'm merely trying to save you grief. You're letting yourself in for great agony, Marquis! Don't confuse this girl with the women you've known! She will not be tempted. You'll never have your way with her!

(Crushed, the Marquis withdraws upstage in a semicircle.)

JACQUES: How spiteful she is, your Marquise.

INNKEEPER: (*To Jacques.*) Don't try to defend your sex, Monsieur Jacques. Have you forgotten so soon how Madame de La Pommeraye loved the Marquis? Why, she's smitten with him even now. His every word is like a dagger in her heart! Can't you see the inferno they both have ahead of them?

(*The Marquis returns to the Innkeeper in a semicircle. She looks up at him.*)

INNKEEPER: Heavens! You look dreadful!

MARQUIS: (*Walking back and forth across the platform.*) I'm haunted. I can't stand it. Can't sleep. Can't eat. For weeks I drank like a fish. Then I turned pious like a monk to catch a glimpse of her in church. . . . Marquise! Find a way for me to see her again! (*The Innkeeper heaves a sigh.*) You're my only friend!

INNKEEPER: I should be only too glad to help you, Marquis, but the situation is delicate. She must never think I'm in collusion with you. . . .

MARQUIS: I beg of you!

INNKEEPER: (*Imitating him.*) I beg of you! . . . What do I care if you're in love or not! Why should I complicate my life? You'll have to manage on your own!

MARQUIS: I implore you! Abandon me now and I am lost. Do it for their sake if not for mine! I warn you, I'm desperate! I'll break down their door, stop at nothing!

INNKEEPER: So be it. . . . As you like. But at least give me time to make the necessary preparations. . . .

(*Servants set chairs around the table upstage as the Marquis exits.*)

Scene 7

INNKEEPER: (*To the Mother and Daughter, who enter upstage.*) Come in, come in. Sit with me at the table, and we'll begin. (*They take their seats at the upstage table. There are now two tables on the stage: one at the foot of the platform, downstage, where Jacques and his Master are sitting, and one on the platform, upstage.*) When the Marquis arrives, we'll all feign surprise. Remember to stay in character.

JACQUES: (*Calling up to the Innkeeper.*) Madame Innkeeper, she's a beast, that woman!

INNKEEPER: (*Calling down to Jacques.*) And the Marquis, Monsieur Jacques, is he an angel?

JACQUES: But no one is asking him to be an angel. Or do you think man has no choice but to be angel or beast? You'd be wiser if you knew the fable of the Knife and the Sheath.

MARQUIS: (*Approaching the women with pretended surprise.*) Oh . . . I hope I am not disturbing you. . . .

INNKEEPER: (*Also surprised.*) In truth . . . we weren't expecting you, Monsieur le Marquis. . . .

MASTER: What actors!

INNKEEPER: But since you're here, please join us for dinner.

(*The Marquis kisses the ladies' hands and takes a seat.*)

JACQUES: This promises to be dull. Let me tell you the fable of the Knife and the Sheath.

MARQUIS: (*Entering into the ladies' discussion.*) I quite agree with you. What are the pleasures of life? Ashes and dust. Can you guess what man I admire most?

JACQUES: Don't listen to him, sir.

MARQUIS: You can't, can you? Well, it's Saint Simeon Stylites, my patron saint.

JACQUES: The fable of the Knife and the Sheath is the moral of all morals and the foundation of all knowledge.

MARQUIS: Just think, dear ladies! Saint Simeon spent forty years of his life praying to God atop a pillar forty meters high.

JACQUES: Listen to me. One day the Knife and the Sheath had a quarrel. "Sheath, darling," said the Knife, "I wish you weren't such a slut, giving refuge every day to new knives." To which the Sheath replied, "Knife, darling, I wish you weren't such a lecher, taking refuge every day in new sheaths."

MARQUIS: Just think, dear ladies, forty years of his life on a pillar forty meters high!

JACQUES: The quarrel broke out while they were at dinner, and a guest sitting between them spoke up. "Dear Sheath," he said, "dear Knife, you do no wrong in changing knives and sheaths. You did commit a fatal error, though, the day you promised not to change. For do you not see, Friend Knife, that God made you to slip into many sheaths?"

DAUGHTER: Tell me, was the column really forty meters high?

JACQUES: "And you, Friend Sheath, do you not see that God made you to accommodate many knives?"

(*The Master has been listening to Jacques without paying attention to the platform. After these words he laughs.*)

MARQUIS: (*With a lover's tenderness.*) Yes, my child. Forty meters high.

DAUGHTER: Didn't Saint Simeon suffer from vertigo?

MARQUIS: No, he did not. And do you know why, my dear child?

DAUGHTER: No.

MARQUIS: Because he never once looked down from the top of his pillar. He never stopped looking upward, to God. And he who looks upward is forever free of vertigo.

THE LADIES: (*Astonished.*) How true!

MASTER: Jacques!

JACQUES: Yes?

MARQUIS: (*Taking leave of the ladies.*) It has been a great honor. . . . (*He exits.*)

MASTER: (*Amused.*) Your fable is immoral, Jacques, and I reject and renounce it, declare it null and void.

JACQUES: But you enjoyed it!

MASTER: That's beside the point! Who wouldn't? Of course I enjoyed it!

(*The Servants remove the table and chairs upstage. Jacques and his Master turn back to watch the platform. The Marquis goes up to the Innkeeper.*)

Scene 8

INNKEEPER: Tell me now, Marquis: Is there another woman in all of France who would do for you what I am doing?

MARQUIS: (*Kneeling before her.*) You are my one true friend. . . .

INNKEEPER: Let's change the subject. What does your heart tell you?

MARQUIS: I'll have that girl or perish.

INNKEEPER: I'd be very glad to save your life.

MARQUIS: I know it will upset you, but I must confess: I sent them a letter. And a jewel box filled with gems. But they sent both of them back.

INNKEEPER: (*Sternly.*) Love is corrupting you, Marquis. What have those two poor women done to you to make you so intent on defiling them? Do you really think that virtue can be bought with a handful of gems?

MARQUIS: (*Still on his knees.*) Forgive me.

INNKEEPER: I warned you. But you're incorrigible.

MARQUIS: Dear friend, I want to make one last try. I'm going to give them one of my houses in town and another in the country. I'm going to give them half of everything I possess.

INNKEEPER: As you wish . . . But honor has no price. I know these women.

(*She walks away from the Marquis, leaving him on his knees, and toward the Mother, who comes up to her from the other side of the platform and kneels before her.*)

MOTHER: Madame la Marquise, don't forbid us to accept his offer! So great a fortune! So great an estate! So great an honor!

INNKEEPER: (*To the Mother, still on her knees.*) Do you imagine I've done what

I've done for the sake of your happiness? You shall go and refuse the Marquis's offer at once.

JACQUES: What is she after now, that woman?

INNKEEPER: (*To Jacques.*) Whatever it may be, it's not likely to further the interests of the two women. They're nothing to her, Monsieur Jacques! (*To the Mother.*) Either you do as I say or I send you straight back to your brothel! (*She turns away from her and back toward the Marquis, who is still on his knees. The Mother rises and exits slowly.*)

MARQUIS: Dear friend, how right you were. They've refused. I'm at my wit's end. What shall I do? Ah, Marquise, do you know what I've decided? I've decided to marry her.

INNKEEPER: (*Feigning surprise.*) A serious move, Marquis. It deserves careful thought.

MARQUIS: To what end, Marquise? I can never be more unhappy than I am at present.

INNKEEPER: Don't be rash, Marquis. A hasty decision could ruin your entire life. . . . (*Pretending to think.*) Though they *are* virtuous, these women. Their hearts are pure as crystal . . . Perhaps you're right. Poverty is no crime.

MARQUIS: Go and see them, I beg of you, and tell them of my intentions.

(*The Innkeeper turns to the Marquis and offers him her hand. He rises, and the two stand face to face. The Marquis smiles.*)

INNKEEPER: Very well, then. I promise to do so.

MARQUIS: Thank you.

INNKEEPER: What wouldn't I do for you?

MARQUIS: (*In a rush of euphoria.*) Then why not, as my only true friend, why not join me and take a husband?

INNKEEPER: Have you someone in mind, Marquis?

MARQUIS: Why, the little count.

INNKEEPER: The dwarf?

MARQUIS: He's wealthy, witty . . .

INNKEEPER: And who will vouch for his fidelity? You, perhaps?

MARQUIS: One can easily do without fidelity in a husband.

INNKEEPER: No, no, not I. I'd be offended. And then, I'm vindictive.

MARQUIS: If you're vindictive, we'll have our revenge together. Yes, not a bad idea! Do you know what? We'll rent a town house and be a happy foursome.

INNKEEPER: Yes, not a bad idea.

MARQUIS: And if your dwarf gets on your nerves, we'll drop him in the flower vase on your bed table.

INNKEEPER: Your proposition is highly attractive, but I will not marry. The only man who could ever be my husband . . .

MARQUIS: Is the Marquis des Arcis?

INNKEEPER: I can admit it to you now fearlessly.

MARQUIS: And why did you say nothing before?

INNKEEPER: By the look of things, I was right not to. The woman you've chosen is much more suited to you.

(*The Daughter appears upstage in a white wedding gown and advances slowly. The Marquis sees her and moves toward her as if in a trance.*)

MARQUIS: Marquise, I'll be grateful to you in the grave. . . . (*When he reaches the Daughter, they freeze in a long embrace.*)

Scene 9

While the Marquis and the Daughter embrace, the Innkeeper moves backward to the other end of the platform without taking her eyes off the Marquis. At last she calls out to him.

INNKEEPER: Marquis! (*The Marquis fails to react. He is lost in his embrace.*) Marquis! (*The Marquis turns his head slightly.*) Were you satisfied with your wedding night?

JACQUES: Good God! And how!

INNKEEPER: I'm so glad. Now listen carefully. Once you had an honorable woman, but you were unable to hold on to her. I was that woman. (*Jacques begins to laugh.*) I have avenged myself by inducing you to marry the sort of woman you deserve. Pay a visit to the Rue de Hambourg and you'll learn how your wife earned her living! Your wife and your mother-in-law! (*She bursts into a devilish laugh.*)

(*The Daughter throws herself at the Marquis's feet.*)

MARQUIS: You vile creature, you! . . .

DAUGHTER: (*At the Marquis's feet.*) Trample me, Monsieur, crush me! . . .

MARQUIS: Out, you vile creature! . . .

DAUGHTER: Do as you will with me! . . .

INNKEEPER: Quickly, Marquis! To the Rue de Hambourg! And while you're there, have a plaque put up, a plaque that says: "The Marquis des Arcis slept here—with one and all." (*She laughs her devilish laugh again.*)

DAUGHTER: (*At the Marquis's feet.*) Have pity on me, Monsieur! . . .

(*As the Marquis kicks her away, she grabs hold of his leg, but he shakes her loose and exits. The Daughter remains on the ground.*)

JACQUES: Just a minute, Madame Innkeeper! That can't be the end of the story!

INNKEEPER: Of course it can. And don't you add one jot to it!

(Jacques leaps up on the platform and takes the place recently vacated by the Marquis. The Daughter grabs hold of his leg.)

DAUGHTER: Monsieur le Marquis, I implore you! Grant me at least the hope that you can forgive me!

JACQUES: Stand up.

DAUGHTER: *(On the ground, clutching his knees.)* Do with me as you see fit! I'll submit to anything!

JACQUES: *(In a sincere voice, moved.)* Please stand up, Madame . . . *(The Daughter does not dare stand.)* So many honorable girls turn into dishonorable women. Why not reverse the process for once? *(Tenderly.)* I firmly believe that debauchery has never tainted, no, never even touched you. Stand up. Don't you hear me? I've forgiven you. Even in the depths of disgrace I never ceased to think of you as my wife. Be honorable, be faithful, be happy, and make me happy. I ask nothing more of you. Stand up, dear wife. Madame la Marquise, stand up! Stand up, Madame des Arcis!

(The Daughter picks herself up, puts her arms around Jacques, and kisses him passionately.)

INNKEEPER: *(Calling out from the other side of the platform.)* She's a whore, Marquis!

JACQUES: Hold your tongue, Madame de La Pommeraye! *(To the Daughter.)* I've forgiven you and want you to know I have no regrets. As for that woman *(he nods in the direction of the Innkeeper)*, not only has she failed to avenge herself; she has done me an immense service. Are you not younger than she, more beautiful, and infinitely more devoted? And now, off to the country, where we're going to have years of happiness. *(He leads her across the platform, then stops and turns to the Innkeeper, dropping the role of Marquis.)* And I must tell you, Madame Innkeeper, they were very happy years. Because nothing on earth is certain, and the meaning of things changes as the wind blows. And the wind blows constantly, whether you know it or not. And the wind blows, and joy turns to sorrow, revenge to reward, and a loose woman becomes a faithful wife with whom none can compare. . . .

Scene 10

Toward the end of Jacques's speech, the Innkeeper comes down from the platform and takes a seat at the table where Jacques's Master is sitting. The Master puts his arm around her waist and drinks with her.

MASTER: Jacques, I don't like the way you've finished off the story! That girl doesn't deserve to be a marquise! She bears a striking resemblance to Agathe! A fine pair of cheats, those two.

JACQUES: You're mistaken, sir!

MASTER: What? I? Mistaken?

JACQUES: Badly mistaken.

MASTER: Since when has a Jacques the right to tell his master whether he's mistaken or not?

(*Leaving the Daughter, who exits during the following dialogue, Jacques leaps down from the platform.*)

JACQUES: I'm not merely "a Jacques." You've even been known to call me your friend.

MASTER: (*Fondling the Innkeeper.*) When I call you my friend, you're my friend. When I call you "a Jacques," you're "a Jacques." Because on high, and you know where that is, on high, as your captain used to say, on high it is written that I am your master. And I command you to retract your version of the story's conclusion, which displeases not only me but also Madame de La Pommeraye, whom I greatly respect (*he kisses the Innkeeper*) as a woman of nobility with a magnificent ass. . . .

JACQUES: Do you really believe, Master, that Jacques would retract a story he told?

MASTER: If his master so wills it, Jacques will retract his story!

JACQUES: That'll be the day, sir!

MASTER: (*Still fondling the Innkeeper.*) If Jacques persists in answering his master back, his master will send Jacques to the shed to sleep among the goats!

JACQUES: Well, I won't go!

MASTER: (*Kissing the Innkeeper.*) Yes you will.

JACQUES: No I won't.

MASTER: (*Loudly.*) Yes you will!

INNKEEPER: Would you do a favor for a lady you've just kissed, Monsieur?

MASTER: Anything her heart desires.

INNKEEPER: Then do stop quarreling with your servant. I realize he's insolent, but isn't that precisely what you need in a servant? It is written on high that the two of you will be unable to do without each other.

MASTER: (*To Jacques.*) Do you hear that, servant? Madame de La Pommeraye says I'll never be rid of you.

JACQUES: Oh, yes you will be rid of me, Master, because I'm off to spend the night with the goats.

MASTER: (*Standing up.*) No you're not!

JACQUES: Yes I am! (*He begins to exit slowly.*)

MASTER: No you're not!

JACQUES: Yes I am!

MASTER: Jacques! (*Jacques continues to exit, but more slowly.*) Jacques, my boy! (*Jacques continues to exit, but very slowly.*) Jacques, dear boy . . . (*The Master runs after him and grabs him by the arm.*) Well, did you hear that? What would I do without you?

JACQUES: All right, then. But to prevent future disputes, let's lay down our principles once and for all.

MASTER: Agreed.

JACQUES: So! Whereas it is written on high that I am indispensable to you, I shall exploit you whenever the opportunity arises.

MASTER: That's not written on high!

JACQUES: All of that was set down the moment our master invented us. It was he who decided that you would have appearance and I would have substance. That you would give the orders and I choose among them. That you would have power and I influence.

MASTER: If that's the case, then we're switching places.

JACQUES: And where would that get you? You'd lose appearance without gaining influence. Stay as you are, sir. And if you're a good master and do as I say, I promise not to be hard on you.

INNKEEPER: Amen. But now that night has fallen, it is written on high that we have drunk our fill and must go to bed.

ACT THREE

Scene 1

The stage is completely bare except for Jacques and his Master.

MASTER: Tell me, where are our horses?

JACQUES: No more silly questions, sir.

MASTER: It's utter nonsense! A Frenchman traveling through France on foot! Do you know who it is who dared rewrite our story?

JACQUES: An imbecile, sir. But now that our story is rewritten, we can't make any changes in it.

MASTER: Death to all who dare rewrite what has been written! Impale them and roast them over a slow fire! Castrate them and cut off their ears. My feet hurt.

JACQUES: Rewriters are never burnt, sir. Everybody believes them.

MASTER: You mean they'll believe the one who rewrote our story? They won't bother to read the original book to find out what we're really like?

JACQUES: Our story, sir, isn't the only thing that's been rewritten. Everything that's ever happened here below has been rewritten hundreds of times, and no one ever dreams of finding out what really happened. The history of mankind has been rewritten so often that people don't know who they are anymore.

MASTER: Why, that's appalling! Then they *(indicating the audience)* will believe we haven't even got any horses and had to trudge through our story like tramps?

JACQUES: *(Indicating the audience.)* They? They'll believe anything!

MASTER: You're in a bad mood today. We should have stayed on at the Great Stag.

JACQUES: Well, I was perfectly willing.

MASTER: Anyway . . . Mark my words. She wasn't born at any inn.

JACQUES: Where then?

MASTER: (*Dreamily.*) I don't know. But the way she spoke, the way she carried herself . . .

JACQUES: I do think, sir, that you're falling in love.

MASTER: (*Shrugging his shoulders.*) If it was written on high . . . (*Pause.*) Which reminds me. You still haven't finished telling me how *you* fell in love.

JACQUES: You shouldn't have given priority yesterday to the story of Madame de La Pommeraye.

MASTER: I let a great lady take precedence yesterday. You'll never understand chivalry. But now that you're alone with me, I give you priority.

JACQUES: Much obliged, sir. Now listen carefully. After I lost my virginity, I went out and got drunk. After I went out and got drunk, my father gave me a beating. After my father gave me a beating, I joined a passing regiment. . . .

MASTER: You're repeating yourself, Jacques!

JACQUES: Me? Repeating myself? Really, sir. There is nothing more shameful than repeating yourself. You shouldn't have said that to me. Now I won't open my mouth till the end of the performance.

MASTER: Please, Jacques, I implore you.

JACQUES: You implore me? Now you're imploring me?

MASTER: Yes.

JACQUES: All right, then. Where was I?

MASTER: Your father had just given you a beating. You joined a passing regiment. You ended up in a hut, where you were taken care of by a big-bottomed beauty. . . . (*He stops suddenly.*) Jacques . . . Listen to me, Jacques. . . . I want you to be frank with me. . . . Completely frank, understand? Is it true that that woman had a big ass, or are you just saying so to make me happy?

JACQUES: Why ask unnecessary questions, sir?

MASTER: (*Melancholy.*) Her bottom wasn't so big, was it?

JACQUES: (*Gently.*) Don't ask questions, sir. You know I don't like lying to you.

MASTER: (*Melancholy.*) So you led me astray, Jacques.

JACQUES: Don't hold it against me.

MASTER: (*Melancholy.*) Of course not, Jacques, my boy. I know you had my best interests at heart.

JACQUES: Yes, sir. I know how much women with big bottoms mean to you.

MASTER: You're a good man, Jacques. You're a good servant. Servants must be good and must tell their masters what they want to hear. Avoid unnecessary truths, Jacques.

JACQUES: Don't worry, sir. I don't like unnecessary truths. I know of nothing more stupid than an unnecessary truth.

MASTER: For example?

JACQUES: For example, that we are mortal. Or that the world is rotten. As if we had to be told. You know the sort who steps on the stage like a hero and cries, "The world is rotten!" Well, the audience applauds, but Jacques isn't interested, because Jacques knew it two hundred, four hundred, eight hundred years before him, and while he and his sort shout, "The world is rotten!" Jacques prefers to please his master. . . .

MASTER: . . . his rotten master . . .

JACQUES: . . . his rotten master, by inventing big-bottomed women of the kind he loves so well. . . .

MASTER: Only I know, I and the one up there, that you are the best servant of all servants who ever served.

JACQUES: So don't ask any questions, don't try to learn the truth. Just listen to me: She had a big bottom. . . . Wait a minute. Which one am I talking about?

MASTER: The one in the hut where they took you in.

JACQUES: Oh, yes. I spent a week in bed there, while the doctors drank up their wine. No wonder my benefactors wanted to get rid of me. Luckily, one of the doctors, a surgeon at the chateau, had a wife, who put in a good word for me, and I went to live with them.

MASTER: So there never was anything between you and the pretty woman from the hut.

JACQUES: No.

MASTER: What a shame. But never mind! Tell me about the doctor's wife, the one who put in the good word for you. What was she like?

JACQUES: Blond.

MASTER: Like Agathe.

JACQUES: Long legs.

MASTER: Like Agathe. And her bottom?

JACQUES: (*Showing him.*) Like this, sir!

MASTER: Agathe all over. (*With indignation.*) Oh, the slut! I'd have treated her a good deal worse than the Marquis des Arcis treated that little cheat of his! Or Young Bigre his Justine!

(*Saint-Ouen has appeared on the platform and is following the conversation between Jacques and his Master with great interest.*)

SAINT-OUEN: And why didn't you?

JACQUES: (*To his Master.*) Do you hear him mock you? He's a scoundrel, sir. I told you so the first time you mentioned him to me.

MASTER: He's a scoundrel, all right, but for the moment he's done no more than what you did to your friend Bigre.

JACQUES: Yet clearly only he is a scoundrel, not I.

MASTER: (*Struck by the veracity of Jacques's remark.*) Why, that's true. You both seduce your best friends' women, yet only he is a scoundrel, and not you. How do you explain that?

JACQUES: I don't know, sir. But I have a feeling that in the depths of that riddle there hides a profound truth.

MASTER: Of course! And I know what it is! The difference between the two of you is not in your deeds but in your souls. You cuckolded your friend Bigre, but then you drowned your sorrows.

JACQUES: I hate to destroy your illusions, but I wasn't drowning my sorrows, I was celebrating. . . .

MASTER: You mean you didn't get drunk out of remorse?

JACQUES: It's shameful, I know, but that's how it is.

MASTER: Jacques, would you do something for me?

JACQUES: For you? Anything you ask.

MASTER: Let's agree that you were drowning your sorrows.

JACQUES: If that is what you wish, sir.

MASTER: That is what I wish.

JACQUES: So be it, sir. I was drowning my sorrows.

MASTER: Thank you. I want to distinguish you as clearly as possible from that scoundrel (*turning toward Saint-Ouen, who is still on the platform*), who, by the way, was not content merely to cuckold me. . . . (*He mounts the platform.*)

Scene 2

SAINT-OUEN: Dear friend! The time has come to think of revenge! And since she has harmed us both, the wretch, I propose we avenge ourselves together!

JACQUES: Yes, I remember. That's where we left off. Well, sir! What did you tell the rat?

MASTER: (*Looking at Jacques from the platform, pathetically.*) What did I tell him? Look at me, Jacques. Look at me, my boy. Look at me and weep at my fate! (*To Saint-Ouen.*) Listen, Saint-Ouen, I'm willing to put your betrayal behind me on one condition.

JACQUES: Good for you, Master! Don't let him push you around!

SAINT-OUEN: Anything you say. Shall I jump out of the window? (*The Master smiles and does not respond.*) Hang myself? (*The Master does not respond.*) Drown myself? (*The Master does not respond.*) Plunge a knife into my breast? Yes, yes! (*He tears open his shirt, picks up a knife, and points it at his chest.*)

MASTER: Put down that knife. (*He grabs it from his hand.*) Come, let's have a drink, and then I'll reveal the severe condition you must satisfy to win my pardon. . . . So Agathe is as passionate as she looks!

SAINT-OUEN: Ah, if only you could know her as I do!

JACQUES: (*To Saint-Ouen.*) Has she got long legs?

SAINT-OUEN: (*To Jacques, softly.*) Not particularly.

JACQUES: And a nice big bottom?

SAINT-OUEN: (*The same.*) Flat as a board.

JACQUES: (*To his Master.*) I see you are a dreamer, sir, and love you all the more for it.

MASTER: (*To Saint-Ouen.*) Let me state my condition. While we empty this bottle, I want you to talk to me about Agathe. You'll tell me what she's like in bed, what she says. How she moves. What she does. Her sighs. You'll tell me, we'll drink, and I'll imagine it. . . . (*Saint-Ouen stares at the Master without responding.*) Well? Are you willing? What's the matter? Speak! (*Saint-Ouen remains silent.*) Do you hear me?

SAINT-OUEN: I do.

MASTER: Do you agree?

SAINT-OUEN: I do.

MASTER: Then why don't you drink?

SAINT-OUEN: I'm looking at you.

MASTER: I can see that.

SAINT-OUEN: We're the same height. In the dark, one of us could easily be mistaken for the other.

MASTER: Well, and what of it? Why don't you start? I want to imagine it! Damn it all, Saint-Ouen, I can't wait! I want you to tell me right now.

SAINT-OUEN: So you want me to describe a night with Agathe?

MASTER: You don't know what passion is! Yes, I want you to! Is that too much to ask?

SAINT-OUEN: On the contrary. It's a mere trifle. Indeed, what would you say if instead of describing the night, I gave you the night itself?

MASTER: The night itself? A real night?

SAINT-OUEN: (*Taking two keys from his pocket.*) The small one opens the front door; the large one, the door to Agathe's antechamber. I've been using them for six months, my friend. I stroll along the street until a potted basil plant appears in the window. I open the door of the house and close it quietly. Quietly I climb the stairs. Quietly I unlock the door. Off the antechamber is an alcove, where I undress. Agathe leaves the door to her bedchamber ajar and awaits me there in her bed, in the dark.

MASTER: And you'd let me take your place?

SAINT-OUEN: With all my heart. I have only one small request. . . .

MASTER: Name it!

SAINT-OUEN: May I?

MASTER: By all means. I want no more than to make you happy.

SAINT-OUEN: You're the best friend a man has ever had.

MASTER: No worse than you. Now then, what can I do for you.

SAINT-OUEN: I'd like you to remain in her arms until morning. Then I'll happen on the scene and surprise you.

MASTER: (*With a rather shocked little laugh.*) Splendid idea! But isn't it a bit cruel?

SAINT-OUEN: Cruel? Not very. Droll, actually. I, too, shall undress in the alcove, and when I surprise you, I'll be . . .

MASTER: Naked! Oh, the perfect profligate! But how shall we manage? We've only one set of keys. . . .

SAINT-OUEN: We enter the house together, undress together in the alcove, but you go in to her first. Then as soon as you're ready, you give me a signal and I join you!

MASTER: An excellent idea! It's divine!

SAINT-OUEN: Then you agree?

MASTER: Of course! But . . .

SAINT-OUEN: But . . .

MASTER: But . . . You see, I . . . No, no, I agree without reservation. Except that, well, since this is the first time, I'd actually prefer to be alone with her. . . . Perhaps later we could . . .

SAINT-OUEN: Ah, I see. You intend to avenge us several times over.

MASTER: The revenge is so sweet . . .

SAINT-OUEN: How true. (*He nods upstage, where Agathe is lying on a step. The Master moves toward her as if under a spell, and she holds her arms out to him.*) Careful! Quiet! The whole house is asleep! (*The Master lies down next to Agathe and takes her in his arms. . . .*)

JACQUES: I congratulate you, sir, but I fear for you.

SAINT-OUEN: (*From the platform, to Jacques.*) According to all the rules, my friend, a servant should rejoice to see his master duped.

JACQUES: My master is a good fellow; he does as I say. I don't like to see other masters, not such good fellows, leading him by the nose.

SAINT-OUEN: Your master is a moron and deserves a moron's fate.

JACQUES: In some ways perhaps he is a fool. But there's a gentle wisdom in his follies, a wisdom I don't find in your cleverness.

SAINT-OUEN: Well, well! A servant enamored of his master! Watch closely and see what this adventure gets him!

JACQUES: In the meantime he's happy, and I'm happy for him!

SAINT-OUEN: We shall see!

JACQUES: In the meantime he's happy, I tell you, and that's good enough for me. What more can one ask than to be happy in the meantime?

SAINT-OUEN: Well, he'll pay dearly for his moment of happiness!

JACQUES: But what if his moment of happiness is so great that even all the misfortunes you've prepared for him will not outweigh it?

SAINT-OUEN: Hold your tongue, servant! If I thought I'd given your dolt of a master more pleasure than pain, I'd indeed run this knife through my heart. (*He calls upstage into the wings.*) Quickly, there! Quickly! It's nearly daybreak!

Scene 3

A great commotion is heard offstage. Then a group of people, including Agathe's Mother and Father in nightclothes, and the Police Officer, rush over to the step where the Master and Agathe lie entwined.

POLICE OFFICER: Quiet, ladies and gentlemen! The evidence is conclusive. Caught in the act. The culprit, if I am not mistaken, is an aristocrat and an honorable man. I trust he will right this wrong on his own rather than wait till the law constrains him to it.

JACQUES: Good God, sir, now they've got you where they want you.

AGATHE'S FATHER: (*Holding back Agathe's Mother, who is trying to beat Agathe.*) Let her be! Everything will turn out for the best. . . .

AGATHE'S MOTHER: (*To the Master.*) You seemed so honorable. Who'd have thought that you would . . .

POLICE OFFICER: (*To the Master, who has in the meantime picked himself up from the step.*) Follow me, sir.

MASTER: And where do you propose to take me?

POLICE OFFICER: (*Leading him off.*) To prison.

JACQUES: (*Stunned.*) To prison?

MASTER: (*To Jacques.*) Yes, Jacques, my boy, to prison . . .

(*The Police Officer exits. The small group that had formed in the vicinity of the step disappears. The Master is alone on the platform. Saint-Ouen rushes over to him.*)

SAINT-OUEN: Oh, my dear, dear friend! How perfectly frightful! You, in prison! How can it be? I've just now come from Agathe's. Her parents refuse to speak to me. They know you're my only friend and blame me for their misfortune. Agathe nearly scratched out my eyes. You understand her position. . . .

MASTER: You alone, Saint-Ouen, can get me out.

SAINT-OUEN: But how?

MASTER: How? By telling the truth.

SAINT-OUEN: Yes, and I've threatened Agathe to do just that. But I can't go through with it. Think of what we two would look like. . . . Besides, it's all your fault!

MASTER: My fault?

SAINT-OUEN: Yes, yours! If you had agreed to my little nastiness, Agathe would have been caught between two men, and she would have ended up the fool. You were too selfish, my friend! You had to have her all to yourself!

MASTER: Saint-Ouen!

SAINT-OUEN: That's how it is, my friend. You're being punished for your selfishness.

MASTER: (*Reproachfully.*) My friend!

(*Saint-Ouen turns on his heel and exits.*)

JACQUES: (*Calling to the Master.*) Damn it all! When are you going to stop calling him your friend? Everybody knows that it was all a trap, that he was the one who denounced you! But no, you'll always be blind! And I'll be a laughingstock for having an imbecile for a master!

Scene 4

MASTER: (*Turning toward Jacques and stepping down from the platform during the speech.*) If only he were just an imbecile, Jacques, my boy. But he was unlucky besides, and that's worse. After I'd been released from prison, I had to cleanse their daughter's tainted honor with a considerable sum. . . .

JACQUES: (*By way of consolation.*) It could have been still worse, sir. Supposing the girl had been pregnant.

MASTER: You've guessed it.

JACQUES: What?

MASTER: Yes.

JACQUES: She was knocked up? (*The Master nods, and Jacques puts his arms around him.*) Master! My poor little master! Now I know the worst of endings of a story.

(*Throughout this scene, the dialogue between Jacques and his Master is imbued with genuine sadness and is completely free of comedy.*)

MASTER: Not only did I pay for that little tart's tainted honor, I was ordered to pay for her confinement, to say nothing of the maintenance and upbringing of a little brat who is the repellent image of my friend Saint-Ouen.

JACQUES: Now I know. The worst of endings of a human story is a brat. The sinister full stop at the end of the adventure. The blot at the end of love. And how old is he now, your son?

MASTER: Nearly ten. He's been in a village all this time, and I plan to stop off there on our travels, settle my account with the people keeping him, and have the little snot apprenticed.

JACQUES: Remember at the beginning when they (*he nods at the audience*) asked me where we were going and I answered, "Which of us knows where we're going?" Well, you knew all along, my sad little master.

MASTER: I think I'll make him a watchmaker. Or a carpenter. Yes, better a carpenter. He will make multitudes of chairs and multitudes of children and the children will make new chairs and new children who will beget new multitudes of children and chairs. . . .

JACQUES: And the world will be cluttered with chairs, and that will be your revenge.

MASTER: (*With disgust.*) The grass will cease to grow, the flowers to bloom, and everywhere there will be only children and chairs.

JACQUES: Children and chairs, chairs and children. It's a grim picture you paint of the future. How lucky we are, sir! We'll die in time.

MASTER: (*Pensively.*) I certainly hope so, Jacques, because there are times when I feel great anxiety at the thought of the continual repetition of children and chairs and all that. . . . You know what I wondered yesterday evening as I listened to the story of Madame de La Pommeraye? Whether it isn't always one and the same story. After all, Madame de La Pommeraye is merely a replica of Saint-Ouen, while I am no more than a version of your poor friend Bigre, who himself is but a counterpart of that dupe of a Marquis. And I see no difference whatever between Justine and Agathe, and Agathe is the double of the little whore the Marquis eventually married.

JACQUES: (*Pensively.*) Yes, sir, it's like a merry-go-round. You know, my grandfather, the one who kept me gagged and read the Bible every night, he didn't always like what he read, he would even say that the Bible repeated itself and that anyone who repeated himself took his listeners for idiots. And you know what I've been wondering, sir? Whether the one who does all the writing on high hasn't repeated himself an incredible amount and whether he, too, doesn't take us for idiots . . . (*Jacques falls silent, and the Master is too sad to respond. After a pause, Jacques tries to console him.*) But good God, sir, don't be so sad. What can I do to cheer you up? I know what, dear little Master. I'll tell you the story of how I fell in love.

MASTER: (*In a melancholy voice.*) Yes, tell me, Jacques, my boy.

JACQUES: The day I lost my virginity, I went out and got drunk.

MASTER: Yes, I know.

JACQUES: Oh, I'm sorry. Then I'll skip ahead to the surgeon's wife.

MASTER: So she's the one you fell in love with?

JACQUES: No.

MASTER: (*Looking around with sudden suspicion.*) Well, then, skip her too, and go on quickly.

JACQUES: Why are you in such a hurry all of a sudden?

MASTER: Something tells me, Jacques, that we haven't much time.

JACQUES: Sir, you scare me.

MASTER: Something tells me you'd better be quick about finishing your story.

JACQUES: Very well, sir. After a week's rest at the surgeon's, I went out for a walk. (*Jacques is absorbed in his story and looks more at the audience than at his Master, who becomes more and more interested in the countryside.*) It was a beautiful day, though I was still limping badly. . . .

MASTER: You know, Jacques, I think we're coming to the village where my bastard lives.

JACQUES: Sir, you're interrupting me at the most beautiful moment! I was still limping badly and my knee still throbbed, but it was a beautiful day, I can see it as if it were now. (*Saint-Ouen appears at the edge of the stage. He does not see the Master, but the Master sees and stares at him. Jacques is now completely absorbed in his story and looks straight out into the audience.*) It was autumn, sir, the trees were all different colors, the sky blue, and as I was walking along a path in the woods, I noticed a girl coming in my direction, and I'm very glad you haven't interrupted me, because it was a beautiful day and she was a beautiful girl, don't interrupt me now, sir, and as she walked toward me, slowly, slowly, I looked at her, and she looked at me, and I saw what a beautiful, melancholy face she had, sir, melancholy, it was, and so beautiful. . . .

SAINT-OUEN: (*Noticing the Master at last, taken aback.*) Oh, it's you, my friend. . . .

(*The Master draws his sword; Saint-Ouen follows suit.*)

MASTER: Yes, it is I! Your friend, the best friend you ever had! (*He lunges at him, and they begin to duel.*) What are you doing here? Come to have a look at your son, eh? Come to see if he's plump enough? If I've been giving him enough to eat?

JACQUES: (*Following the duel in terror.*) Careful, sir! Watch out! (*Before long, Saint-Ouen, run through by the Master, collapses. Jacques leans over him.*) I think he's had it. Oh, sir, why did this have to happen?

(*Jacques is still leaning over Saint-Ouen when a group of Peasants rushes onstage.*)

MASTER: Quickly, Jacques! Run! (*He runs off.*)

Scene 5

Jacques does not manage to escape. He is caught by several Peasants, who tie his hands behind his back. His hands bound, he stands at the edge of the stage while the Bailiff looks him up and down.

BAILIFF: Tell me, friend, what do you think of the prospect of being thrown into prison, tried, and hanged?

JACQUES: All I can tell you is what my captain used to tell me: Everything that happens here below is written first on high.

BAILIFF: A great truth . . . (*He and the Peasants exit slowly, leaving Jacques alone for his monologue.*)

JACQUES: Now, the value of what is written on high—that's another matter entirely. Oh, Master! I'm going to the gallows because you fell in love with that idiot Agathe. Where is the wisdom in that, Master? Now you'll never know how I fell in love. That beautiful, melancholy girl was a servant at the chateau, and then I too was hired as a servant there, but you'll never know the end of the story because I'm going to be hanged, her name was Denise and I loved her dearly, loved her as I never loved again, but we were together only a fortnight, can you imagine, sir, only a fortnight, a fortnight because my master at the time, who was both my master and hers, gave me to the Comte de Boulay, who then gave me to his elder brother, the Captain, who gave me to his nephew, the public prosecutor of Toulouse, who gave me to the Comte de Trouville, and the Comte de Trouville gave me to the Marquise du Belloy, who ran off to London with an Englishman, which caused quite a scandal, but just before fleeing she took the time to commend me to the Capitaine de Marty, yes, sir, the very captain who used to say that everything was written on high, and he gave me to Monsieur Herissant, who placed me with Mademoiselle Isselin, whom you, sir, were keeping at the time, but who got on your nerves because she was lean and hysterical, and whenever she got on your nerves I would make you laugh with my chatter, so you took a liking to me and would certainly have provided for me in my old age, because you promised to, and I know you'd have kept your word, we'd never have parted, we were made for each other. Jacques for his master, his master for Jacques. And here we are, separated, and for such a stupid prank! Good God, what do I care if you let that scoundrel get the better of you! Why must I hang for your good heart and bad taste! The stupidities written on high! Oh, Master, he who wrote our story on high must have been a very bad poet, the worst of bad poets, the king, the emperor of bad poets!

(*During Jacques's last few lines, Young Bigre appears at the edge of the stage. He stands staring at him questioningly, then calls to him.*)

YOUNG BIGRE: Jacques?

JACQUES: (*Without looking at him.*) Shove off, damn you!

YOUNG BIGRE: Is that you, Jacques?

JACQUES: Shove off, all of you! I'm talking to my master!

YOUNG BIGRE: Damn it, Jacques, don't you recognize me? (*He grabs hold of Jacques and turns him round to face him.*)

JACQUES: Bigre . . .

YOUNG BIGRE: Why are your hands tied?

JACQUES: They're going to hang me.

YOUNG BIGRE: Hang you? No . . . My friend! Fortunately there are still friends around who don't forget their friends! (*He undoes the rope binding Jacques's hands, swings him round to face him again, and puts his arms around him. They are still embracing when Jacques bursts out laughing.*) What are you laughing about?

JACQUES: Here I was, telling off a bad poet for being such a bad poet, and what does he do but quickly send me you to correct his bad poem. And I tell you, Bigre, even the worst of poets couldn't have come up with a more cheerful ending for his bad poem!

YOUNG BIGRE: I don't understand a word you're saying, my friend, but it doesn't matter! I've never forgotten you. Remember the attic? (*Now it is his turn to laugh. He gives Jacques a slap on the back. Jacques laughs with him.*) Do you see it? (*He points upstage to the attic.*) That's no attic, my boy! It's a chapel! It's a temple of true friendship! You have no idea, Jacques, how happy you made us! You enlisted in the army, remember? And, well, a month later I found out that Justine . . . (*He pauses significantly.*)

JACQUES: What about her?

YOUNG BIGRE: That Justine . . . (*he makes another eloquent pause*) . . . was going to have . . . (*He pauses once more.*) Well, guess! . . . A baby.

JACQUES: And it was a month after I enlisted that you found out about it?

YOUNG BIGRE: What could my father say? He had no choice but to let me marry her. And eight months later . . . (*He makes an eloquent pause.*)

JACQUES: What was it?

YOUNG BIGRE: A boy!

JACQUES: How is he doing?

YOUNG BIGRE: (*Proudly.*) Fine, just fine! We named him Jacques in your honor! And believe it or not, he even looks a little like you. You'll have to come and see him! Justine will be thrilled!

JACQUES: (*Looking back.*) Dear little Master, our stories look laughably alike . . . . (*Young Bigre leads him off with great glee.*)

Scene 6

MASTER: (*Entering the bare stage and calling out unhappily.*) Jacques! Jacques, my boy! (*He looks around.*) Ever since I lost you, the stage is as bare as the world and the world as bare as an empty stage. . . . What I wouldn't give to hear you tell the fable of the Knife and the Sheath again. That disgusting fable. Then I could reject and renounce it and declare it null and void, and you could tell it again and tell it each time as if it were the first. . . . Oh, Jacques, my boy, if only I could reject the story of Saint-Ouen like that! . . .

But only your wonderful stories can be revoked; my stupid intrigue is ir-revocable. And I'm in it by myself, without you and the splendid asses you evoked with your sweet rambling lips. . . . (*He dreamily recites the following line as if it were from an ode.*) Hail, voluptuous rumps! Hail, resplendent full moons! . . . (*In his usual voice.*) You were right, you know. None of us knows where we're going. I thought I'd have a look at my bastard, and in-stead lost my dear little Jacques.

JACQUES: (*Coming up to the Master from the other side.*) My little Master . . .

MASTER: (*Turning toward Jacques, amazed.*) Jacques!

JACQUES: Remember what that noble female of an innkeeper with the big bottom said about us: We can't live without each other. (*The Master is over-come with emotion. He falls into Jacques's arms, and Jacques comforts him.*) There, there. Now tell me, where are we going?

MASTER: Which of us knows where we're going?

JACQUES: Nobody knows.

MASTER: No one.

JACQUES: You lead the way, then.

MASTER: How can I lead the way if we don't know where we're going?

JACQUES: Because it's written on high. You are my master and it's your duty to lead.

MASTER: True, but haven't you forgotten what's written a bit farther on? That the master gives the orders, but Jacques chooses among them. Well? I'm waiting!

JACQUES: All right, then. I want you to lead me . . . forward. . . .

MASTER: (*Looking around, highly embarrassed.*) Very well, but where is forward?

JACQUES: Let me tell you a great secret. One of mankind's oldest tricks. For-ward is anywhere.

MASTER: (*Turning his head round in a circle.*) Anywhere?

JACQUES: (*Making a large circle with one arm.*) Anywhere you look, it's all for-ward!

MASTER: (*Without enthusiasm.*) Why, that's splendid, Jacques! That's splendid! (*He turns around slowly in place.*)

JACQUES: (*Melancholy.*) Yes, sir. I find it quite wonderful myself.

MASTER: (*After a brief bit of stage business, sadly.*) Well then, Jacques, forward!

(*They exit diagonally upstage.*)

END

Protest

Václav Havel

translated and adapted by Vera Blackwell

Martha Swope

PROTEST
[Public Theater, New York, U.S.A]
Directed by Lee Grant

Stanek's ground-floor study in his house on the outskirts of Prague. The house is surrounded by a garden.

Doorbell. The front door is opened.

STANEK: (*Loud, cordial.*) Vanek!—Hello!

(*The front door is closed.*)

VANEK: (*Noncommittal.*) Hello, Mr. Stanek—
STANEK: Come in, come in! (*Pause. Sudden outburst of emotion.*) Vanek! My dear
    fellow! (*Pause. Conversationally.*) Did you have trouble finding it?
VANEK: Not really—
STANEK: Forgot to mention the flowering magnolias. That's how you know
    it's my house. Superb, aren't they?
VANEK: Yes—
STANEK: I managed to double their blossoms in less than three years, com-
    pared to the previous owner. Have you magnolias in your garden?
VANEK: No—
STANEK: You must have them! I'm going to find you two quality saplings and
    I'll come and plant them for you personally. (*Crosses to the bar.*) How about
    some brandy?
VANEK: I'd rather not, Mr. Stanek, if you don't mind—
STANEK: Come on, Vanek! Just a token one. Eh?

(*Two drinks are poured.*)

VANEK: (*Sighs.*)

STANEK: Here we are. Well—here's to our reunion!

VANEK: Cheers—

(*Both drink.*)

VANEK: (*Shudders slightly. Emits a soft groan.*)

STANEK: I was afraid you weren't going to come.

VANEK: Why?

STANEK: Well, I mean, things got mixed up in an odd sort of way—What?— Won't you sit down?

VANEK: (*Sits down in an armchair, placing his briefcase on the floor beside him.*) Thanks—

STANEK: (*Sinks into an armchair opposite Vanek with a sigh.*) That's more like it! Peanuts?

VANEK: No, thanks—

STANEK: (*Helps himself. Munching.*) You haven't changed much in all these years, you know?

VANEK: Neither have you—

STANEK: Me? Come on! Getting on for fifty, going gray, aches and pains set-ting in—Not as we used to be, eh? And the present times don't make one feel any better either, what? When did we see each other last, actually?

VANEK: I don't know—

STANEK: Wasn't it at your last opening night?

VANEK: Could be—

STANEK: Seems like another age! We had a bit of an argument—

VANEK: Did we?

STANEK: You took me to task for my illusions and my over-optimism. Good Lord! How often since then I've had to admit to myself you were right! Of course, in those days I still believed that in spite of everything some of the ideals of my youth could be salvaged and I took you for àn incorrigible pessimist.

VANEK: But I'm not a pessimist—

STANEK: You see, everything's turned around! (*Short pause.*) Are you—alone?

VANEK: How do you mean, alone?

STANEK: Well, isn't there somebody—you know—

VANEK: Following me?

STANEK: Not that I care! After all, it was me who rang you up, right?

VANEK: I haven't noticed anybody—

STANEK: By the way, suppose you want to shake them off one of these days, you know the best place to do it?

VANEK: No—

STANEK: A department store. You mingle with the crowd, then at a moment

when they aren't looking you sneak into the loo and wait there for about
two hours. They become convinced you managed to slip out through a side
entrance and they give up. You must try it out sometime!

VANEK: (*Pause.*) Seems very peaceful here—

STANEK: That's why we moved here. It was simply impossible to go on writing
near that railway station! We've been here three years, you know. Of
course, my greatest joy is the garden. I'll show you around later—I'm
afraid I'm going to boast a little—

VANEK: You do the gardening yourself?

STANEK: It's become my greatest private passion these days. Keep puttering
about out there almost every day. Just now I've been rejuvenating the
apricots. Developed my own method, you see, based on a mixture of
natural and artificial fertilizers plus a special way of waxless grafting. You
won't believe the results I get! I'll find some cuttings for you later on—
(*Opens a large silver box on coffee table between them.*) Would you like a cigarette?

VANEK: Thanks—

(*Clicking of lighter.*)

VANEK: (*Exhales.*)

STANEK: (*Sips his brandy.*) Well now, Ferdinand, tell me—How *are* you?

VANEK: All right, thanks—

STANEK: Do they leave you alone—at least now and then?

VANEK: It depends—

STANEK: (*Short pause.*) And how was it in there?

VANEK: Where?

STANEK: Can our sort bear it at all?

VANEK: You mean prison? What else can one do?

STANEK: As far as I recall you used to be bothered by hemorrhoids. Must have
been terrible, considering the hygiene in there.

VANEK: They gave me suppositories—

STANEK: You ought to have them operated on, you know. It so happens a
friend of mine is our greatest hemorrhoids specialist. Works real miracles.
I'll arrange it for you.

VANEK: Thanks—

STANEK: (*Short pause.*) You know, sometimes it all seems like a beautiful
dream—all the exciting opening nights, private views, lectures, meetings
—the endless discussions about literature and art! All the energy, the
hopes, plans, activities, ideas—the wine-bars crowded with friends, the
wild booze-ups, the madcap affrays in the small hours, the jolly girls
dancing attendance on us! And the mountains of work we managed to get
done, regardless!—That's all over now. It'll never come back!

(*Pause. They both drink.*)

STANEK: Did they beat you?

VANEK: No—

STANEK: Do they beat people up in there?

VANEK: Sometimes. But not the politicals—

STANEK: I thought about you a great deal!

VANEK: Thank you—

STANEK: (*Short pause.*) I bet in those days it never even occurred to you—

VANEK: What?

STANEK: How it'll all end up! I bet not even you had guessed that!

VANEK: Mmnn—

STANEK: It's disgusting, old boy, disgusting! The nation is governed by scum! And the people? Can this really be the same nation which not very long ago behaved so magnificently! All that horrible cringing, bowing and scraping! The selfishness, corruption and fear wherever you turn! Good Lord! What have they made of us, old boy? Can this really be us? Is this still ourselves at all?

VANEK: I don't believe things are as black as all that—

STANEK: Forgive me, Ferdinand, but you don't happen to live in a normal environment. All you know are people who manage to resist this rot. You just keep on supporting and encouraging each other. You've no idea the sort of environment I've got to put up with! Makes you sick at your stomach!

VANEK: You mean television?

STANEK: In television, in the film studios—you name it.

VANEK: There was a piece by you on the box the other day—

STANEK: You can't imagine what an ordeal that was! First they kept blocking it for over a year, then they started changing it around—changed my whole opening and the entire closing sequence! You wouldn't believe the trifles they find objectionable these days! Nothing but sterility and intrigues, intrigues and sterility! How often I tell myself—wrap it up, chum, forget it, go hide somewhere—grow apricots—

VANEK: I know what you mean—

STANEK: The thing is though, one can't help wondering whether one's got the right to this sort of escape. Supposing even the little one might be able to accomplish today can, in spite of everything, help someone in some way, at least give him a bit of encouragement, uplift him a little—Let me bring you a pair of slippers.

VANEK: Slippers? Why?

STANEK: You can't be comfortable in those boots.

VANEK: I'm all right—

STANEK: Are you sure?

VANEK: Yes. Really—

(*They both drink.*)

STANEK: (*Pause.*) How about drugs? Did they give you any?

VANEK: No—

STANEK: No dubious injections?

VANEK: Only some vitamin ones—

STANEK: I bet there's some funny stuff in the food!

VANEK: Just bromine against sex—

STANEK: But surely they tried to break you down somehow!

VANEK: Well—

STANEK: If you'd rather not talk about it, it's all right with me.

VANEK: Well, in a way, that's the whole point of pre-trial interrogations, isn't it? To take one down a peg or two—

STANEK: And to make one talk!

VANEK: Mmnn—

STANEK: If they should haul me in for questioning—which sooner or later is bound to happen—you know what I'm going to do?

VANEK: What?

STANEK: Simply not answer any of their questions! Refuse to talk to them at all! That's by far the best way. Least one can be quite sure one didn't say anything one ought not to have said!

VANEK: Mmnn—

STANEK: Anyway, you must have steel nerves to be able to bear it all and in addition to keep doing the things you do.

VANEK: Like what?

STANEK: Well, I mean all the protests, petitions, letters—the whole fight for human rights! I mean the things you and your friends keep on doing—

VANEK: I'm not doing so much—

STANEK: Now don't be too modest, Ferdinand! I follow everything that's going on! I know! If everybody did what you do the situation would be quite different! And that's a fact. It's extremely important there should be at least a few people here who aren't afraid to speak the truth aloud, to defend others, to call a spade a spade! What I'm going to say might sound a bit solemn perhaps, but frankly, the way I see it, you and your friends have taken on an almost superhuman task: to preserve and to carry the remains, the remnant of moral conscience through the present quagmire! The thread you're spinning may be thin, but—who knows—perhaps the hope of a moral rebirth of the nation hangs on it.

VANEK: You exaggerate—

STANEK: Well, that's how I see it, anyway.

VANEK: Surely our hope lies in all the decent people—

STANEK: But how many are there still around? How many?

VANEK: Enough—

STANEK: Are there? Even so, it's you and your friends who are the most exposed to view.

VANEK: And isn't that precisely what makes it easier for us?

STANEK: I wouldn't say so. The more you're exposed, the more responsibility you have towards all those who know about you, trust you, rely on you and look up to you, because to some extent you keep upholding their honor, too! (*Gets up.*) I'll get you those slippers!

VANEK: Please don't bother—

STANEK: I insist. I feel uncomfortable just looking at your boots.

(*Pause. Stanek returns with slippers.*)

VANEK: (*Sighs.*)

STANEK: Here you are. Do take those ugly things off, I beg you. Let me— (*Tries to take off Vanek's boots.*) Won't you let me—Hold still—

VANEK: (*Embarrassed.*) No—please don't—no—I'll do it— (*Struggles out of his boots, slips on slippers.*) There—Nice, aren't they? Thank you very much.

STANEK: Good gracious, Ferdinand, what for?— (*Hovering over Vanek.*) Some more brandy?

VANEK: No more for me, thanks—

STANEK: Oh, come on. Give me your glass!

VANEK: I'm sorry, I'm not feeling too well—

STANEK: Lost the habit inside, is that it?

VANEK: Could be—But the point is—last night, you see—

STANEK: Ah, that's what it is. Had a drop too many, eh?

VANEK: Mmnn—

STANEK: I understand. (*Returns to his chair.*) By the way, you know the new wine-bar, "The Shaggy Dog"?

VANEK: No—

STANEK: You don't? Listen, the wine there comes straight from the cask, it's not expensive and usually it isn't crowded. Really charming spot, you know, thanks to a handful of fairly good artists who were permitted—believe it or not—to do the interior decoration. I can warmly recommend it to you. Lovely place. Where did you go, then?

VANEK: Well, we did a little pub-crawling, my friend Landovský and I—

STANEK: Oh, I see! You were with Landovský, were you? Well! In that case, I'm not at all surprised you came to a sticky end! He's a first class actor, but once he starts drinking—that's it! Surely you can take one more brandy! Right?

VANEK: (*Sighs.*)

(*Drinks poured. They both drink.*)

VANEK: (*Shudders, emits a soft groan.*)

STANEK: (*Back in his armchair. Short pause.*) Well, how are things otherwise? You do any writing?

VANEK: Trying to—

STANEK: A play?

VANEK: A one-actor—

STANEK: Another autobiographical one?

VANEK: More or less—

STANEK: My wife and I read the one about the brewery the other day. We thought it was very amusing.

VANEK: I'm glad—

STANEK: Unfortunately we were given a rather bad copy. Somewhat illegible.

VANEK: I'm sorry—

STANEK: It's a really brilliant little piece! I mean it! Only the ending seemed to me a bit muddy. The whole thing wants to be brought to a more straightforward conclusion, that's all. No problem. You can do it.

(*Pause. Both drink. Vanek shudders.*)

STANEK: Well, how are things? How about Pavel? Do you see him?

VANEK: Yes—

STANEK: Does he do any writing?

VANEK: Just now he's finishing a one-actor, as well. It's supposed to be performed together with mine—

STANEK: Wait a minute. You don't mean to tell me you two have teamed up also as authors!

VANEK: More or less—

STANEK: Well, well!—Frankly, Ferdinand, try as I may, I don't get it. I don't. I simply can't understand this alliance of yours. Is it quite genuine on your part? Is it?—Good heavens! Pavel! I don't know! Just remember the way he started! We both belong to the same generation, Pavel and I, we've both —so to speak—spanned a similar arc of development, but I don't mind telling you that what he did in those days—Well! It was a bit too strong even for me!—Still, I suppose it's your business. You know best what you're doing.

VANEK: That's right—

(*Pause. Both drink.*)

STANEK: Is your wife fond of gladioli?

VANEK: I don't know. I think so—

STANEK: You won't find many places with such a large selection as mine. I've got thirty-two shades, whereas at a common or garden nursery you'll be lucky to find six. Do you think your wife would like me to send her some bulbs?

VANEK: I'm sure she would—

STANEK: There's still time to plant them, you know. (*Pause.*) Ferdinand—

VANEK: Yes?

STANEK: Weren't you surprised when I suddenly rang you up?

VANEK: A bit—

STANEK: I thought so. After all, I happen to be among those who've still managed to keep their heads above water and I quite understand that—because of this—you might want to keep a certain distance from me.

VANEK: No, not I—

STANEK: Perhaps not you yourself, but I realize that some of your friends believe that anyone who's still got some chance today has either abdicated morally, or is unforgivably fooling himself.

VANEK: I don't think so—

STANEK: I wouldn't blame you if you did, because I know only too well the grounds from which such prejudice could grow. (*An embarrassed pause.*) Ferdinand—

VANEK: Yes?

STANEK: I realize what a high price you have to pay for what you're doing. But please don't think it's all that easy for a man who's either so lucky, or so unfortunate as to be still tolerated by the official apparatus, and who—at the same time—wishes to live at peace with his conscience.

VANEK: I know what you mean—

STANEK: In some respects it may be even harder for him.

VANEK: I understand.

STANEK: Naturally, I didn't call you in order to justify myself! I don't really think there's any need. I called you, because I like you and I'd be sorry to see you sharing the prejudice which I assume exists among your friends.

VANEK: As far as I know nobody has ever said a bad word about you—

STANEK: Not even Pavel?

VANEK: No—

STANEK: (*Embarrassed pause.*) Ferdinand—

VANEK: Yes?

STANEK: Excuse me— (*Gets up. Crosses to the tape recorder. Switches it on. Soft, nondescript background music under the following dialogue. Stanek returns to his chair.*) Ferdinand, does the name Javurek mean anything to you?

VANEK: Our pop bard? I know him very well—

STANEK: So I expect you know what happened to him.

VANEK: Of course. They locked him up for telling a story during one of his performances. The story about the copper who meets a penguin in the street—

STANEK: Ridiculous, isn't it? It was just an excuse, that's all. The fact is, they hate his guts because he sings the way he does. Good Lord! The whole thing is so cruel, so ludicrous, so base!

VANEK: And cowardly—

STANEK: Right! And cowardly! Look, I've been trying to do something for the lad. I mean, I know a few chaps at the town council and at the prosecutor's office, but you know how it is. Promises, promises! They all say they're going to look into it, but the moment your back is turned they drop it like a hot potato, so they don't get their fingers burnt! Sickening, the way everybody looks out for number one!

VANEK: Still, I think it's nice of you to have tried to do something—

STANEK: My dear Ferdinand, I'm really not the sort of man your friends obviously take me for! Peanuts?

VANEK: No, thanks—

STANEK: (Short pause.) About Javurek—

VANEK: Yes?

STANEK: Since I didn't manage to accomplish anything through private intervention, it occurred to me perhaps it ought to be handled in a somewhat different way. You know what I mean. Simply write something—a protest or a petition? In fact, this is the main thing I wanted to discuss with you. Naturally, you're far more experienced in these matters than I. If this document contains a few fairly well-known signatures—like yours, for example—it's bound to be published somewhere abroad which might create some political pressure. Right? I mean, these things don't seem to impress them all that much, actually—but honestly, I don't see any other way to help the lad. Not to mention Annie—

VANEK: Annie?

STANEK: My daughter.

VANEK: Oh? Is that your daughter?

STANEK: That's right.

VANEK: Well, what about her?

STANEK: I thought you knew.

VANEK: Knew what?

STANEK: She's expecting. By Javurek—

VANEK: Oh, I see. That's why—

STANEK: Wait a minute! If you mean the case interests me merely because of family matters—

VANEK: I didn't mean that—

STANEK: But you just said—

VANEK: I only wanted to say, that's how you know about the case at all; you were explaining to me how you got to know about it. Frankly, I wouldn't have expected you to be familiar with the present pop scene. I'm sorry if it sounded as though I meant—

STANEK: I'd get involved in this case even if it was someone else expecting his child! No matter who—

VANEK: I know—

STANEK: (*Embarrassed pause.*) Well, what do you think about my idea of writing some sort of protest?

VANEK: Where did I leave my briefcase?

STANEK: (*Puzzled.*) By your chair—

VANEK: Oh, yes, of course— (*Opens his briefcase, rummages inside, finds what he was looking for, hands the document to Stanek.*) I guess this is the sort of thing you had in mind—

STANEK: What?

VANEK: Here—

STANEK: (*Grabs the document.*) What is it?

VANEK: Have a look—

STANEK: (*Glances at it.*) Good Lord! (*Reads carefully, clearly suprised, getting excited. Mumbles as he reads. Finishes his reading, flabbergasted.*) Well! Well, well! (*Jumps up, begins to pace about in some agitation, the document in his hand.*) Now isn't it marvelous! Marvelous!—That's a laugh, isn't it? Eh?—Good Lord! Here I was cudgeling my brains how to go about it, finally I take the plunge and consult you—and all this time you've had the whole thing wrapped up and ready! Isn't it marvelous? I knew I was doing the right thing when I turned to you! No question about it! (*Sits down, glances at the document, slams it with his hand.*) There! Precisely what I had in mind! Brief, to the point, fair, and yet emphatic. Manifestly the work of a professional! I'd be sweating over it for a whole day and I'd never come up with anything remotely like this!

VANEK: (*Mumbles in shy appreciation at the compliment.*)

STANEK: Listen, just a small point—here at the end—do you think "wilfulness" is the right word to use? Couldn't one find a milder synonym, perhaps? Somehow seems a bit misplaced, you know. I mean, the whole text is composed in very measured, factual terms—and this word here suddenly sticks out, sounds much too emotional, wouldn't you agree? Otherwise it's absolutely perfect. Maybe the second paragraph is somewhat superfluous, in fact it's just a rehash of the first one. Except for the reference here to Javurek's impact on nonconformist youth. Excellent! Well done! This must stay. How about putting it at the end instead of your "wilfulness"? Wouldn't that do the trick?—But these are just my personal impressions. Good heavens! Why should you listen to what I have to say! On the whole the text is excellent and no doubt it's going to hit the mark. Let me say again, Ferdinand, how much I admire you. Your knack for expressing the fundamental points of an issue, while avoiding all needless abuse, is indeed rare in these parts!

VANEK: Come on—you don't really mean that—

STANEK: Great piece of work! Thank you for letting me see it. Here— (*Hands the document back to Vanek.*) You better put it back in your briefcase. (*Drinks. Short pause.*) Anyway, it's good to know there's somebody around whom one can always turn to and rely on in a case like this.

VANEK: Good gracious, it's only natural, isn't it?

STANEK: It may seem so to you. But in the circles where I've to move such things aren't in the least natural! The natural response is much more likely to be the exact opposite. When a man gets into trouble everybody drops him as soon as possible, the lot of them. And out of fear for their own positions they try to convince all and sundry they've never had anything to do with him; on the contrary, they sized him up right away, they wouldn't have ever touched him with a barge pole! But why am I telling you all this, you know best the sort of thing that happens! Right? When you were in prison your long-time theatre pals held forth against you on the box. It was revolting!

VANEK: I'm not angry with them—

STANEK: But I am! And what's more I told them so. In no uncertain terms! You know, a man in my position learns to put up with a lot of things, but—if you'll forgive me—there are limits! I appreciate it might be awkward for you to blame the lads, as you happen to be the injured party. But listen to me, old boy. You've got to distance yourself from the affair, that's all! Just think! Once we, too, begin to tolerate this sort of muck—we're *de facto* assuming co-responsibility for the entire moral marasmus and indirectly contributing to its deeper penetration. Am I right?

VANEK: Mmnn—

STANEK: (*Short pause.*) Have you sent it off yet?

VANEK: We're still collecting signatures—

STANEK: How many have you got so far?

VANEK: About fifty—

STANEK: Fifty? Not bad! (*Short pause.*) Well, never mind, I've just missed the boat, that's all.

VANEK: You haven't—

STANEK: But the thing's already in hand, isn't it?

VANEK: Yes, but it's still open—I mean—

STANEK: All right, but now it's sure to be sent off and published, right? By the way, I wouldn't give it to any of the agencies, if I were you. They'll only print a measly little news item which is bound to be overlooked. Better hand it over directly to one of the big European papers, so the whole text gets published, including all the signatures!

VANEK: I know—

STANEK: (*Short pause.*) Do they already know about it?

VANEK: You mean the police?

STANEK: Yes.

VANEK: I don't think so. I suppose not—

STANEK: Look here, I don't want to give you any advice, but it seems to me you ought to wrap it up as soon as possible, else they'll get wind of what's going on and they'll find a way to stop it. Fifty signatures should be enough! Besides, what counts is not the number of signatures, but their significance.

VANEK: Each signature has its own significance!

STANEK: Absolutely, but as far as publicity abroad is concerned, it is essential that some well-known names are represented, right? Has Pavel signed?

VANEK: Yes—

STANEK: Good. His name—no matter what one may think of him personally—does mean something in the world today!

VANEK: No question—

STANEK: (*Short pause.*) Listen, Ferdinand—

VANEK: Yes?

STANEK: There's one more thing I wanted to discuss with you. It's a bit delicate, though—

VANEK: Oh?

STANEK: Look here, I'm no millionaire, you know, but so far I've been able to manage—

VANEK: Good for you—

STANEK: Well, I was thinking—I mean—I'd like to—Look, a lot of your friends have lost their jobs. I was thinking—Would you be prepared to accept from me a certain sum of money?

VANEK: That's very nice of you! Some of my friends indeed find themselves in a bit of a spot. But there are problems, you know. I mean, one is never quite sure how to go about it. Those who most need help are often the most reluctant to accept—

STANEK: You won't be able to work miracles with what I can afford, but I expect there are situations when every penny counts. (*Takes out his wallet, removes two banknotes, hesitates, adds a third, hands them to Vanek.*) Here—please —a small offering.

VANEK: Thank you very much. Let me thank you for all my friends—

STANEK: Gracious, we've got to help each other out, don't we? Peanuts?

VANEK: Not for me—

STANEK: (*Helps himself. Munching.*) Incidentally, there's no need for you to mention this little contribution comes from me. I don't wish to erect a monument to myself. I'm sure you've gathered that much by now, eh?

VANEK: Yes. Again many thanks—

STANEK: Well now, how about having a look at the garden?

VANEK: Mr. Stanek—

STANEK: Yes?

VANEK: We'd like to send it off tomorrow—

STANEK: What?

VANEK: The protest—

STANEK: Excellent! The sooner the better!

VANEK: So that today there's still—

STANEK: Today you should think about getting some sleep! That's the main thing! Don't forget you've a bit of a hangover after last night and tomorrow is going to be a hard day for you!

VANEK: I know. All I was going to say—

STANEK: Better go straight home and unplug the phone. Else Landovský rings you up again and heaven knows how you'll end up!

VANEK: Yes, I know. There're only a few signatures I've still got to collect—it won't take long. All I was going to say—I hope you'll agree with me—I mean, don't you think it would be helpful—As a matter of fact it would be sensational! After all, practically everybody's read your *Crash*!

STANEK: Oh, come on, Ferdinand! That was fifteen years ago!

VANEK: But it's never been forgotten!

STANEK: What do you mean—sensational?

VANEK: I'm sorry, I had the impression you'd actually like to—

STANEK: What?

VANEK: Participate—

STANEK: Participate? Wait a minute. Are you talking about the signatures? Is that what you're talking about?

VANEK: Yes—

STANEK: You mean I should—

VANEK: I'm sorry, but I had the impression—

STANEK: Good Lord! I'm going to have some more brandy. How about you?

VANEK: No, thanks—

STANEK: Suit yourself— (*Crosses to bar, pours himself a drink. Returns to his chair. Drinks. Pause.*) Now that's a laugh, isn't it?

VANEK: What's a laugh?

STANEK: For heaven's sake, can't you see how absurd it is? Eh? I ask you over hoping you might write something about Javurek's case, you come here and produce a finished text and what's more, one furnished with fifty signatures! I'm bowled over like a little child, can't believe my eyes and ears, I worry about ways to stop them from ruining your project—and all this time it hasn't occurred to me to do the one simple, natural thing which I should have done in the first place! I mean, at once sign the document myself! Well, you must admit it's absurd!

VANEK: Mmnn—

STANEK: Listen, Ferdinand, isn't this a really terrifying testimony to the situation into which we've been brought? Isn't it? Just think: even I, though I know it's rubbish, even I've got used to the idea that the signing of protests is the business of local specialists, professionals in solidarity, dissidents! While the rest of us—when we want to do something for the sake of ordinary human decency—automatically turn to you, as though you were a sort of service establishment for moral matters. In other words, we're here simply to keep our mouths shut and to be rewarded by the relative peace and quiet, whereas you're here to speak up for us and to be rewarded by kicks on earth and glory in the heavens! Perverse, isn't it?

VANEK: Mmnn—

STANEK: Of course it is! And they've managed to bring things to such a point that even a fairly intelligent and decent fellow—which, with your permission, I still think I am—is more or less ready to take this situation for granted! As though it was quite normal, perfectly natural! Sickening, isn't it? Sickening the depths we've reached! What do you say? Makes one puke, eh?

VANEK: Well—

STANEK: You think the nation can ever recover from all this?

VANEK: Hard to say—

STANEK: What can one do? What can one do? Well, seems clear, doesn't it? In theory, that is. Everybody should start with himself. What? However! Is this country inhabited only by Vaneks? It really doesn't seem that everybody can become a fighter for human rights.

VANEK: Not everybody, no—

STANEK: Where is it?

VANEK: What?

STANEK: The list of signatures, of course.

VANEK: (Embarrassed pause.) Mr. Stanek—

STANEK: Yes?

VANEK: Forgive me, but—I'm sorry, I've suddenly a funny feeling that perhaps—

STANEK: What funny feeling?

VANEK: I don't know—I feel very embarrassed—Well, it seems to me perhaps I wasn't being quite fair—

STANEK: In what way?

VANEK: Well, what I did—was a bit of a con trick—in a way—

STANEK: What are you talking about?

VANEK: I mean, first I let you talk, and only then I ask for your signature—I mean, after you're already sort of committed by what you've said before, you see—

STANEK: Are you suggesting that if I'd known you were collecting signatures for Javurek, I would never have started talking about him?

VANEK: No, that's not what I mean—

STANEK: Well, what do you mean?

VANEK: How shall I put it—

STANEK: Oh, come on! You mind I didn't organize the whole thing myself, is that it?

VANEK: No, that's not it—

STANEK: What is it then?

VANEK: Well, it seems to me it would've been a quite different matter if I'd come to you right away and asked for your signature. That way you would've had an option—

STANEK: And why didn't you come to me right away, actually? Was it because you'd simply written me off in advance?

VANEK: Well, I was thinking that in your position—

STANEK: Ah! There you are! You see? Now it's becoming clear what you really think of me, isn't it? You think that because now and then one of my pieces happens to be shown on the box, I'm no longer capable of the simplest act of solidarity!

VANEK: You misunderstand me—What I meant was—

STANEK: Let me tell you something, Ferdinand. (*Drinks. Short pause.*) Look here, if I've—willy-nilly—got used to the perverse idea that common decency and morality are the exclusive domain of the dissidents—then you've—willy-nilly—got used to the idea as well! That's why it never crossed your mind that certain values might be more important to me than my present position. But suppose even I wanted to be finally a free man, suppose even I wished to renew my inner integrity and shake off the yoke of humiliation and shame? It never entered your head that I might've been actually waiting for this very moment for years, what? You simply placed me once and for all among those hopeless cases, among those whom it would be pointless to count on in any way. Right? And now that you found I'm not entirely indifferent to the fate of others—you made that slip about my signature! But you saw at once what happened, and so you began to apologize to me. Good God! Don't you realize how you humiliate me? What if all this time I'd been hoping for an opportunity to act, to do something that would again make a man of me, help me to be once more at peace with myself, help me to find again the free play of my imagination and my lost sense of humor, rid me of the need to escape my traumas by minding the apricots and the blooming magnolias! Suppose even I prefer to live in truth! What if I want to return from the world of custom-made literature and the proto-culture of the box to the world of art which isn't geared to serve anyone at all?

VANEK: I'm sorry—forgive me! I didn't mean to hurt your feelings—Wait a minute, I'll—Just a moment— (*Rummages in his briefcase, extracts the list of signatures from among his papers and hands it to Stanek.*) Here you are, Mr. Stanek—

STANEK: What is it? The signatures?

VANEK: Yes—

STANEK: Ah! Good. (*Peruses the list, mumbles, nods, gets up, begins to pace around.*) Let me think aloud. May I?

VANEK: By all means—

STANEK: (*Halts, drinks, begins to pace again as he talks.*) I believe I've already covered the main points concerning the subjective side of the matter. If I sign the document, I'm going to regain—after years of being continually sick at my stomach—my self-esteem, my lost freedom, my honor, and perhaps even some regard among those close to me. I'll leave behind the insoluble dilemmas, forced on me by the conflict between my concern for my position and my conscience. I'll be able to face with equanimity Annie, myself, and even that lad when he comes back. It'll cost me my job. Though my job brings me no satisfaction—on the contrary, it brings me shame—nevertheless, it does support me and my family a great deal better than if I were to become a night watchman. It's more than likely that my son won't be permitted to continue his studies. On the other hand, I'm sure he's going to have more respect for me that way, than if his permission to study was bought by my refusal to sign the protest for Javurek. He happens to worship Javurek, as a matter of fact. He's crazy about him! (*Sighs with some exasperation.*) —Well then. This is the subjective side of the matter. Now how about the objective side? What happens when—among the signatures of a few well-known dissidents and a handful of Javurek's teenage friends—there suddenly crops up—to everybody's surprise and against all expectation—my signature? The signature of a man who hasn't been heard from regarding civic affairs for years! Well? What? Let's think about it. My co-signatories—as well as many of those who don't sign documents of this sort, but who nonetheless deep down side with those who do—are naturally going to welcome my signature with pleasure. The closed circle of habitual signers—whose signatures, by the way, are already beginning to lose their clout, because they cost practically nothing. I mean, the people in question have long since lost all ways and means by which they could actually pay for their signatures. Right? Well, this circle will be broken. A new name will appear, a name the value of which depends precisely on its previous absence. And of course, I may add, on the high price paid for its appearance! So much for the objective "plus" of my prospective signature. Now what about the authorities? My signature is going to surprise, annoy and upset them for the very reasons which will bring joy to the other signatories. I mean, because it'll make a breach in the barrier the authorities have been building around your lot for so long and with such effort. All right. Let's see about Javurek. Concerning his case, I very much doubt my participation would significantly influence its outcome. And if so, I'm afraid it's more than likely going to have a negative effect. The authorities will be anxious to prove they haven't been panicked. They'll want to show that a surprise of this sort can't make them lose their cool. Which brings us to the consideration of what they're going to do to me. Surely, my signature is bound to have a much more significant influence on what happens in my case. No doubt, they're going to punish me far more cruelly than you'd expect. The point being that my punishment will serve them as a warning signal to all those who might be tempted to follow my example in the future, choose freedom, and thus swell the ranks of the dissidents. You may be sure they'll want to teach them a lesson! Show them what the score is! Right? The thing is—well, let's face it—they're no longer worried all that much about dissident activities within the confines of the established ghetto. In some respects they even seem to prod them on here and there. But! What they're really afraid of is any semblance of a crack in the fence around the ghetto! That's what really scares them! So they'll want to exorcize the bogey of a prospective epidemic of dissent by an exemplary punishment of myself. They'll want to nip it in the bud, that's all. (*Drinks. Pause.*) The last question I've got to ask myself is this: what sort of reaction to my signature can one expect among those who, in one way or another, have followed what you might call "the path of accommodation." I mean people who are, or ought to be, our main concern, because—I'm sure you'll agree—our hope for the future depends above all on whether or not it will be possible to awake them from their slumbers and to enlist them to take an active part in civic affairs. This is what really matters, isn't it? Well, I'm afraid that my signature is going to be received with absolute resentment by this crucial section of the populace. You know why? Because, as a matter of fact, these people secretly hate the dissidents. They've become their bad conscience, their living reproach! That's how they see the dissidents. And at the same time, they envy them their honor and their inner freedom, values which they themselves were denied by fate. This is why they never miss an opportunity to smear the dissidents. And precisely this opportunity is going to be offered to them by my signature. They're going to spread nasty rumors about you and your friends. They're going to say that you who have nothing more to lose—you who have long since landed at the bottom of the heap and, what's more, managed to make yourselves quite at home in there—are now trying to drag down to your own level an unfortunate man, a man who's so far been able to stay above the salt line. You're dragging him down—irresponsible as you are—without the slightest compunction, just for your own whim, just because you wish to irritate the authorities by creating a false impression that your ranks are being swelled! What do you care about losing him his job! Doesn't matter, does it? Or do you mean to suggest you'll find him a job down in the dump in which you yourselves exist? What? No—Ferdinand! I'm sorry. I'm afraid, I'm much too familiar with the way these people think! After all, I've got to live among them, day in day out. I know precisely what they're going to say. They'll say I'm your victim, shamelessly abused, misguided, led astray by your cynical appeal to my humanity! They'll say that in your ruthlessness you didn't shrink even from making use of my personal relationship to Javurek! And you know what? They're going to say that all the humane ideals you're constantly proclaiming have been tarnished by your treatment of me. That's the sort of reasoning one can expect from them! And I'm sure I don't have to tell you that the authorities are bound to support this interpretation, and to fan the coals as hard as they can! There are others, of course, somewhat more intelligent perhaps. These people might say that the extraordinary appearance of my signature among yours is actually counter-productive, in that it concentrates everybody's attention on my signature and away from the main issue concerning Javurek. They'll say it puts the whole protest in jeopardy, because one can't help asking oneself what was the purpose of the exercise: was it to help Javurek, or to parade a new-born dissident? I wouldn't be at all surprised if someone were to say that, as a matter of fact, Javurek was victimized by you and your friends. It might be suggested his personal tragedy only served you to further your ends—which are far removed from the fate of the unfortunate man. Furthermore, it'll be pointed out that by getting my signature you managed to dislodge me from the one area of operation—namely, backstage diplomacy, private intervention—where I've been so far able to maneuver and where I might have proved infinitely more helpful to Javurek in the end! I do hope you understand me, Ferdinand. I don't wish to exaggerate the importance of these opinions, nor am I prepared to become their slave. On the other hand, it seems to be in the interests of our case for me to take them into account. After all, it's a matter of a political decision and a good politician must consider all the issues which are likely to influence the end result of his action. Right? In these circumstances the question one must resolve is as follows: what do I prefer? Do I prefer the inner liberation which my signature is going to bring me, a liberation paid for—as it now turns out—by a basically negative objective impact—or do I choose the other alternative. I mean, the more beneficial effect which the protest would have without my signature, yet paid for by my bitter awareness that I've again—who knows, perhaps for the last time—missed a chance to shake off the bonds of shameful compromises in which I've been choking for years? In other words, if I'm to act indeed ethically—and I hope by now you've no doubt I want to do just that—which course should I take? Should I be guided by ruthless objective considerations, or by subjective inner feelings?

VANEK: Seems perfectly clear to me—
STANEK: And to me—
VANEK: So that you're going to—
STANEK: Unfortunately—
VANEK: Unfortunately?
STANEK: You thought I was—
VANEK: Forgive me, perhaps I didn't quite understand—
STANEK: I'm sorry if I've—
VANEK: Never mind—

STANEK: But I really believe—
VANEK: I know—

(*Stanek hands Vanek the list of signatures, crosses to the tape recorder, switches it off, returns to his chair, sits down.*)

VANEK: (*Puts papers back in his briefcase.*)

(*Both drink.*)

VANEK: (*Shudders. Emits a soft groan.*)
STANEK: (*Embarrassed pause.*) Are you angry?
VANEK: No—
STANEK: You don't agree, though—
VANEK: I respect your reasoning—
STANEK But what do you think?
VANEK: What should I think?
STANEK: That's obvious, isn't it?
VANEK: Is it?
STANEK: You think that when I saw all the signatures, I did, after all, get the wind up!
VANEK: I don't—
STANEK: I can see you do!
VANEK: I assure you—
STANEK: Why don't you level with me?! Don't you realize that your benevolent hypocrisy is actually far more insulting than if you gave it to me straight?! Or do you mean I'm not even worthy of your comment?!
VANEK: But I told you, didn't I, I respect your reasoning—
STANEK: I'm not an idiot, Vanek!
VANEK: Of course not—
STANEK: I know precisely what's behind your "respect"!
VANEK: What is?
STANEK: A feeling of moral superiority!
VANEK: You're wrong—
STANEK: Only, I'm not quite sure if you—you of all people—have any right to feel so superior!
VANEK: What do you mean?
STANEK: You know very well what I mean!
VANEK: I don't—
STANEK: Shall I tell you?
VANEK: Please do—
STANEK: (*Emphatic.*) Well! As far as I know, in prison you talked more than you should have!

VANEK: (*Gasps, jumps up, wildly staring at Stanek.*)
STANEK: (*Stares back in triumph.*) Right? (*Short tense pause.*)
VANEK: (*Almost inaudible.*) What??

(*The telephone rings.*)

VANEK: (*Broken, sinks back in his chair.*)
STANEK: (*Crosses to the phone, lifts the receiver.*) Hello—Yes—What?—Good
Lord! You mean—Wait a minute—I see—I see—Where are you?—Yes,
yes, of course—Absolutely!—Good!—You bet!—Sure—I'll be here
waiting for you! Bye bye. (*Replaces the receiver. Pauses. Returns to his chair. To
Vanek.*) You can go and burn it downstairs in the furnace!
VANEK: What?
STANEK: He's just walked into the canteen! To see Annie.
VANEK: Who did?
STANEK: Javurek! Who else?
VANEK: (*Jumps up.*) Javurek? You mean he was released? But that's wonderful! So your private intervention did work, after all! Just as well we didn't
send off the protest a few days earlier! I'm sure they would've got their
backs up and kept him inside!
STANEK: (*Pause. Stares at Vanek. Then suddenly cordial.*) My dear fellow, you
mustn't fret! There's always the risk that you can do more harm than good
by your activities! Right? Heavens, if you should worry about this sort of
thing, you'd never be able to do anything at all! Come, let me get you those
saplings—

END

Fire in the Basement

a fiery farce

Pavel Kohout

translated by Peter Stenberg and Marketa Goetz-Stankiewicz

Klaus Herzog

FIRE IN THE BASEMENT
[Stadttheater Aachen, Aachen, West Germany]
Directed by Volker K. Bauer

Dark. A sudden scream, which gradually dies away. Quiet. A light cuts across the foot board of a large double bed. A pair of naked legs, obviously female, are hanging over it. Far off in the distance the whine of a fire truck siren.

HIS VOICE: Grrr!
HER VOICE: Miow!
HIS VOICE: Grrr, grrr!
HER VOICE: Miiiiiow!
HIS VOICE: Grr, grr, grrr!
HER VOICE: (*Moaning.*) Miiowiiooowwwwooo!

(*The legs jerk up, give in, gradually sink and disappear behind the bedboard. The fire truck siren is much closer. A young man shows up behind the bedboard. Exhausted he leans his chest against the board and stretches out his hand. Light illuminates the whole set: a tiny basement room, a door on each side, in the back a window onto the street or courtyard, which lets in a little daylight. The room is very sparsely furnished; the walls are decorated with posters, and aside from the bed the only piece of furniture is a table. On it a glass and some empty soda and beer bottles as well as a pile of banana and orange peels. A bridal gown and a wedding suit are hanging on a clothes stand behind the bed. The young man rummages around in the banana peels until he finds a whole banana. He begins to peel it.*)

HER VOICE: Mrrrrra!

(*The young man stares at a fixed point; he is completely concerned with something behind the bedboard. But he continues to peel his banana.*)

ENGL: Quaquaqua . . .
HER VOICE: Mrrra, mrrrraaa!
ENGL: Quaquaquac . . .
HER VOICE: Mmmrrrraaaaaa!
ENGL: Yauyauyauyauhooooo!

(*He yells and disappears behind the bedboard. The siren wails again, this time very close by. The bed seems to be dancing to the craziest sounds, which come from it. This time two pairs of naked legs, remarkably intertwined, appear for a moment behind the bedboard just as the doorbell rings sharply. The legs freeze. The bell rings again. The legs plummet. His head and her head take their place above the bedboard. Both young people are about twenty. In contrast to the young man, who seems to be a small innocuous guy, she seems like a pretty big, tough girl; she has the banana in her mouth. The bell keeps ringing, though not continuously.*)

ENGL: Who's that?
JARTCHI: (*Throws the rest of the banana on the table.*) It must be your dopey
    friends.
ENGL: Ah come on. Where did you get that idea? Why them?
JARTCHI: You said they'd probably try something or other.
ENGL: All I said was that we should have invited them.
JARTCHI: Especially the chorus girls, right?

(*Pounding on the door.*)

JARTCHI: Nice friends you've got there!
ENGL: How do you know who's there?
JARTCHI: You don't know? So go open up. You can invite them right into
    bed.
ENGL: Why should I invite them into bed?
JARTCHI: You did say, we should have invited them, didn't you?
ENGL: Yeah, but I didn't say anything about bed.
JARTCHI: But why not? I'm sure they'd enjoy a return visit to such a familiar
    spot.
ENGL: Okay, okay, I'll open up, and then you can see for yourself about these
    fabled girls from the theatre, who I never had anything to do with.
JARTCHI: So it is them. It didn't take them long to find you, did it?
ENGL: How am I supposed to know if it's them!
JARTCHI: I thought you said you were going to open up.
ENGL: I only said that because you said . . . Jartchi, how can you be jealous
    already?
JARTCHI: Me? Jealous? Are you kidding? (*Disappears behind the bedboard.*)
ENGL: (*Listening.*) They're gone . . . Jartchi. Why would I want anybody else

when I've got you?! You know? Grrrrr . . . ! Well? Grrrrrr . . . ! What about it?

JARTCHI: Grouuuuu!

(*She drags him behind the bedboard. Her head and shoulders appear, this time from behind. Again meaningless noises, and the bed begins to shake. At this moment a metal pole sinks down through the basement window, and a fireman in full regalia comes sliding down. A powerful searchlight is attached to his helmet.*)

JARTCHI: (*Terrified.*) Help!

(*At the same time she pulls the covers out from under Engl, so abruptly that he flies on the floor. She throws the covers over her head and disappears behind the bedboard. Engl tries to cover up as quickly as possible and also hides behind the bedboard. The fireman runs around him to the door, and rattles the doorknob.*)

VODICKA: Keep it calm! Don't panic! (*Bends over the lock and yells in the direction of the basement window.*) Hurnik!
HURNIK: I'm listening.

(*Every time a fireman in the room speaks with one outside, he flips on the microphone, which is attached to the strap of his helmet at his throat. The voice is projected through a loudspeaker built into his helmet.*)

HURNIK: (*Above.*) Yeah!
VODICKA: The door splitter!
HURNIK: Roger. Will do!
VODICKA: (*Turning to Engl.*) Is there a child in there?
ENGL: (*Speechless, shakes his head.*)
VODICKA: Brothers or sisters?
ENGL: (*Shakes his head.*)

VODICKA: Any old folks?
ENGL: (*Shakes his head.*)

(*A gigantic fireman comes sliding down the pole. He is carrying a very large and very savage-looking axe.*)

VODICKA: Hurry up, Hurnik!
HURNIK: Will do! (*Runs to the door.*)
VODICKA: Relatives or friends?
ENGL: (*Shakes his head.*)
VODICKA: Subletters? Anybody else? Let's go, man!

ENGL: (*Finally manages to blurt out something.*) No . . .

(*While Hurnik fumbles around with the lock, another fireman comes sliding down the pole. His regalia is slightly less impressive than Vodicka's, and he is the only one who isn't wearing gloves. Instead he is holding between his teeth a roll of documents tied together with a string.*)

VODICKA: (*Immediately starts reporting to him.*) Imperiled persons—two!
TVRZNIK: Roger. Notice taken. Janik!
JANIK: (*From above.*) I'm listening.
TVRZNIK: To UPOR! Imperiled persons—two!
JANIK: Roger. Will be reported.

(*Hurnik smashes the axe into the door.*)

ENGL: What are you doing?
VODICKA: Don't worry! We got here just in time.
TVRZNIK: (*Pushes aside the pile of banana and orange peels on the table, unrolls his documents and straightens them out. They consist of a series of forms attached to a clipboard.*) Do you have a dog in there?
ENGL: What? No.
TVRZNIK: A cat?

(*Hurnik begins a rhythmical smashing of the door.*)

ENGL: Wait a minute! (*Jumps up, but ducks back behind the bedboard in the nick of time.*)
TVRZNIK: A cat?
ENGL: The key is in the lock!
VODICKA: Well, why didn't you say so in the first place? (*Unlocks the door, we see a staircase, which leads from the basement to the upstairs.*) There's no fire here! (*Locks it again, and followed by Hurnik, races to the other door.*)
TVRZNIK: A cat??
ENGL: What?
TVRZNIK: Do you have a cat in there??
ENGL: No, for God's sake!
VODICKA: (*Examining the lock.*) Janik!
JANIK: (*From above.*) I'm listening.
VODICKA: Lock explosives!
JANIK: Right away!
TVRZNIK: Canary?
ENGL: No.
TVRZNIK: Goldfish?

ENGL: No. Listen here, what the hell is . . .

(*A ladder is dropped down through the basement window. As Hurnik climbs up it, a young fireman with another savage-looking axe comes sliding down the pole. He and Hurnik have simple uniforms with a differing number of wires and helmets with searchlights.*)

VODICKA: Let's go, Janik!
JANIK: All set.
TVRZNIK: Other animals?

(*Janik smashes the second door with his axe.*)

ENGL: But that one's not even locked!
VODICKA: Well, why didn't you say so right off? (*Opens the door a hair, slams it immediately, and blows on his fingers, although he is wearing gloves.*) Oh boy!
TVRZNIK: Other animals?
VODICKA: Hurnik!
HURNIK: (*From above.*) I'm listening.
VODICKA: The asbestos stuff!
HURNIK: Will do!
ENGL: (*Finally getting control of himself.*) Jesus Christ, Jartchi! There's a fire in here! (*Shakes her behind the bedboard.*) Please help me out with her!
TVRZNIK: First things first. Other animals?
ENGL: No we're alone . . . Jartchi!
VODICKA: (*Holds a thermometer up to the door, yells at the window.*) Hurnik!
HURNIK: I'm listening.
VODICKA: Put on the Fahrenheit defense system! With boots!
HURNIK: Will do.
TVRZNIK: (*Has replaced the old form with a new one.*) Do you have any originals in here?
ENGL: What kind of . . .
TVRZNIK: a) paintings b) sculptures c) others?
ENGL: No, no we don't . . .
TVRZNIK: Objets d'art?
ENGL: No . . . Jartchi. I beg you to . . .

(*Janik climbs up the ladder as Hurnik slides down the pole. He is wearing an asbestos suit over his head and body, an eyeshield and asbestos boots. Various objects are dangling from his armor—things like asbestos pouches, etc.*)

TVRZNIK: Antiques?
ENGL: No.
TVRZNIK: Persian rugs or gobelins.

ENGL: Where would we get them? Can you hear me, Jartchi?

VODICKA: Do you use gas in there?

ENGL: Yes, I mean, no, not gas, we have . . .

TVRZNIK: Manuscripts or inventions?

ENGL: No.

VODICKA: Kerosene oven?

ENGL: No, but . . .

TVRZNIK: Family jewels?

ENGL: No.

VODICKA: Propane-butane?

ENGL: No, I mean, yes! We have a propane-butane!

VODICKA: (*Whistling in surprise.*) Stove?

ENGL: And an oven . . .

VODICKA: Janik!

JANIK: (*From above.*) I'm listening.

VODICKA: Jock strap.

JANIK: Will do.

TVRZNIK: Gold or silver?

ENGL: No, well—silverware.

TVRZNIK: Where?

ENGL: In the kitchen cabinet.

VODICKA: (*Below the basement window. Takes the jock strap and puts it on Hurnik.*) Yell, Hurnik!

HURNIK: (*Nods.*)

TVRZNIK: Value?

ENGL: Jartchi inherited it . . . Jartchi!

VODICKA: Bombs?

ENGL: What do you mean bombs?

VODICKA: The propane-butane! Gas bottles!

ENGL: Yes, Two! Jesus Christ . . .

VODICKA: (*Bellowing.*) Janik!

JANIK: (*From above.*) I'm listening.

VODICKA: The armor shield too.

JANIK: (*Whistles in disbelief.*) Right away.

TVRZNIK: Savings books?

ENGL: The bombs could go up any minute, couldn't they?

TVRZNIK: Savings books?

ENGL: (*Shaking the bedcovers.*) Jartchi, stop the baloney! We've got to get out of here.!—She's out like a light . . .

VODICKA: Listen, be glad. Somebody will turn her back on soon enough. Is it too tight, Hurnik?

HURNIK: (*Shakes his head.*)

(*Janik comes sliding down the pole and gives Hurnik something which looks like a medieval shield.*)

VODICKA: Ready, Hurnik?

HURNIK: (*Gives the thumbs-up sign.*)

TVRZNIK: Are there any savings books in there?

ENGL: No, there aren't.

VODICKA: Janik, the timing device! (*Janik takes a large alarm clock with a horn from his belt and hangs it on a hook next to the door.*) Timing device ready for action.

ENGL: Can't you at least help me to carry her out!

TVRZNIK: First things first. Other valuable items?

VODICKA: Set it at thirty.

JANIK: Set at thirty.

VODICKA: Hurnik, if the butane goes off, get out fast!

HURNIK: (*Nods.*)

TVRZNIK: Other valuable items?

ENGL: No, no . . .

VODICKA: Ready! three,—two—

JARTCHI: (*Bolts up behind the bedborad, and pokes her head out from under the bedcovers.*) What do you mean, no? All the money we have is in there!

VODICKA: (*Stops counting.*)

TVRZNIK: How much?

JARTCHI: More than five thousand! (*To Engl.*) I can't even afford to faint around here! You won't take care of anything!

TVRZNIK: Where?

JARTCHI: In the clothes closet! There's a kind of handbag with a chain on it. Please, try and get it!

VODICKA: Did you year that, Hurnik. Try to fight your way through to the handbag!

HURNIK: (*Nods and gives the thumbs-up sign.*)

VODICKA: Ready! Three-two-one-now!

(*Janik presses the alarm, the horn sounds. Vodicka opens the door slightly, and with Janik's help, pushes Hurnik in, and slams the door behind him. Janik climbs back up the ladder.*)

JARTCHI: I told you to put the money in the bank! Didn't I say that?

ENGL: Yeah sure, but how the hell was I supposed to know that . . .

JARTCHI: What are you, a man or a mouse? What if it all goes up in smoke?

TVRZNIK: (*Placing another form on the clipboard.*) Name?

ENGL: What? Oh . . . Engl.

TVRZNIK: Full name.

ENGL: Engl Jaroslav.

TVRZNIK: Papers!

ENGL: Papers . . . (*Searches around on his naked body.*)

TVRZNIK: Do you have your papers?
ENGL: Of course. Just a second.

(*Covers up with a pillow, gets out of bed and backs himself up to the clothes stand. With his free hand he rummages through the pockets of his wedding jacket.*)

JARTCHI: He lets five thousand crowns just burn up!
ENGL: But—
JARTCHI: Will you please just shut up!—What is it that caught fire?
JANIK: (*From above.*) Janik here, sir.
VODICKA: I'm listening.
JANIK: UPOR wants to know if we'll need the roof winch?
VODICKA: They can keep it for the time being.
JANIK: Roger.
VODICKA: Also all the floor winches and stuff.
JANIK: Roger.
VODICKA: The basement winch will be enough, if it's working.
JANIK: In working order, sir.
VODICKA: Bon. In a few minutes I will give the positional announcement.
JANIK: Roger. Will be reported.
ENGL: I must have left it on the kitchen cabinet.
JARTCHI: You're just impossible!
TVRZNIK: This is getting serious.
JARTCHI: He lets his papers just burn up!
TVRZNIK: Who's going to vouch for your identity?
ENGL: She will, of course! Jartchi . . . !
TVRZNIK: Hold it. I'll ask the questions around here.

(*The horn blows. Vodicka opens the door slightly. Hurnik, accompanied by a cloud of black smoke, stumbles out. Vodicka immediately slams the door behind him.*)

VODICKA: How does it look?
HURNIK: (*Gives the thumbs-down sign and begins to mumble incomprehensibly.*)
VODICKA: (*Puts his ear to the plexiglass shield, and listens attentively.*) Gotcha.
JARTCHI: Did he get the handbag?
TVRZNIK: First things first. (*To Engl.*) Start counting.
ENGL: What?
TVRZNIK: Start counting out loud, so you don't hear her. I want to check you over.
VODICKA: (*To Hurnik.*) Gotcha.
HURNIK: (*Mumbles on.*)
ENGL: Here, it's on my business card!
TVRZNIK: In so far as it's yours.

ENGL: Why shouldn't it be mine?

TVRZNIK: You're acting as if the fire were somewhere else. Keep counting.

ENGL: My God . . . (*Starts counting.*)

TVRZNIK: Louder!

ENGL: (*Counts more loudly.*)

VODICKA: Gotcha. Will be reported. Quiet here!

TVRZNIK: Quiet!!

ENGL: (*Stops counting.*)

JARTCHI: Did he find the handbag?

VODICKA: Janik!

JANIK: (*From above.*) I'm listening.

VODICKA: Communication for UPOR: Position report number one. Epicenter kitchen, steps six to seven, progressive tendency, visibility zero = zero, cause as yet undetermined, measures taken to localize. Commander Vodicka.

JANIK: Roger. Will be reported.

ENGL: What did that all mean?

VODICKA: That things are getting hot around here. Janik!

JANIK: I'm listening.

VODICKA: Hydrants and hoses. At least three rolls.

HURNIK: Will do.

(*Three sets of hoses come unrolling through the window. Vodicka disentangles them and gives Hurnik the nozzles.*)

JARTCHI: (*Leaps up. The bedsheet covers her like a toga.*) I hope you're not planning on shooting that thing around in here!

ENGL: They've got to put it out, Jartchi.

JARTCHI: (*Ignoring him.*) Listen, Commander, it's already so damp in here, we'll never get it dry. Isn't there any other way of putting it out?

VODICKA: Bon. (*Calls up.*) Come back, Hurnik! Take the Valkyrie!

JANIK: Will do.

(*Slides down the pole wearing on his back an apparatus that looks like a flamethrower.*)

VODICKA: Swiss invention. We don't like to use it much. Refills use up too much foreign currency. It smothers the flame, and finally you just sweep up the fire.

JARTCHI: You're a real pal. We'll repay you somehow.

VODICKA: I'm sure you will. We sure are pulling out all the stops for you!

JARTCHI: (*To Engl.*) Do you hear that? And you would have let them flood us out.

TVRZNIK: Keep counting!

ENGL: (*Starts counting again.*)

TVRZNIK: (*To Jartchi.*) What's your name?

JARTCHI: Jaroslava Englova.

TVRZNIK: (*To Engl.*) That'll do.

ENGL: (*Stops counting.*)

TVRZNIK: (*Pointing to Jartchi.*) What's her name?

ENGL: Jaroslava Schoberova.

JARTCHI: How could you forget that we're married?

ENGL: Englova! Sorry, in all this . . . I'm just . . .

JARTCHI: You really are hopeless.

ENGL: We just got married.

TVRZNIK: Do you have a marriage certificate?

ENGL: Of course . . . (*Searches through his jacket pocket again.*)

VODICKA: (*With Janik's help he has fastened the apparatus on Hurnik's back and now hands him the nozzle.*) Janik, adjustments!

JANIK: (*Turns a nozzle on the tank.*) Adjustments concluded.

VODICKA: Ready, Hurnik?

HURNIK: (*Gives the thumbs-up sign.*)

VODICKA: Timing device at one hundred twenty.

JANIK: (*Sets the alarm.*) One hundred and twenty it is.

JARTCHI: Please the handbag. It has a kind of chain on it.

VODICKA: Did you hear that, Hurnik? Try to fight your way through to the handbag.

HURNIK: (*Nods and gives the thumbs-up sign.*)

VODICKA: Three, two, one, now!

(*Janik presses the alarm. The horn sounds. Vodicka opens the door slightly. Smoke pours out. Janik and Vodicka shove Hurnik in and slam the door behind him. Janik climbs back up.*)

ENGL: (*Suddenly remembering.*) You've got it in the handbag!

TVRZNK: This is getting serious.

JARTCHI: Didn't I tell you to keep it yourself? Didn't I say that, huh?

ENGL: How was I supposed to know . . .

TVRZNIK: Sir!

VODICKA: I'm listening.

TVRZNIK: These people cannot produce any identification.

JARTCHI: He just lets the marriage certificate burn up!

VODICKA: Oh, oh, that looks bad.

JARTCHI: I can swear that he's really my husband.

TVRZNIK: In so far as you're his wife.

ENGL: But she is my wife.

TVRZNIK: In so far as you're her husband.

ENGL: But why should we want to lie to you?

VODICKA: No offense, Mister—okay what do I care—Engl. Have you ever heard of something called arson?

JARTCHI: Come on Commander. We wouldn't set fire to our own apartment!

TVRZNIK: In so far as it's your apartment!

ENGL: But of course it's our apartment!

TVRZNIK: Do you at least have the lease?

ENGL: Of course . . . Jartchi where's the lease?

JARTCHI: You had it!

ENGL: Then I gave it to you.

JARTCHI: To me?

ENGL: In your—in your handbag.

JARTCHI: Christ Almighty. Is there anything you didn't put in the handbag to burn up? He just . . .

TVRZNIK: First things first. Who's the apartment manager here?

ENGL & JARTCHI: (*To each other.*) Who's the apartment manager here?

TVRZNIK: Do you know any of the neighbors?

ENGL: We just moved in three days ago.

TVRZNIK: You must have run into somebody in three days.

ENGL: We haven't been out.

TVRZNIK: You were sick?

ENGL: No, we . . .

JARTCHI: (*To Vodicka.*) You must know by now what caught fire in there!

VODICKA: (*Listening at the door. Calls up.*) Janik!

JANIK: I'm listening.

VODICKA: Call UPOR. Tell them to send an ambulance fast in case the butane goes up.

JANIK: Will do. Will be reported.

ENGL: Shouldn't we get out of here?

TVRZNIK: Why haven't you been out in the last three days?

JARTCHI: (*Completely returned to normal.*) Is that so important right now? Why don't you help them put it out?

ENGL: Jartchi . . . !

VODICKA: My colleague Tvrznik is the fire damage inspector. He has nothing to do with the fires as such, just with their causes and consequences.

ENGL: Please, we didn't mean anything, it's just that it's all so . . .

VODICKA: Okay okay, we understand. It's not every day you have a fire.

JARTCHI: I'd like to know how the fire could break out in the kitchen! (*The sheet has slipped down over one of her shoulders.*)

TVRZNIK: Why don't you put some clothes on?

JARTCHI: Now just a second . . . Jarda!

TVRZNIK: You're her husband?

ENGL: That's right.

TVRZNIK: And you don't care if, and with strangers around, too . . .

VODICKA: My colleague Tvrznik just got married too. So you've got to be shown some understanding yourself.

ENGL: Please, put something on!

JARTCHI: What, may I ask? All my stuff is in the other room.

TVRZNIK: (*Pointing to the clothes stand.*) And who might this belong to?

JARTCHI: But that's my wedding dress!

VODICKA: If I were you, I'd put it on. Then at least you'll have something for the new start in case the butane goes up.

ENGL: Please, hurry up. (*Begins to get dressed himself.*)

JARTCHI: (*Getting unsteady; forces herself to the clothes stand, still wrapped up in the sheet.*) A great idea to put the clothes in the kitchen!

ENGL: But that was your . . .

JARTCHI: For Christ's sake, can't you stop talking. Why don't you tell me what could have caught fire in the kitchen!

JANIK: (*From above.*) Janik here, sir.

VODICKA: I'm listening.

JANIK: UPOR wants to know if we need lifesaving nets.

VODICKA: They can keep them.

JANIK: Roger.

VODICKA: And they can keep the chutes, too.

JANIK: Roger.

VODICKA: But we need all the outflow blockers and the sewer pipe rammer!

JANIK: Roger. Will be reported.

(*In the meantime Engl and Jartchi, squatting behind the bed, have put on their wedding clothes, which under the circumstances look pretty pathetic.*)

JARTCHI: Pull up my zipper at least!

ENGL: (*Doing it.*) Listen, shouldn't we get out of here?

TVRZNIK: Why didn't you go out for three days?

JARTCHI: Is that so difficult to figure out when we were married the day before yesterday.

TVRZNIK: In so far as you are married.

JARTCHI: Did you notice the clothes we're wearing?

TVRZNIK: In so far as they belong to you.

ENGL & JARTCHI: What?

TVRZNIK: In so far as the real groom and the real bride are not also . . . (*Points to the kitchen.*)

ENGL: But that's . . . that's really . . . Commander!

VODICKA: Mister—Okay, let's say—Engl, fire is the best detective because it often turns up at the right place at the right time. Once we had a case where a guy had knocked off his aunt, and just as he was pouring gas all over her, there's Hurnik hanging in his window in order to tell him that the house was on fire underneath him.

(*While Engl and Jartchi are speechless, the horn sounds twice. Vodicka opens the door a crack. Hurnik staggers out, accompanied by a cloud of black smoke. Vodicka slams the door behind him and supports Hurnik.*)

VODICKA: How does it look?
HURNIK: (*Gives the thumbs-down sign and mumbles.*)
VODICKA: (*Puts his ear to the plexiglass and listens.*) Gotcha.
JARTCHI: Did he get the handbag?
TVRZNIK: First things first. Miss—okay let's say Mrs. Englova, in so far as you are Mrs. Englova—, you must know what's behind this door.
JARTCHI: The kitchen, of course.
VODICKA: Is that right, Hurnik?
HURNIK: (*Nods.*)
TVRZNIK: What's in the kitchen?
JARTCH: Clothes cabinet, kitchen cabinet, refrigerator, and . . . the oven.
VODICKA: Hurnik?
HURNIK: (*Nods.*)
TVRZNIK: What's in the oven?
JARTCHI: Nothing.
TVRZNIK: And in the refrigerator?
JARTCHI: Vodka, beer and a roast duck.
VODICKA: This?

(*Hurnik lifts his hand. In it he is holding a charcoal object which might have been a bird at some point.*)

JARTCHI: Christ Almighty . . . is that what it's like in there . . . I thought you claimed you would just sweep it up . . . !
VODICKA: Where was this duck, Hurnik?
HURNIK: (*Mumbles.*)
VODICKA: Understood. Will be reported. Janik!
JANIK: (*From above.*) I'm listening.
VODICKA: To UPOR: Position report number two. Cause of fire: Oven with duck not turned off.
JANIK: Roger. Will be reported.
JARTCHI: (*Yelling.*) No! No! That's not . . .
VODICKA: Wait a second, Janik! Hold that report!
JANIK: Roger. I'm waiting.
JARTCHI: I'm absolutely sure that I turned off . . . that the duck . . .

(*Hurnik again holds up the charcoal skeleton, and Jartchi breaks down in despair. Engl on the other hand takes the opportunity to show himself to be master of the house.*)

ENGL: I told you to take the duck out. Did I tell you that or didn't I?

JARTCHI: (*Breaks into tears.*)

ENGL: And then she asks how the fire started!!

VODICKA: Oh don't blame the little woman too much, Mr. Engl. Things like this happen to people with more experience, too, you know. Once we had a case where a lady forgot to turn off the oven. She erred, she confessed and promised it'll never happen again. Right, young lady?

JARTCHI: (*Cries even more.*)

TVRZNIK: (*In the meantime he has filled out a sheet and hands it to Engl on the clipboard.*) Bottom left.

ENGL: Yes . . . (*Takes the pen from him and wants to sign.*)

TVRZNIK: Don't you want to read it through?

ENGL: No, what's the point . . . ?

VODICKA: Read it out loud, Tvrznik. You see how excited the two of them are.

TVRZNIK: Roger. (*Reads.*) ''The fire was caused by reckless neglect of the female renter of the apartment in failing to switch off duck in oven.''— Right?

ENGL: But that's pretty . . . Couldn't you somehow . . .

VODICKA: Somehow what?

ENGL: Somehow tone it down. For Jartchi's sake . . .

VODICKA: I like that, Mr. Engl. I like it when a family sticks together. Tvrznik, cut out ''in oven.'' It's not necessary.

TVRZNIK: Roger. (*Crosses something out.*)

VODICKA: How does it read now?

TVRZNIK: (*Reads.*)''The fire was caused by reckless neglect of the female renter of the apartment in failing to switch off duck.''

VODICKA: Okay. Satisfied, Mr. Engl?

ENGL: Yeah, sure, but . . . Does Jartchi have to be . . . I mean so directly . . .

VODICKA: I really like you for that, Mr. Engl. I wouldn't leave my wife in the lurch either. Tvrznik, cross out ''female renter of apartment.'' We don't have to know that.

TVRZNIK: Roger. (*Crosses something out.*)

VODICKA: How does it read now?

TVRZNIK: (*Reads.*) ''The fire was caused by reckless neglect in failing to switch off duck.''

VODICKA: Well, see. Everything's okay now, right?

ENGL: Yeah, sure . . . only . . .

VODICKA: Come on, out with it! Only what?

ENGL: Only if it wasn't so clearly stated that . . . that somebody was negligent.

VODICKA: I see. You know, Mr. Engl, our motto is: live and let live. We don't want to be harder on you than the fire was. If it will make you happy—Tvrznik, cross out "reckless neglect in failing to switch off."

TVRZNIK: Roger. (*Crosses something out.*)

VODICKA: And how does it read now?

TVRZNIK: (*Reads.*) "The fire was caused by duck"

VODICKA: Good. Let them try and figure that out!

ENGL: That's really nice of you.

TVRZNIK: (*Again hands him the paper with the clipboard.*) Bottom left, Mr . . . You are really Mr. Engl?

ENGL: (*Intently.*) I swear it! I wouldn't lie to you when you've been so decent to us! (*Signs.*)

TVRZNIK: I believe you. (*Handing the paper to Jartchi.*) Bottom left, Mrs . . . you are Mrs. Englova, aren't you?

JARTCHI: (*Nods while crying.*)

TVRZNIK: I believe you.

(*Jartchi signs. Vodicka tries the light switch on the wall. A light goes on and illuminates the whole mess.*)

VODICKA: You've got lights! Why didn't you say so right away?

(*Janik slides down the pole and helps Hurnik to take off his asbestos suit. Then the two of them begin to roll up the hoses.*)

ENGL: Could you please tell us how the clothes cabinet looks?

VODICKA: Hurnik?

HURNIK: I'm listening.

VODICKA: The clothes cabinet?

HURNIK: Kindling wood.

ENGL: And the kitchen cabinet?

HURNIK: Ashes.

JARTCHI: (*Holding back tears.*) And my handbag?

(*Hurnik gives Vodicka a piece of blackened chain, which he hands on to Jartchi. She starts crying again.*)

VODICKA: Don't cry, little lady . . . the insurance company will pay off for those few crowns and the other junk without a second look.

JARTCHI; (*Sobbing, to Engl.*) I told you to take care of the . . .

VODICKA: (*Whistling in amazement.*) What? You're not . . . ohohoh!

(Hurnik and Janik are alternatively sliding down the pole and climbing up the ladder. Gradually they clear the room of all the paraphernalia which they had previously brought in.)

ENGL: *(Again deflated.)* We had nothing worth . . .

JARTCHI: And for two years we saved up for this nothing! *(Starts crying again.)*

VODICKA: Tvrznik!

TVRZNIK: I'm listening.

VODICKA: Could we ah . . .

TVRZNIK: You're the boss, sir.

VODICKA: I think so. They're nice young people. We should try and help them out.

TVRZNIK: *(Bows, takes another form from his file, fastens it to the clipboard and hands it to Engl.)* Bottom right.

ENGL: *(Not believing his eyes.)* But that's a . . . Jartchi, it's an insurance policy!

JARTCHI: *(Stops crying, takes the form.)* Let me see that!

VODICKA: My colleague Tvrznik also moonlights for the insurance company as an assessor. It's only reasonable. One can't live by fires alone.

ENGL: But you can't do that—after the fact . . .

VODICKA: Who said anything about after the fact? Only the date is given, not the hour. You could have taken out the policy just before the fire broke out! Once we had a case where lightning struck during the actual signing.

JARTCHI: And they recognized the validity?

VODICKA: And how. My colleague Tvrznik enjoys complete confidence. And we testified as well.

ENGL: Only . . . this didn't happen before the fire . . .

VODICKA: Okay, if that's the way you want it, Mr. Engl. *(To Jartchi.)* Is he really your husband?

JARTCHI: Jarda, if you don't accept this offer . . .

VODICKA: Cool off—be glad that Mr. Engl has principles, young lady. Of course nobody would notice anything, but the more expensive the principles, the more you can enjoy them.

(Tvrznik starts to put the form away, but Jartchi stops his hand, takes the form from him and hands it to Engl.)

JARTCHI: I told you I'd only marry you if you stopped acting like an idiot. And you promised you would. Did you promise or not?

TVRZNIK: Bottom right.

ENGL: *(Signs.)*

JARTCHI: Me too?

VODICKA: The head of the family is sufficient—and I assume that that is Mr. Engl. The main thing is that you don't forget to pay the first premium, which is due today, and comes to . . .

TVRZNIK: Three hundred and twelve crowns.

ENGL: And where are we supposed to get that?

JARTCHI: I told you to put the money in the bank. I told you . . .

VODICKA: But listen kids. You're already burned out. What's the sense of fighting about it? Somebody will lend you the few crowns.

ENGL: If you hadn't chased away all my friends . . .

VODICKA: Wait a minute, wait a minute! Where there's smoke there doesn't have to be fire!

JARTCHI: Don't worry. I'll get the money somewhere, even if I have to start walking the streets. I'm just sorry the fire didn't reach this room. At least we could have bought a bed that hadn't been used!

VODICKA: Young lady, you know, I like you. That's why I want to tell you the following: You've been here for only three days, and nobody has even visited you. So we're the only ones who know what actually burned up.

JARTCHI: What do you mean?

VODICKA: Tvrznik . . .

TVRZNIK: I'm listening.

VODICKA: Could we . . .

TVRZNIK: You're the boss, sir.

VODICKA: Well, I just want the best for these two, because they're so nice and decent. It's actually surprising that you two don't own anything other than a refrigerator, a kitchen cabinet, a clothes cabinet and an oven with duck. We saw a bunch of other things here.

ENGL: What kind of things.

VODICKA: For example—Tvrznik!

TVRZNIK: (*Placing another form on the clipboard and reading aloud.*) An Empire trumeau.

ENGL: What's that?

TVRZNIK: (*Reads.*) A small antique table with mirror. Value about 8000 crowns.

VODICKA: It was over there next to the door, right? Hurnik!

HURNIK: I'm listening. (*Opens a pouch.*)

VODICKA: What's left of it?

HURNIK: The fittings. (*Takes out a piece of blackened metal.*)

VODICKA: (*Looking at it.*) That's really too bad. Go on!

TVRZNIK: (*Reads.*) The Portrait of a Lady by the academy painter Chily. Approximate value 10,000 crowns.

VODICKA: Grandma, I suppose. Hurnik!

HURNIK: (*Hands him a scorched piece of wood.*) A piece of the frame.

VODICKA: (*Looks at it.*) It's enough to make you cry, no?

TVRZNIK: (*Reads.*) One three quarter length fur coat, chinchilla, purchase price 6021 crowns.

HURNIK: Here are the buttons.

VODICKA: And so forth, etc. You'll read through it later, right?

HURNIK: (*Shakes out a pile of burned objects on the table.*) Here's the rest of it.

TVRZNIK: (Reads.) The total damage comes to 57,344 point 20 crowns. (*Hands the list and the pen to Engl.*) Upper left.

JARTCHI: (*As if in a dream.*) Fifty-seven thousand . . .

VODICKA: Well, do you want it?

ENGL: But it's . . .

VODICKA: What?

ENGL: But it's just . . .

VODICKA: Well, what's the matter, Mr. Engl? Did you want to say: fraud? You did, didn't you? And you'd be surprised: of course it's fraud! But the insurance itself is a hundred times as big a fraud. My colleague Tvrznik could tell you how many people stuff it like a piggy bank for as long as they live and never get even a single fire out of it. One pensioner has figured out that with all that insurance money, he could have . . . what was it he could have done?

TVRZNIK: Made a trip around the world.

VODICKA: And?

TVRZNIK: He went crazy.

VODICKA: You see, thanks to our efforts there are so few real fires that getting insurance is like throwing your money down the drain. We work ourselves to the bone and they pocket the premiums. So you shouldn't be surprised if we try and double-cross them once in a while. Of course, if you're not interested . . .

(*Tvrznik starts to put the form away, and Hurnik shoves the burned stuff back in his pouch. Jartchi lays her hand on the paper.*)

JARTCHI: Wait a minute. (*To Engl.*) Go count for a while! (*To Vodicka.*) Just so we understand each other, Commander, can we do anything for you in return?

VODICKA: Why, of course you can, young lady. We should all get a piece of the pie.

JARTCHI: And how big might the slices be?

VODICKA: Ah, that's a good woman for you. You've made a fine choice, Mr. Engl.—Just like we were home, right? Everyone gets the same size slice. There are four of us and two of you. So—one third for you. That makes . . .

TVRZNIK: 19,114 point 73 crowns.

JARTCHI: That doesn't seem fair to me.

VODICKA: What? Why not?

JARTCHI: You delivered the goods, but we cooked it up right here.

VODICKA: Very good. I like that. You should really get half.

TVRZNIK: 28,672 point 10 crowns.

JARTCHI: (*Shakes her head.*)

VODICKA: Still too little? How come?

JARTCHI: Everyday can be a holiday for you, but for us it comes only once a lifetime.

VODICKA: Isn't she adorable? You don't know how lucky you are, Mr. Engl, that I'm no longer as combustible as I once was. Okay. Keep two thirds. That makes . . .

TVRZNIK: 38,229 point 46 crowns.

VODICKA: No, no, no, that will have to do. I've got expenses, and then my boys here might go off and take a better offer, probably right from the insurance people. Right, Hurnik?

HURNIK: Right, sir.

VODICKA: Okay, agreed?

JARTCHI: And the five thousand?

VODICKA: What five thousand?

JARTCHI: The ones that burned. You can't slice that up.

VODICKA: You win. Tvrznik. Add that to it.

TVRZNIK: 43,229 point 46 crowns.

JARTCHI: Did you hear that, Jarda? Think about it: we'd have to save for eight years to get that much together.

ENGL: (*Stubbornly.*) Four . . . !

TVRZNIK: (*Ceremoniously hands the form to Vodicka.*) Commander, the registry of the damages.

JARTCHI: But we'd be eating pork and beans for four years, too.

ENGL: (*Stubbornly.*) I like them.

VODICKA: Let's see . . . (*Goes through the list.*) Trumeau, Chily, chinchilla . . . (*Reads incomprehensibly.*)

JARTCHI: Jarda, don't be an idiot! Almost everybody does it!

ENGL: Well, I'm sorry, but maybe I'm not just everybody . . .

VODICKA: He agrees. (*Signs.*) Hurnik! Janik!

HURNIK: (*Below.*) I'm listening.

JANIK: (*Above.*) I'm listening.

VODICKA: Sign here!

(*Janik slides down, both step simultaneously to the table.*)

BOTH: Right. (*They sign.*)

JARTCHI: So you're not everybody! And just who do you think you are? Onassis?

ENGL: You married me. So you must know . . .

JARTCHI: I don't care if you're just a chauffeur, but when you break your word . . . you swore you would do anything for me. Did you say that or not?

ENGL: But not fraud . . .

JARTCHI: Then you should have said that. You should have said: sweetheart, I'll do anything for you, except commit fraud. But you didn't say that. You were even ready to kill somebody.

ENGL: Me?

JARTCHI: Didn't you say you'd kill Kubr if he didn't stop calling me?

ENGL: (*Spreading his hands helplessly.*) But that's the kind of thing you just *say* . . .

JARTCHI: You just *say* everything!

VODICKA: Come on, kids, what's the matter? In that case just forget it. The money involved isn't worth it if it ruins your honeymoon.

JARTCHI: We're not talking about the money, we're talking about the principle of it.

VODICKA: I'd be careful if I were in your place. Once we had a case where a school burned down because the principal on principle wouldn't let us in with street shoes on.

JARTCHI: Is it valid if I sign it by myself?

ENGL: Jartchi!

VODICKA: Your signatures are only a formality anyhow. Fire victims aren't taken seriously. They're always asking for the moon. What counts is the signature of the official authorities—and that's us.

JARTCHI: May I? (*Tvrznik hands her pen and paper.*)

TVRZNIK: Upper left.

ENGL: If you do that . . .

JARTCHI: (*Belligerent, but somewhat uncertain.*) What then??

ENGL: Then I don't want to know anything about it.

JARTCHI: (*Turns away in disdain and signs.*)

TVRZNIK: (*Takes the form from her and hands it to Vodicka.*) The forms, Commander.

VODICKA: (*Tears out the carbon copy, and bowing, gives it to Jartchi, while Tvrznik replaces the original with another form.*) If you please, young lady . . . (*But when the carbon copy is at the tip of her fingers, he grabs it back and gives her the other paper with his other hand.*) Pardon me, this here too . . .

JARTCHI: What's this?

VODICKA: Confirmation that you have received a private loan from the four of us in the amount of 14,114 point 74 crowns. To be paid back immediately upon receipt of 57,344 point 20 crowns from the insurance company. The rest—43,229 point 46 crowns belongs to you. In order, young lady?

JARTCHI: (*Studies the paper.*) Yes, I think so . . .

TVRZNIK: In the middle.

JARTCHI: (*Signs, exchanges the paper for the other ones, which she stares at as if it were a valuable prize.*) We should drink to that, shouldn't we? If it weren't for the fire, I could offer you something . . . (*She looks and notices for the first time that almost all the fire-fighting equipment has disappeared.*) Is the fire already out?

VODICKA: But, young lady, that's what the fire department is for! You know what we say: "Does your fire need some aid?

JANIK & HURNIK: Call on Vodicka's Brigade!"

VODICKA: My colleague Tvrznik wrote that himself.

TVRZNIK: (*Bows.*)

JARTCHI: I'm so happy! (*Kisses Vodicka on the cheek.*)

VODICKA: You certainly are fiery, young lady. You should have married a fireman.

JARTCHI: The least you can do is thank them, Jarda!

ENGL: (*Stubborn.*) I didn't set any fire.

JARTCHI: What's that supposed to mean? You should thank them and me as well. Otherwise you'd be getting pretty desperate for cigarettes and beer after eight years. (*Notices that Janik and Hurnik are gnawing at the banana peels, and Vodicka is sucking out the last drop from the glass.*) My God, you must be hungry and thirsty . . . maybe something survived in the refrigerator!

(*She runs to the kitchen. Hurnik gets in her way. At first it looks like a clumsy accident, but then Janik cuts her off, too.*)

VODICKA: Leave that to my boys, young lady. They're equipped for it. After you use the Valkyre, it hangs in the air of an hour. Your dress would look like a Swiss cheese. Janik!

JANIK: I'm listening.

VODICKA: Go get some . . . didn't somebody say something about vodka?

JARTCHI: Tell him to take anything he can get his hands on.

JANIK: (*Unlocks the kitchen door and reaches for the door knob.*)

VODICKA: Janik!

JANIK: I'm listening.

VODICKA: (*Reprimanding.*) At least take the armor shield!

JANIK: Roger. Will do.

(*Hurnik lets him and his armor shield in. A thin waft of smoke comes out. In the meantime Engl has sat down on the bed. Overjoyed Jartchi kneels at his feet and attempts a reconciliation.*)

JARTCHI: Jarda! (*Gives him a kiss.*) Are you really mad?

ENGL: Oh no . . .

JARTCHI: Don't get angry. Be happy! With forty-three thousand we can turn this dump into a palace and . . . You know what else? We'll be able to afford a . . . (*Whispers in his ear.*) What do you think?

VODICKA: See? Fire is a stern master but an obedient servant. I hope you'll
take us for a ride too some day.

JARTCHI: I didn't mean a car . . .

VODICKA: No, well what then?

(Janik comes out of the kitchen. He's carrying bottles on his shield as if it were a tray. Hurnik locks the door behind him.)

VODICKA: Well, Janik?

JANIK: Contents of the refrigerator not damaged, Commander. Vodka, beer
and . . . *(as he puts the shield on the table he turns it around. Behind the bottles is a pan)* a duck. *(Engl and Jartchi stare at the duck as if they had seen a ghost.)*

VODICKA: Congratulations! I can see you're not overburdened with chairs.
It's about time you got burned out. Hurnik!

HURNIK: I'm listening.

VODICKA: Turn the bed sideways!

HURNIK: Will do.

VODICKA: You'll have to excuse us, Mr. Engl . . .

(Engl gets up mechanically, Hurnik leans against the bed and turns it sideways, until it stands next to the table like a long bench.)

VODICKA: Let's go boys. Sit down.

(All the firemen sit down next to each other on the bed. Janik and Hurnik on the ends, Tvrznik and Vodicka in the middle. Vodicka takes the duck, rips it to pieces, and passes it around.)

VODICKA: All work makes Jack a dull boy. It's lucky that a refrigerator like
that is a *de facto* fireproof safe. Once we had a case—I hope it's all right,
young lady, for us to eat with our fingers like we do at home—where all the
personnel and the customers at a meat outlet had saved themselves in a big
freezer like this, a total of—

TVRZNIK: Three men and eighteen women.

VODICKA: And not a single one of them had gotten so much as a blister. It was
just too bad for them that we didn't find them until a month later. But who
could have expected them to be in there, huh? A delicious duck! *(To Engl.)*
Don't you want some?

ENGL: *(Beaten down.)* Okay . . .

VODICKA: Well then sit down with us!

(Engl starts to obey, but Jartchi holds him back and finally says something.)

JARTCHI: Hold it!

VODICKA: And just take what you want, young lady. Do you want a piece of the tail?

JARTCHI: I want to look in the kitchen.

(*The firemen continue eating and drinking good-naturedly. But Engl is very nervous.*)

ENGL: What do you want to see in there?

VODICKA: Come on, young lady, don't spoil the meal. First it's got to die out completely in any case.

JARTCHI: I'll put on the asbestos!

VODICKA: That wouldn't do you any good. No, no, young lady. It's a man's job.

JARTCHI: (*To Engl.*) Then you go look!

ENGL: Me? Why?

JARTCHI: You're a man, aren't you. I want you to go and look.

ENGL: But I . . .

VODICKA: Tvrznik!

TVRZNIK: I'm listening.

VODICKA: Couldn't we—

TVRZNIK: Whatever you say, Commander.

VODICKA: I'm very much for it. Mr. Engl is a grown-up, he's rational, and he has principles, he loves his wife—Why shouldn't he take a look in? I think we'll make an exception and look the other way.

ENGL: Not for my sake . . .

VODICKA: Just to satisfy the little lady, Mr. Engl. She is your wife, isn't she?

ENGL: Yes, but—

VODICKA: Well then. Why not take a look in if it will make her happy? That would make you happy, young lady, wouldn't it?

JARTCHI: (*Becomes uncertain.*) Yes . . .

ENGL: I don't want to!

VODICKA: But, but what is that supposed to mean, Mr. Engl? We have to hold the little lady back by force, and you're afraid to go in at all? That's a great prospectus for your marriage.

ENGL: I'm not afraid.

VODICKA: Well, congratulations. Janik!

JANIK: I'm listening.

VODICKA: Give him the asbestos stuff and the boots. And Hurnik!

HURNIK: I'm listening.

VODICKA: Go with him, and take care of him.

JANIK & HURNIK: Will do.

VODICKA: (*While Engl is being dressed.*) Don't stay in there too long, Hurnik. Just long enough for Mr. Engl to look around.

HURNIK: Roger.

VODICKA: As for you, Mr. Engl, chin up! Thanks to your little wife you'll look back on this calamity as if it was Christmas. Ready, Mr. Engl?

HURNIK: (*Indicating to Engl that he should put his thumbs up.*)

ENGL: (*Already wearing the equipment, hesitatingly puts his thumbs up.*)

VODICKA: Okay, then—Off you go!

(*He opens the door, and with Janik's help, pushes Engl in. Hurnik follows with the axe. Vodicka slams the door and blows away some smoke with his hand. Jartchi makes a motion in the direction of the kitchen.*)

JARTCHI: Jarda!

VODICKA: (*Steps in her way.*) Don't worry, young lady. Hurnik will make sure that he doesn't roast.

JARTCHI: Let me by!

VODICKA: (*Scolding.*) Not like that, young lady. I don't like you at all like this. We come to you as friends and you treat us like strangers.

(*The door opens and Engl comes out, accompanied by Hurnik: Janik locks it behind them.*)

VODICKA: Now see. Nothing happened to us. We're back already. Janik, Hurnik, quick, get that stuff off him before he collapses on us!

BOTH: Will do. (*Takes off his helmet, chest protector, and boots.*)

ENGL: (*Smoothes out his hair, is very upset.*)

JARTCHI: Well??

VODICKA: A real mess, eh, Mr. Engl?

JARTCHI: How does it look?

VODICKA: Not a nice sight, eh?

JARTCHI: Say something, Jarda!

ENGL: It's like this, Jartchi . . .

JARTCHI: Like what??

ENGL: The clothes cabinet is . . .

VODICKA: . . . Kindling.

ENGL: (*Nods.*)

JARTCHI: And the kitchen cabinet?

ENGL: Ashes. Everything is . . .

VODICKA: Well, what do you say, Mr. Engl? Were you lucky or not?

ENGL: Yeah. (*Sinks heavily onto the bed.*)

(*All the firemen sit down again. Engl sits between Vodicka and Tvrznik. They have great difficulty all fitting on the bed. The firemen fish out their portions from the pan and continue eating.*)

VODICKA: Well, you see? Don't think about it anymore. Have a bite to eat instead. I saved a wing for you. (*Hands him a portion.*) Just so you can fly away in case the little lady tries to beat you up.

(*All the firemen laugh. Engl begins to gnaw mechanically; Jartchi is the only one still standing. She is thinking things through.*)

VODICKA: Sit down with us, young lady. At least you'll get warm. Come on, boys. Shove over!

JARTCHI: Wait a minute.

VODICKA: Now what?

JARTCHI: If the duck got all burned up, what's this thing here? (*Vodicka and the other firemen stop chewing.*)

VODICKA: (*Harshly.*) Well, Mr. Engl, can you clear this up for us?

ENGL: I . . .

VODICKA: Just among us women folk: isn't it likely that there were two ducks?

JARTCHI: Two?

VODICKA: Didn't you just happen to roast the second one yourself as a little surprise for the little lady? Huh?

ENGL: Yes . . .

JARTCHI: When for heaven's sake? I would have known that!

VODICKA: Didn't it just happen to be in the middle of the night?

ENGL: That's right . . .

JARTCHI: . . . But why didn't you say anything to me about it?

VODICKA: Well? Why didn't you inform the little lady, Mr. Engl?

ENGL: I forgot . . .

VODICKA: Come on, come on. At your age? You better watch out, young lady—Once we had a case where some clown like this forgot to save his mother-in-law, his wife and his two kids from a fire. (*All the firemen laugh loudly and continue chewing.*)

JARTCHI: I was sure I had turned off the oven and put the duck in the refrigerator . . . But that means . . .

VODICKA: (*His mouth full.*) You're getting warmer, young lady.

JARTCHI: That means—that you're the one who didn't turn off the oven!

VODICKA: Now it's getting really hot, eh Mr. Engl?

ENGL: Prabably . . .

JARTCHI: And you were going to just sit there and let me take the blame?

VODICKA: That's not true either, I'm on Mr. Engl's side here. Don't you remember how stoutly he defended you when we made up the official report? He has no cause to have a guilty conscience. And furthermore if you want to be fair: now the one who really earned this . . .

TVRZNIK: 43,289 point 46 crowns.

VODICKA: . . . is him. Right?

JARTCHI: That was just sheer luck!—And now tell me why you're roasting a duck in the middle of the night when there's already one in the fridge?

ENGL: I . . .

VODICKA: Didn't you happen to want to have some friends over in private, Mr. Engl?

JARTCHI: (*Understanding.*) Jarda! You were . . . (*As if spellbound she looks at each of the firemen in turn.*) Wait a second!

(*She starts moving and the others notice too late that she's headed for the kitchen. All but Engl jump up, their hands and mouths full of duck, but Jartchi reaches the door with a jump, turns the key and opens it. The scene freezes for a second. Then Jartchi goes into the kitchen. Engl closes his eyes. Pause. Jartchi comes back out, carrying in her hand a metal canister, which is still sending out a bit of smoke: a smoke bomb. She starts laughing. She laughs so hard that she has to lean on the door. Vodicka joins in laughing. Then the other firemen. The room echoes with laughter.*)

JARTCHI: (*Finally catching her breath.*) Well, you really put me on! You know you really put the fear of God in me for a while.

VODICKA: Oh no, really?

JARTCHI: I even cry at the movies, when I know they're just acting. How was I supposed to guess here in my own place that you guys get all this (*pointing to their uniforms*) from the theatre?

VODICKA: Yeah sure!

JARTCHI: Jarda was always saying: If you don't let me keep on acting in the theatre group, they'll pay you back. But as soon as somebody yells "Fire," everybody goes crazy!

VODICKA: Yeah sure!

JARTCHI: You know I think I'll let him go back to it. He's a better actor than I thought.

VODICKA: So you see . . .

JARTCHI: Sit down, don't stand around. Please just make yourselves at home.

(*The firemen sit down and begin eating again. They drink freely from the bottles.*)

JARTCHI: But there's one thing I won't forgive you for. I could already smell the money. That's right, love, you'll feel sorry about the beautiful fire, too, when you're eating pork and beans for the third straight year! (*The firemen roar with laughter.*) Forty-three thousand . . . You really pushed it to the limit! (*To Engl.*) Wouldn't you like to introduce me to your friends?

ENGL: (*Softly.*) I've never seen them before in my life.

(*The firemen stop chewing. Once again the scene freezes.*)

JARTCHI: Come on, enough's enough. Or I might get really scared!

ENGL: They're not from the theatre group . . .

(*Hurnik and Janik stand up. Jartchi, terrified, moves back, but Hurnik just goes to the door to the stairway, and Janik to the basement window. They take up positions there as if they were standing guard. Vodicka and Tvrznik wipe off their hands.*)

JARTCHI: (*Anxiously.*) Who are you?

VODICKA: Don't be so nervous, young lady. We're the firemen!

JARTCHI: And . . . what do you want here?

VODICKA: What do we want? We've just been doing our duty.

JARTCHI: But there wasn't any fire here!

VODICKA: What! No? Come on, young lady! Women certainly tend to be forgetful, don't they, Mr. Engl?

JARTCHI: Let him alone. He's just as normal as I am!

VODICKA: Well, I'll grant you that, young lady!

JARTCHI: Who do you want to convince that there was a fire here??

VODICKA: Why should we want to convince anyone of anything? You're both normal people, and we've got your signed statements. That'll do.

TVRZNIK: (*Opens his file, and reads.*) The fire was caused by us. Jaroslav Engl, Jaroslava Englova.

JARTCHI: What a lie!

ENGL: (*Particularly harassed, since he is still squeezed in between Vodicka and Tvrznik.*) Jartchi . . .

JARTCHI: But what we signed said: "The fire was caused by duck!"

VODICKA: But young lady, you can't have something that stupid in an official statement! Look for yourself, Mr. Engl.

TVRZNIK: (*Shows him the statement.*)

JARTCHI: What you quoted wasn't what we signed!

VODICKA: Let's not quibble about words, young lady. The fact is that you signed this statement about a fire. Or didn't you?

JARTCHI: But that's not worth anything! That's fraud!

ENGL: Just a second, Jartchi . . . Gentlemen, would you mind telling us what you actually—

JARTCHI: Will you please be quiet! You've already let them make an ass of you! How can you be so thick! Can't you see that they're trying to blackmail us!

VODICKA: We blackmail you? That's really too much, young lady.

JARTCHI: But you won't get away with it. That promissory note isn't valid, either.

VODICKA: Which one?

JARTCHI: The one for fourteen thousand.

VODICKA: Fourteen thousand? Oh you mean the one for—

TVRZNIK: 14,114 point 74 crowns.

JARTCHI: Yeah, that one.

VODICKA: And why do you think it's not valid?

JARTCHI: Because nothing burned down here, not to kindling and not to ashes. Absolutely nothing. Not even the duck!

VODICKA: Really? What about the—

TVRZNIK: (*Takes out another form and reads.*) Empire trumeau.

JARTCHI: I don't even know what that is!

TVRZNIK: Portrait of a Lady by the academic painter Chily.

JARTCHI: We never had anything like that on our walls!

TVRZNIK: One three quarter length fur coat, chinchilla.

JARTCHI: How could we afford that?

VODICKA: Well, in that case why did you sign this statement which claims that everything was there this morning? I hope it wasn't in order to collect . . .

TVRZNIK: 57,344 point 20 crowns.

VODICKA: . . . from the insurance company?

JARTCHI: That was your idea!

VODICKA: Better be careful, young lady, don't do anything too drastic. That is after all a serious charge. How do you propose to go about substantiating it?

JARTCHI: Jarda . . .

VODICKA: This document containing your signatures states that the items were here. If they were not here, that certainly would be fraud—on your part, of course. A case of fraud, which according to—

TVRZNIK: Paragraph 132, section 1, letters a through c.

VODICKA: —is punishable with . . .

TVRZNIK: Imprisonment for no less than two years nor more than five.

VODICKA: Which I really would not like to believe, young lady. (*Brightening up.*) But—if the things really were here, that's proof enough that there really was a fire. Right? (*Quiet. Tvrznik carefully ties his file back up.*)

JARTCHI: For God's sake, Jarda. Say something!

ENGL: What am I supposed to say?

JARTCHI: Christ Almighty! What kind of man are you? Call somebody or just throw them out. If we tell them what really happened, nobody could blame us.

ENGL: Maybe we'd better come to some kind of agreement, Jartchi.

VODICKA: I like that, Mr. Engl. There's nothing you couldn't learn how to swallow. Right?

JARTCHI: Do you know what I think you are? (*Goes behind the back of the bed.*) A great big zero. And do you know what I'm going to do now? (*With a leap she is at the bed, rips the file out of Tvrznik's hands, runs under the basement window, through which Janik has just climbed, and starts to yell.*) Help! Help!

ENGL: (*Jumps up.*) Jartchi, for God's sake!

(*Vodicka and Tvrznik remain calmly seated. Then we hear Janik's voice over the loudspeaker.*)

JANIK: Sir, UPOR is calling.
JARTCHI: (*Stops yelling.*)
VODICKA: Go ahead.
JANIK: UPOR wants to know if we still need the ambulance.
VODICKA: No, they can keep it.
JANIK: Roger.
JARTCHI: Heeeelp!
VODICKA: But tell them to send the hearse. We probably won't be able to force our way through to the people in time. I can hear them screaming.
JANIK: Roger. Will do.

(*Jartchi has stopped screaming and, terrified, is looking at Vodicka.*)

VODICKA: Hurnik!
HURNIK: I'm listening.
VODICKA: The Valkyrie.
HURNIK: Will do.

(*Janik comes sliding down the pole again and helps Hurnik put the familiar apparatus on his back.*)

VODICKA: Were you in the military, Mr. Engl?
ENGL: Yes.
VODICKA: Rank?
ENGL: Private first class.
VODICKA: So, now that the excitement has died down, you will surely be able to tell us what the Valkyrie *de facto* is.
ENGL: A flame-thrower.
VODICKA: Very good, private. (*To Tvrznik.*) Take his name down, Tvrznik.—I'll make sure you'll be a Corporal any day now. I assume you know what a flame-thrower is used for?
ENGL: (*Shakes his head.*)
VODICKA: Sometimes we have cases where the people are gradually suffocating, and we can't get to them. Or they panic and are threatening the others. During a really big fire, Private, martial law goes into effect, and what is best for the majority is by definition the most humane course of action. Since the little lady claims that there hasn't been any fire . . . Hurnik!
HURNIK: Will do.

(*Steps into the middle of the room and aims the nozzle at Jartchi. Vodicka and Tvrznik have finally stood up and move as far as possible behind the bed, as does Janik.*)

VODICKA: You better come back here, Private. There's an average of two deaths per basement holocaust, but we grieve for every single life.

ENGL: (*Pulls himself together, jumps up, and yells.*) Wait!

VODICKA: Yes? I'm waiting, Private.

ENGL: (*Goes to Jartchi, who is frozen with fear, and takes the documents from her.*) Will you spare us if I give this back to you?

VODICKA: Why not?

ENGL: What's our guarantee?

VODICKA: The best one you could hope for. After all you owe us . . .

TVRZNIK: 14,114 point 73 crowns.

VODICKA: Of course, that's only after you receive your—

TVRZNIK: 57,344 point 20 crowns.

VODICKA: We're fair people to deal with, Private. And naturally we don't intend to harm ourselves either.

ENGL: Why are you doing it?

VODICKA: (*Stretching out his hand.*) The papers!

(*Engl goes and gives them to him. Vodicka hands them to Tvrznik. Hurnik lowers the nozzle. Janik takes the apparatus from him.*)

VODICKA: I'll tell you why, Corporal. Everybody's got to live, right? We firemen live off fires. The more fires, the more firemen, the better the positions, higher salaries, improved equipment. But—the more firemen and the more effective the equipment, the fewer the fires . . . You understand?

ENGL: (*Nods numbly.*)

VODICKA: So what choice do we have left to us if the only thing we know how to do is put out fires. When your business is putting out fires, you may find that you have to start up a holocaust or two now and then. Right, boys?

HURNIK & JANIK: Will do. (*They start carrying things up the ladder again.*)

VODICKA: But we take care of the others too—, as long as they don't spoil the fun. The young lady got it straight, even if she got her wires crossed later on. But we'll consider that over and done with, right, young lady? We have a successful mission and you have a dowry.

JARTCHI: (*Goes to the bed, sits down exhausted and leans her head on the bedboard.*)

VODICKA: Bon. The main thing is you stood by her when it counted. But that's why people get married. So there's only one detail left: when there's a fire, and we are not quite sure how it started, and afterwards the victims seem to be upset, the rule is that we leave a fire-guard behind at the burned location. Not necessarily forever, but for as long as is needed to make sure that everything is nice and quiet again. Hurnik and Janik are the most logical candidates. Pick out which one you like the best.

(*Hurnik and Janik come sliding down the pole with a folding cot and other equipment.*)

They stand at attention next to each other. Jartchi's shoulders begin to quiver.)

VODICKA: Little lady, you don't have to worry. The guard will stay in the kitchen and be quiet as a mouse. That has the advantage that if you roast a duck again . . . oh, let's forget it.

ENGL: Commander, Sir.

VODICKA: I'm listening, Corporal.

ENGL: Maybe you could come up with another suggestion?

VODICKA: (*Turns to the firemen.*) Did you hear that? Bravo, Corporal. I think I'll promote you to Platoon Leader!

TVRZNIK: (*Opens the papers and notes it down.*)

VODICKA: As a Platoon Leader, you see, you could stay here by yourself.

ENGL: I'm—

VODICKA: A Platoon Leader of the fire department can fulfill the function of fire guard without assistance.

ENGL: But I'm not . . .

VODICKA: Everybody—Attention!

(*Janik and Hurnik stand at attention. Tvrznik opens the file and hands it to Vodicka. Instinctively Engl also snaps to attention.*)

VODICKA: Corporal Engl Jaroslav, I herewith promote you to the position of Platoon Leader of the fire department. At ease! (*Gives the file back to Tvrznik.*)

TVRZNIK: (*Hands Engl the file and a pen.*) Anywhere.

VODICKA: We're making an exception, mainly to calm down the young lady. By the way she'll have to stand guard herself, of course, when you're at work. From now on you'll receive an additional salary of 2000 crowns every month.

JARTCHI: (*Stops crying and dazed, lifts her head.*)

VODICKA: Well, Mr. Engl?

ENGL: (*Without saying a word, he signs.*)

VODICKA: My congratulations, Platoon Leader. (*Shakes his hand, embraces him and kisses him.*)

(*After that Janik, Hurnik, and Tvrznik shake his hand. Then Janik takes the folding cot back out.*)

VODICKA: With this signature you have formally recognized your obligations. And now as for your rights . . .

TVRZNIK: (*Hands him various vouchers from his file.*) Voucher for the helmet . . . For the uniform . . . For the equipment . . . As well as a cash advance of 312 crowns. (*Pays him in bills and coins.*)

VODICKA: Well, look at that! That happens to be just enough for the insurance premium.

JANIK: (*From above.*) Commander, UPOR is calling.

VODICKA: I'm listening.

JANIK: UPOR wants to know why we've been here so long.

VODICKA: Why? Is there a fire somewhere?

JANIK: No.

VODICKA: Report to UPOR. Action successfully concluded. Departure shortly. Receiver remains on.

JANIK: Roger. Will be reported.

VODICKA: We will proceed according to plan.

JANIK: Roger. Will not be reported. (*Outside a motor starts turning over. It starts up.*)

VODICKA: Everyone—Forward march!

FIREMEN: Roger. Will do.

TVRZNIK: (*Ties up the papers, takes them between his teeth and climbs up.*)

VODICKA: Platoon Leader Engl!

ENGL: (*Standing at attention.*) I'm listening.

VODICKA: You take over the fire watch.

ENGL: Will do.

VODICKA: Best of luck in your new job and marriage.

ENGL: Roger.

(*Vodicka climbs out. Hurnik, who is carrying the flame thrower on his back again, aims the nozzle at Engl and Jartchi, makes a hissing noise, and then makes believe he is setting the whole room on fire like a kid playing soldier. Then he too climbs out. Right after that the ladder and pole are pulled up. The truck starts away. The fire siren sounds and moves away quickly. Engl has been standing at attention until this point. Now he rushes desperately to the stairway door. It is locked, and the key has disappeared. He runs to the basement window and tries to jump up and pull himself up in vain.*)

ENGL: (*Screams.*) Jartchi! Come and help!

(*Desperately he tries to shove the clothes stand through the window, and see if he can climb out like that. That also doesn't work. Jartchi doesn't move. He drops everything and runs to her.*)

ENGL: Do you hear? We've got to go to the police right away!

JARTCHI: (*Lost in thought, she just shakes her head.*)

ENGL: You were right. They'll understand that we had no choice. They were capable of anything . . . So hurry up!

JARTCHI: (*Without saying a word, she takes off her wedding dress.*)

ENGL: What are you doing?

JARTCHI: (*Wearing only panties and bra, she takes a bucket, a broom, and some rags from the corner.*)

ENGL: What are you doing now?

JARTCHI: Cleaning up.

ENGL: What . . . ? For God's sake!

JARTCHI: What do you mean . . . ! The clothes cabinet is kindling . . . the kitchen cabinet is ashes . . .

ENGL: Jartchi, have you gone crazy?

JARTCHI: (*Begins to clean up.*) On the contrary.

ENGL: What do you mean, on the contrary? Stop it. (*Tries to grab the broom.*) I'm telling you, we've got to go to the police!

JARTCHI: (*Defending herself.*) Let me go!

ENGL: Jartchi . . .

JARTCHI: (*Pulls away from him, sharply.*) Did you get three hundred and twelve crowns from them?

ENGL: Yes, but—

JARTCHI: So what do you want the police for? Hurry up and pay the insurance premium, so that you get today's date on it!

ENGL: But we're not going to accept this money!

JARTCHI: Forty three thousand? And why not? Can you tell me that?

ENGL: So that we'll be completely in their power?

JARTCHI: You idiot! You idiot! You should get down on your knees and thank me. They had us so completely in their power that if it weren't for their fear they would calmly have burned down the whole damned place, everything, us included, just to chalk up Brownie points with the authorities. Come on! We got off easy!

ENGL: Now you probably expect me to stand guard?

JARTCHI: And why not? They probably won't bother you if you're one of them.

ENGL: Jartchi, be reasonable! Think what you're asking me to do! Come on . . .

JARTCHI: Why don't you try and be reasonable. You're not a little baby. You have a wife, you want to have a family . . . Well, do something for them. What good are the police, if the firemen come back?

(*The fire truck signal is heard in the distance. Terrified Jartchi immediately leaps into the bed and covers herself with the sheet. The siren dies away. Engl stands next to the bed, unsure of what to do next. Then he kneels down in front of her.*)

ENGL: Jartchi . . . I love you . . . I don't want you to have to be afraid . . . Are you listening? . . . I'll do whatever you think is right. Do you hear me? I'll pay the insurance. I'll put our money in the bank, and then everything will be like before.

JARTCHI: (*Under the covers.*) Then get going! Hurry up!

(*Engl stands up, goes quickly into the kitchen. Pause. Then he laughs shrilly. He comes to the doorway and laughs like a crazy man. In one hand he's holding an empty silverware-chest, in the other an open handbag with a chain.*)

JARTCHI: (*Can't stand it any longer and looks out from under the covers.*) What's the matter with you?

ENGL: The money—the silverware—everything gone! They were . . . just thieves!

(*Stunned she stands up in the bed, then he grabs her and whirls her madly around the room, until she is caught up in the feeling of relief, and joins in enthusiastically in the romp. Then they both fall on the bed, and the laughter changes into sudden passion.*)

JARTCHI: (*Hisses like a tigress.*)

ENGL: (*Hisses like a lion.*)

JARTCHI: (*Hisses more strongly and rips off his jacket.*)

ENGL: (*Hisses even more strongly, rips off her bra and stops short.*) And what if they're not really thieves?

JARTCHI: (*Uneasy again.*) What if it's just as a bonus that they . . .

BOTH: (*Unison.*) —steal?

END

A Blue Angel

Milan Uhde

translated by Vera Pech
adapted to the American idiom by Peter Stenberg

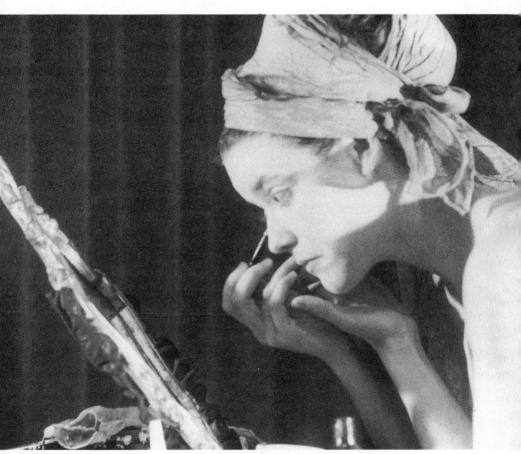

A BLUE ANGEL
[Théâtre au Boudufil, Geneva, Switzerland]
Directed by Yan Kaplan

(*Sound of a moving train.*)

Why are you staring at me like that? I'm not much to look at. It's true, right? An old bag. Not too bad? Don't give me that. If I could shed twenty years. Maybe fifteen. You would be surprised. My hair used to hang down to my waist. I was like Goldilocks. I looked great. Really. Would you believe I used to be a stewardess? For three years. Actually four. Man, the letters I used to get. Love letters. Offers of marriage. One guy wrote all the way from Stockholm. From the embassy there. I threw it all away. You're laughing, right? My husband always makes believe he's laughing. Actually he's the jealous type. A little bit. He cares about me. The guy who was helping me to get on the train, that was my husband. He didn't want to let me go. He keeps saying: It doesn't make sense. —I say: Sweetheart, we can't give up now. —Do you know where I am going? To the Supreme Court. Why? To seek justice. And I'm not kidding. I'll fight to the end, no matter what it costs. Look at this, all these papers. Three kilos, at least. Solid stuff. Dynamite. I am not telling you any more. If I can't get it the easy way, I'll get it the hard way. When my uncle was dying, I said to my brother: You know, kid, there is a lot of stuff for us in that place of his. Let's make a list up now, so we don't fight about it later. But he says he doesn't want any inheritance from my uncle. I can go if you want to. So I didn't go. But my brother went. The very same evening. Hauled off a whole bunch of stuff. For three days he was dragging it away. Then my uncle died. I say, for God's sake, kid, aren't you ashamed of yourself? The manager phoned me the minute she saw you. You can't deny it. Half of that stuff is mine. He says: I am not going to fight with you. Go see my lawyer, he's got the list of things. I was there today—I say: all the best things are gone. China. The stamp collection. Altogether at least fifty thousand crowns' worth. Of course, my dear little brother said he didn't take anything. I say: Listen kid, do you really have the heart to wreck my last chance? He says: If you need some cash, just say so. I can probably scratch up five thousand. But just watch how you handle me. That did it. Brothers and sisters should stick together, for God's sake. Even more, when they've been orphans since they were fourteen and sixteen. I would have given my life for him and I thought he felt the same way about me. For instance, I had a key to his place. He gave it to me, just in case. Times were tough. People were getting picked up all the time. And it started with that key. I say to myself: When he's out you're gonna go, and look it over, and if you find those stamps and the china, you're gonna wait for him and say: Okay, kid, thanks a lot. I know what you're going to say: A man's house is his castle. But I was really frantic. And he saw it coming and got it all cut. No trace of stamps, china, or anything anywhere. I was just furious. I always suspected he had quite a few things of his own, but I had no idea he had so much. Antique vases, sculptures, gold spoons, even pure gold. I swear I didn't want to do it. But I had nothing to put it in. So I used his luggage and crammed it all in. It was like I was in a trance. It was only back home that I sobered up. I wake up during the night and say to myself: Well, old girl, you really did it this time. Chills run up and down my spine. This really wasn't my style. I've always let the people take advantage of me. So, right away the next morning I called him. I wanted to return everything. But, he says, I'm a thief. I say: Listen, kid, I don't give a damn about your things. I just wanted to let you feel how I felt when you treated me like dirt.—But he hung up. And, he sued me. So, I sued him in return. Of course, they didn't accept my complaint. Who knows if the stamps and the china really existed at all, they said. But his accusations were valid, they said. You have to understand, he is an officer. He's got friends everywhere, used to tour wine cellars with the State Prosecutor. My husband says: The court will make you give it all back in the end, just wait. I never had anything to do with courts, but when I realized how scared he was, I said: You wait and see.—

And I went to see the Chief Judge. I say: My maiden name is Richlerova, if that means anything to you. Oh, yes, the General, says he. And I say: A name known the world over. I am his niece. And I happen to know something about the law, too.—Well, then you know the law applies to everybody, says he. I am sure your uncle wouldn't like his name being used to influence this court. He cut me short like that, the bastard. My husband says: Your clothes might have had something to do with it. Too flashy. I say: Darling, a fortuneteller told me in 1944: Your color is blue, Ma'm. Wear this color and you can't go wrong.—I will stick with that.—And I went to see somebody else. Well, I have my connections. I say: Slavku, I have got to put the squeeze on this bastard who makes believe judges can't be bribed. I know a lot about him, but I think I suspect even more, all I need is a few little details. But Slavek says: Listen love, forget it. I say: Do you mean to tell me there's nothing on him?—In this country you can always find something on everybody, Slavek says, but not the way you would like it, that's out. We serve the state. Well, I say—and don't I belong to the state? Since when is justice a private matter? By the way, Slavek, where was it we met for the first time? Which bar was it—the Adria? 1942? Maybe, says Slavek. You used to keep nice company.—Those were good girls, I say. They were agency models from Vesely's. I am not talking about the girls, says Slavek. I am talking about the guys. They were there on their own, I say, and a bar is a public place. But you, dear Slavek, you were there while on duty and the money you were spending, was dirty money. Bloodstained money.—Try to prove it, he says. I say: Well, your bosses have it down somewhere black on white. And Slavek: They know all sorts of things about you too. I say: One difference. I never worked for the Gestapo, never. And I don't work for the police. It won't do any harm if they investigate me. But, it could be the end of you.—Just try it, he says. I say: Don't get so excited or you'll wet your pants. You know very well that I'm not going to see your boss, or his boss. I'm going to find somebody who is out to get you and don't tell me there's nobody like that around. And don't start crying later on because I didn't warn you.—

That's the way I handled him. You find that hard to believe, don't you? I can hardly believe it myself. It was a nightmare. At first the judge didn't take me seriously either, when I turned up again. Says he: Lady, we went through all this before, we are just wasting time. It's up to you, your Honor, I say. Somebody else is going to waste some time with you. They might even ask, how is your cousin in America doing? Is he there legally? Or did he just forget to return from his business trip abroad? And didn't they slap three years on him for it? Did you list his name in the questionnaire? The part that says: relative abroad? You didn't, did you? And what about that house you sold for the estimated price? Hundred and twenty thousand. How much did you really get? Twice as much, right? They started to investigate, but there was the usual cover up. But nothing can be buried so deep that it cannot be dug up again. What would your wife say about all that? She is an honest person. By the way, how come she goes to church on the other side of town? Is she ashamed to be one of the believers? It's her right, isn't it? On the other hand, it looks bad for a judge to have a wife with such outdated views. Especially since he himself lectures all over the place about how wonderfully we're getting on without the help of God. And now, your Highness, just imagine, all this coming to light. Those gentlemen who do the selecting of judges would make sure that you would have time on your hands till your dying day.—I went at him like that for at least fifteen minutes; naturally, there was much more I could have told him. In the end, all he said, was: Get out. For the last time, get out. You make me sick, get out.—I say: I am going. But you just think it over. He did. And for a whole year, there wasn't a peep out of him. Now, tell me, what do you think of me? That I'm a bitch? You are right. When I woke up that night, I felt like I was watching a movie.—Jesus, I say, I think I'm listening to a rehearsal with Milan Dvoraček as director: Jesus stop it, I can't watch this any longer. So, right away, I wrote to my brother, asked him to have a heart and give me a break and let me have at least some of those things he took from my uncle. But instead, he did everything he could to get the whole court procedure going again. He even contacted the Office of the President. His wife told me all about it after another one of their fights.—I say to her: Look, you must have seen all that china and all those stamps.—She says: I didn't. He didn't have anything like that at home. I say: You said yourself, right out of the blue that he bought this cottage for fifty thousand. She says: That's normal with him. For a while he's got nothing and then he's Mister Moneybags. You know him yourself, a big wheeler-dealer. Well, my brother's not easy to catch off guard. In the end, he sent off an anonymous letter full of accusations. He claimed . . . , well he made up some really awful stories. When the police started questioning me, I thought I'd go crazy. My brother: the wartime prison warden, until he switched uniforms and now he had the nerve to sling mud at me. That really ticked me off. I hopped on the train and went to see Zorka. We used to work together in the theatre. Her old man's an officer at the Ministry. I say: Zorka, you have to help me. My dear little brother is a thief. Do you know how he does it? For instance, they load the truck full of old shoes and coats and take it to the main depot. There they get a certificate that the stuff is no longer usable. It's supposed to go to the dump but instead they take it back to the barracks and give it to the soldiers. And the newly issued clothes they sell to civilians. My brother claims: In the villages around the garrison every other person wears combat boots and dyed coats. My dear girl, Zorka says, that's nothing new, everybody does that. Well, so what? say I. Here and there, they can punish somebody, can't they? You know what, there's something to that, says Zorka. Vikynek won't want to start any trouble, but that's all right. He has a skeleton in his closet too. A fresh one. He went on a business trip. The jerk. With some lady photographer. Within two days it all came out into the open. Where is that brother of yours stationed exactly?—I haven't slept a wink all night. To do the dirty on your own brother! I say to myself: In the morning, you ask her to forget the whole thing. But she just laughed. Apparently, by then, she'd already fixed it all up. So, for the last time in my life I went to see him. Jirko, I say to him, cancel the litigation and give me what belongs to me. For God's sake, try to be human. Of course, he replies: Sis, I swear, I haven't seen any stamps or china. Have you? I say: As sure as I'm looking at you right now. There seem to be three possibilities, he says, either our dear uncle played a joke on us and gave it all to somebody else, or he was robbed or—. Do you know what he told me?—Or you are a nut. I say: Listen kid, here was I and there was uncle and he says to me: Milo, you've stood by me during the hard times, and now I have something for you. He got up, opened a cabinet and there was twelve shelves full of china and at the bottom two drawers full of stamp albums. And he says: Books mean nothing to you, so I'm giving those to the University, but all this is to be divided between you and Jirka, so you would have something to remember me by. I can see it if it were today. I even thought to myself. So we're getting finally something out of you. But, actually, it would have been better if it had never happened. The best thing that could have happened to us would have been if he had just forgotten all about us. Anyway, when my mother died two years after my father, old uncle took us in. Actually, his housekeeper took us in, telling us all the time how lucky we were to live with the good doctor and how wonderful of him not to stick us in an orphanage. I know now, that he couldn't have done it in any case. The town just wanted us off their backs; there would have been legal squabbles for sure. Three times a day the menu included how he works from morning till night and how careful he is about his reputation, especially when it comes to his clients. At the same time, the old bag wanted to know if my brother is drinking.—My dad used to drink, my brother said once. And the old bag shot back: It's not nice to talk that way about the dead.—But it was quite clear she was the one who talked about our father first, because he was a drop-out and didn't dare to show his face in public. The first two years, we hardly saw our uncle. The old bag brought us a a letter now and then. Pure baloney. He dictated it to his secretary. About how one should live and so on. Of course, he himself didn't practice what he preached. That place of his had two entrances. One led to a kitchen and three lousy rooms—there lived my brother and me and the old bag. The other one led to his rooms and we were not allowed to enter them. Why? Look, he was almost forty and single. Do you know what I mean? I saw quite a few young things going in and out of there. Good looking girls. He was no saint. I remember how he asked me once to come in. Into his office, of course. I hear, Milo—I was baptized Milada—that you like going to the movies. I say: I'm not allowed to?—I knew right away what was going to come next. The old bag was always complaining about me. Somebody told her that I'm hanging around with the boys, and that we're sitting in the balcony—well, when you're sixteen you know what's going on up in the balcony. So, I say: These guys are from our high school. And what about the girls? he shot back. There are no girls there, right? Well, well. Five or six young men and you alone, what's that supposed to mean? I say: Why not? At least they don't get fresh.—That was a lie, of course. They did get fresh, and I knew that he knew. But it was funny to watch him not being able to say it outright. Only later on I realized that he wasn't reluctant, he just didn't care. He says: All right, until you shape up, no more pocket money. It didn't faze me. Two of the boys I went with had quite a bit of money. All he managed to do was make sure I didn't care about what happened next. One day I found the old gal going crazy, crying away in the kitchen—the good doctor phoned from London that he's not coming back to Prague for a while. And I couldn't care less. She took care of the house, he either left her some money or was maybe sending some. He wrote to her and she was always weeping and wailing when she read it. Then came Hitler, she was picked up after high school, I decided to stand up on my own two feet and move out. The boy, the name is Vesely—you didn't know Vesely?—lingerie, dresses, ladies' accessories—he persuaded his father to take me on as a model. That was great. However, my uncle returned in 1945 as a colonel with an English wife and got in touch with me. I say: Look here, uncle, in 1938 you didn't care what might happen to me. You left and that was it. So you don't need to bother now either. But, he started right away on how he took part in the Nuremberg Nazi trials, how he might become a Minister and how painful it is for him to hear about how I'm behaving here. And so I say: So what? What was I supposed to do—just go under? Old man Vesely was a fine man. According to you a collaborator. But if it were not for him, I would have ended up in Germany or maybe even in a concentration camp. In England, you made all those fancy speeches on the radio, everybody was illegally listening to it, but people on the street here avoided me. Old man Vesely wasn't scared. And so when he asked me to entertain a few people in the bar, should I have said maybe: Mister Vesely, would you kindly provide me with a list of those people who are not collaborators or from the Gestapo? And when old man Vesely died and his distinguished offspring told me to take a walk, I went straight to the theatre. For God's sake, says my uncle, which one? I say: What do you think we could put on in 1944 in Prague? And if somebody told you that we did our acts in the nude, that's a lie. In a bathing suit, sure. But just between you and me, why shouldn't a woman perform in the nude. You don't have to look, if you don't want to. They say the Gestapo liked the place. Well, I had my own opinion of them, but they paid their bills. So, what? I wasn't the one sitting in London free to curse them. Anyway, my beloved uncle, you didn't seem to be so fussy yourself, or do you mean to tell me that you didn't know what you were getting Vendralova into? That was the name of the housekeeper. I said: Then you disappear from sight but first you bribe her to be your messenger, get her involved in all sorts of illegal stuff, make a big show when she is sent to a camp and cry crocodile tears when she catches typhus and packs it in. In those days, I was a real dummy, but one thing was clear to me. I had to get out of your place presto or I was going to be next. You don't see it that way? Pardon me, you are my father's brother, but I just can't see how you could make charges against anybody or pass any judgment. You have no idea about anything. Or, maybe you do and that's even worse. When I think of you being a Minister, I could puke. And that's what I am going to tell anybody who asks.—Man, I really shot off my big mouth that time. Actually, cross my heart, I really didn't mean a thing. But he, who at first was full of national pride, and all for the punishment of traitors, was suddenly full of understanding and willing to do anything to help. Man, believe it or not, he was scared of me. Of me, a two-bit actress from a defunct theatre, who carried all her worldly possessions in two bags. And he set up my job with the airlines. Everybody was wondering how come I didn't manage to get something better out of him. Except, I didn't want to. By the way, being a stewardess is a real drag. I know now, I should have never taken it. Why did I take it? I imagined the blue uniform and said to myself: Maybe it's fate. But I never felt right there. You know, the best times were always in the theatre after the performance. We all went partying, and early next morning, I'd get somebody to drive me home, always got out a few blocks from where I lived, so people wouldn't talk; well, they did anyway. Carried shoes in my hand so I didn't wake up the landlady, then took a shower and crawled into bed without a care in the world. Boy, I slept like a log. On the other hand, in the airplane, how shall I explain it to you? The truth is, I can see through people. Let's take Pokorny. Everybody says: Excellent pilot. But, I look at him, and can tell you exactly what he is thinking about and how he's feeling. He boozes all night and then he is supposed to fly to Brussels and Paris. Gee! I had to have a double scotch. And that costs money. Later on, it wasn't helping anyway. I say: Riso, let somebody else take your place. Why? says he. I say: You know very well why. He pretended he didn't know what I was talking about. So, I explained it to him. I didn't exactly like doing that. People don't like it when you touch a raw nerve. But the thing is in this case he wasn't the only one involved. Naturally, he started abusing me. I thought, to hell with it. What else could I do? But he denounced me. Flirting with the passengers, according to him. The whole case came up before with the boss. In the end I told them to their faces everything I didn't like. There was a lot. And what do you think happened? I was reprimanded. I knew that in advance. The boss says: Well, Sweetie, what's with you? And suddenly it was clear as a bell. They cooked it all up together, to protect each other. So I say: If you want a reprimand, it will be a reprimand. And I submitted a complaint. It was received by the Deputy Head of the department. A decent man, I knew right away, he wasn't mixed up in it with the others. He asked about my uncle and then he said: Everything you say here, Miss, is true. It might all be even worse than you think. But people are people. Are we supposed to throw them all out? Nobody's perfect. And planes have to fly. I say: Sir, you have this marvelous ability to see through things, too. He says: Well, a little bit. Except I know how to keep it under control. I simply don't use it. And I advise you to do the same. I think you could use some rest. The question is, can you find it with the Airlines?— Well, we came to an agreement. I was posted with the Military, to a Recreation Center for Officers. Beautiful country. Mountains. I was supposed to be a supervisor. They wanted a married woman only. I said: No thanks. Not that I was hard up for men. Of course, when you have an x-ray for a brain, love is pretty hard to find. You don't just have a body. You've got a soul too. But you can't turn off those damned x-rays. I could go out with some guy and know right away he wasn't for me. But what was worse was I thought I would be able to make a clean break and get away from my uncle, but it didn't happen.

About half a year later, I got a summons—from the Secret Police. By that time, my uncle wasn't working at the Ministry anymore, but in a factory. In the legal department. He sent his wife back to England, he was a nobody and nothing could help him. They wanted me to tell them what kind of a man he was. At that time, I had no idea he was in the hospital. In a prison hospital. They came for him during the night, he recognized their car and jumped from the window. They saved his life though and he was supposed to stand trial. I told them: I hardly knew him. They screamed at me, telling me they knew all about how terrible he was and didn't believe I wouldn't know anything about it. They claimed the Nazis helped him to get to England in 1938 when he promised to work for them and said that was the reason why he was such a lenient prosecutor in Nuremberg. But, apparently, the English found out and forced him to work for them after the war here. I said: Not a peep from him to me about any of this. Boy, did they rough me up. Claimed I was helping him and said I could save myself by telling them everything I knew. Anybody else would have done just that. But, I am different. You can treat me anyway you want to, I said, I know nothing. They kept me there for a few days till I folded and get this, in the end, they let me go. He got fifteen years, my uncle, that is, and I was sacked. Not because of him, of course. Where there's a will, there is a way. The guests are complaining that the cultural programs are not interesting, they said. And they also don't approve of my conduct and the way I dress. I say: The programs I arranged were no good, but they were too good for those officers. And when it comes to my conduct, I am single and I can wear whatever I please. And I walked out. Actually, the whole thing was no joke. All this happened so fast that I had no time to find any other job. I didn't even have a place to sleep. I threw together my luggage, got on the bus, rode to the terminal and collapsed on a bench. I couldn't think straight. The bus driver, who knew me by sight, started up a conversation when he finished his shift. That was a miracle! The first human being, my x-ray eyes told me, pure as the driven snow. To make a long story short—he took me home with him and we got married. Not right away. He was divorced, didn't want to rush into anything and neither did I. However, his mother, she went crazy. Accusing me of luring him off to live in sin. What will people say and all that kind of stuff. So, in the end, we gave in, except for one thing. I said: Mommy, I have to call her that—you can complain all you want, but I am not going to wear anything else. And she replied: If you only had two blue outfits, I wouldn't mind. But everything—including the coat and hat—what does it look like? A nuthouse. What bothered her most, of course, was that I didn't have anything. I mean money of course. She says: Dear girl, you are thirty. How come you haven't saved any money? Honza has to pay alimony, I own the apartment—how are you going to live?—Of course, I went to work right away with Honza—that's my husband—as a conductor for a bus company, but that wasn't good enough for her. In the end I got so ticked off, I thought about leaving. But I enjoyed living with Honza. Not that I was in love with him. He's younger than I am and at the beginning, he struck me as a little bit of a drip. Except for that mother of his, living with him was really peaceful. But I couldn't get over all that stuff with those soldiers. So, I say: I am going to write up what kind of place that Recreation Center was. I'll send it to the State Prosecutor and also to the Ministry of Justice. The manager of the Recreation Center, the caretaker—the old bag—and some of the therapeutic personnel and maybe even some higher-ups, I'll get them all. And Honza says: For God's sake, what good will that do? Do you think I've got no tales to tell? It's like a giant pyramid. The biggest bastard sits on top of the smaller one and so on and on. You can't change that. And I say: Maybe you can't. But I am going to try. He says: So what? Let's say, you dynamite the pyramid. Will anybody feel better because of that? Will you? Tomorrow, everything will start all over again, maybe it will be even worse. I tell you what, let's take a walk, have dinner somewhere, a little bit of wine, see some nice people, how about it?—Well, there's something to that. For instance, I go to a store and say: I need blue stockings. They say: We don't have any now and are not going to have any in the future. Call the manager, I say. Honza grabs my elbow and whispers: What do you want him for? I say: I am going to test him, just a little bit and then I'll put the squeeze on him. For God's sake, says Honza, it's not his fault. He is not the one who makes the stockings. But he talks nicely to the manager, slips him a little bottle—and in a month or two we stop by, and there's a dozen pair of stockings waiting for me under the counter. Sometimes, I lose some sleep over all this business. I have to get up and walk around the kitchen. You can't imagine the horror when I realize how much I actually know, even about his silly mother, it's volumes, and something should be done about it. But in the end, I go back to bed. Peace and quiet is really much more important.—

When my uncle was released from jail and got a piece of paper announcing his innocence, he asked me to come over and told me he wasn't feeling very well, he also said that I will get the china and the stamps. And right away, I was all mixed up again. Should I go for it or not? By that time I knew what it meant to be in love. It's not just the feeling. That happens when you are seventeen. But Honza and I, we lived through a lot together. For twelve years we always stuck with each other. That's called love. And I began to get worried. His Ma ruined one marriage already, and when I couldn't find work and we were all the time broke, she put me through the mill. And poor Honza kept repeating: The worst thing is, there is no peace.—Did you ever sit on a bench at a terminal and realize that you own nothing and don't know a soul? You can live like that if you are a cat. But I am not a cat. And haven't been one for a long time. And those damned stamps and the china could be the answer. I could see it clearly. I would come and say: Mommy, here is twenty five thousand. Either you stop hassling Honza about me, or I am moving out. Do you understand that? I told my brother last time I talked with him: For God's sake, try to understand or I'm not responsible for what happens. He says: Don't threaten me. I don't scare easily. Believe it or not, I started crying. For him, because he was so hard. For Honza's mother, for myself, knowing the whole dirty mess I'm getting myself in, simply for all of us. I guess, I really cried an awful lot, because in the end he said: Yeah, the fact is, you've suffered much more than I have. I will withdraw the charge against you and we'll straighten things out, somehow. It won't be twenty five thousand, but I won't gyp you either. My God, was I ever happy. It was just like the old Jirka. I said: Jirko, I was always on your side. When they went after you, asking: What was your brother doing during the war? I said: He helped the prisoners. Yeah, as a jailer. It could have cost him his neck. Of course, I told him right away what was in store for him, Zorka's husband, inspection of the warehouse, we forgave each other everything and had a drink to celebrate. But my brother surprised me once more. Imagine this: As soon as the inspection was over, instead of giving me what he promised, he started the lawsuit as if nothing happened. It came before a new judge, I got the summons and lost. What do you think of that? Honza says: Mili, that uncle of yours will be the death of us yet. Give back all that junk, we'll pay and keep going as usual. I say: We will pay? Where's the money supposed to come from? Are you going to sell the furniture? He says: Why not? Look at it this way. It's a beautiful day. Everything blue. I say: So much more reason. We will appeal and I am sure we will win. I was just so furious at my brother and also at myself, for being so stupid. Right away, I mailed the appeal. But during the night it came to haunt me. I say: Old girl you are lost. But there is no other way. I say: That's it. If Honza wants to leave you, he'll leave you no matter what. He must be just sick of you by now. Do what he says, he is right.—But you cannot stop an avalanche halfway down the mountain. And I had one sure ace up my sleeve. The last one. A man who told me once: If you are ever in a tough spot, call. So, I wrote to him. A little voice whispered: Go, talk it over face to face—. But Honza kept saying a letter is sufficient and I was myself reluctant to get into this mess. In a way, I hoped God would take care. My brother, on the other hand, had different ideas. All of a sudden, there he is, waving this document, showing he worked during the war with the underground. I said: Your Honor, he sure did. In return for gold and jewelry. The prisoners had families and they sure forked over. They paid for every little favor.—Man, was he mad. My darling kid brother. I was a Gestapo whore, mentally handicapped—it runs in the family, according to him, because our Dad committed suicide and Mother died in a mental institution. That's not true, she had a tumor and was in a regular hospital. I had to leave the job with the Airlines, he claimed, because I was going cuckoo, and when it comes to the china and the stamps, I made it all up. I am not of sound mind and that is the reason I was pensioned off early and there is no truth to my saying that he acknowledged the inheritance, only I came to him once drunk and he promised something in order to get rid of me, and in the end he wanted them to have me declared legally incompetent. Well, I said: Unsound mind? True, there was an accident. When I worked for those buslines. A big smash up it was, too. Eight months I spent in the hospital. They nearly gave up on me, but I survived. Just look, my hands, feet, everything fine. Only the headaches remained. That's the reason I was given disability. But be honest. Do I look like a nut? Not even my brother succeeded in persuading them of that, although he bribed both the doctors on the commission. However, he succeeded in the rest. They tried to confuse the caretaker, so that in the end she wasn't really sure if she saw him entering my uncle's apartment, and our appeal was turned down. Honza pleaded again, but there was no other way for me. I took everything away and didn't pay a cent. And so, the day before yesterday, the bailiff rang the bell. To confiscate the furniture, he came. I say: Nothing doing. Except, he brought with him some policemen, they stuck labels on everything, everything Honza and I bought together, radio, fridge, labels everywhere, and if I don't come to some agreement with my brother, they'll sell it at an auction and impound my pension and Honza's salary, they said. Honza was speechless, but you should hear his mother. Christ, she wouldn't let go. I say: Don't you worry, Mommy, they'll be back to apologize. Because now, I'll really get going.—

I pulled myself together and off I went. Wait a minute, I know just what you are going to say. She isn't competent. Right? The famous Supreme Court. It's all crystal clear to me. I am not going to be in this all by myself. I will have somebody on my side. That's my ace. You know who? General Pavlica. You are familiar with the name, I hope. His son works there. Yes, at the Supreme Court. Aha! How about that? I'll win this one. Pavlica will take care of it for me. Why? Because at one time, I meant something to him. Maybe. And when I tell him what I know—here, I wrote it all down, the whole life, just to make sure, so he could see that this story is dynamite—it could be all wrapped up in a week. Part of it his son and part him. Aren't you bowled over? You can't believe it? You think, he hasn't seen her all those years, hasn't answered her letter, he is a big cheese now, he wouldn't give her the time of day.—Maybe you're right. It might go like this. He will try. Won't answer the phone. Or maybe he'll come and say: Sweetie, who's not badly off today? But if you ever get into a really tough spot, just let me know.—I know all about that. Except, I know his chauffeur. He still works for him, I made sure of that. I am going to tell him: Freddy, where are you taking the old boy tonight? And you can bet your bottom dollar that I'm going to find out, because Freddy—well, that's another story. So, Pavlica can't hide from me even if he buried himself underground. But he will try to wiggle out of it. Look, Sweetie, how am I supposed to force your brother to do anything? I am just a small fry.—How do I react to that? Pavlica, I'll help your memory. You used to come to see me at the Recreation Center, Nine Cliffs. I called you from there when I was sacked. You made some promises then, do you remember? You don't? And before that, who swore to chuck his career? Those were the days, do you remember? And all that booze. One girl actually died. Helenka. Do you remember? You don't? Would you like to read it right here?—And he says: Bluebell—that's right, that's what he called me—Bluebell, you wouldn't do that to me? And I say: If I don't get what belongs to me, Pavlico, I am going to see Kilinger and spill the beans. You know I can do it. He knows that damn well. And he sure knows who Franta Kilinger is. Everything is going to work out. You don't believe it? Let's have a bet. There are moments when I have terrific powers. In my eyes and in my head. I see through everything. You're laughing. You want me to try it? Should I? On you? I don't want to offend you. By the way, why are you staring like that all the time? Do you know me from somewhere? You were also in a fix, am I right? Should I tell you what kind of a fix? Wait a moment. I have to concentrate. Somebody, who was important to you left you in the lurch. Am I right? You are mad at him. No? At whom then? Nobody? Don't lie. You are also part of a pyramid. Everybody is. You wouldn't repay them in kind if you could? Don't you have nightmares? Well, I don't think you realize what you are capable of. One day you might find out.—Man, my head is just throbbing. We better quit. I always get a headache. That's because I remember everything. Everything. Even you. I used my x-ray on you. I have it now. It's nothing, you don't need to worry. When this whole thing is done with, I promise myself to live the way Honza does. I won't be able to manage it a hundred percent, but he won't know. He thinks I go to the kitchen to have a smoke during the night. Do you know what I do there? I pray. It helps. I have a blue nightgown. Long, down to my heels. I didn't used to go to church, but he who hears confessions, prays afterwards, I am sure. He only knows what people confess. I, on the other hand, have to pray a thousand times more. Otherwise, I would go crazy. And then you really don't know yourself. Many a time, I hear a voice whispering: Don't fool around with it. Chuck it all out. Lash out at everyone you can, let it all explode, let everything be buried in the debris, everything, everything, everything.—And just like Honza I say: God will solve it all. But the voice replies: God is great, yet, he sent the flood on us all.—You see, dear Sir, that's what I have to live with. You probably think: What a bunch of crazy ideas and this creature in blue.—But, were it not for that, today, I might be up for murder. And not just for one. Do you know what I mean? Nobody knows. One of Honza's friends used to call me Blue Angel. To him, it was just a joke.

(The sound of a train slowing down.)

Well, we are here. And just look at it, what a day it turned out to be. All blue. Do you want to wish me luck? You don't want to. Well, you don't have to. I'll manage. If not, God Almighty, I'd rather not think about it.

(Sounds of a railway station.)

Have yourself a nice day. By the way,—what's your color? You don't know? You better find out. Good bye.

END

The Detour

Pavel Landovský

translated by Ewald Osers
adapted to the American idiom by Donald Soule

CHARACTERS:

Ted Hevrle, nicknamed ''Butts,'' a prisoner under escort (48).
Victor Fidler, State Security (33)
Ferdinand Novak, State Security (30)
Jan Malek, driver, guard, dog-handler (25)
Major Makovsky, Camp Commandant (55)
Kubelka, a prisoner (21)
Sonya, Fidler's mistress and wife of his boss (29)
Jane, her friend, a clerk-typist (29)
Frank, a womanizer (25)
Vince, his admirer (23)
Several anonymous voices (prisoners, master-of-ceremonies, loudspeaker,
    band and guests at the dance).

[Translator's Note: Hevrle is pronounced something like Hevileh. The stress
is always on the first syllable.]

1.

OFFICE OF THE LABOR CAMP COMMANDANT

Through the open window come the background noises of a labor camp. A dog is heard barking in the distance. Immediately outside the window a group of prisoners clatters past in nailed boots. A croaking announcement is heard over the camp loudspeaker system.

VOICE: Hut 4, departure for washroom postponed to 15.30 hours. Night shift Energo-3 project, departure for the building site delayed by one hour. Additional rations of dried food will be given out on the site. I repeat, Hut 4, departure for . . .

FIDLER: Malek, shut the window and then get to the canteen. My eardrums are bursting.

MALEK: Done, Comrade Lieutenant.

FIDLER: Lieutenant, State Security—fat lot of use that is to us here. We've been kept waiting for three solid hours! (*The window is closed: the loudspeaker is muffled.*)

MALEK: I'd better drive into town to fill up the tank. By the look of things we'll have a bit of a rush. Should have left at two.

FIDLER: Get going then. We'll leave the moment he's handed over to us.

MALEK: Sure.

NOVAK: And get some cigarettes while you're at it—but get a kind you can smoke. Sparta would be best—if they've got any.

MALEK: I'll try the bar. (*Footsteps, sound of a door being opened and shut.*)

FIDLER: You know what, Ferdie—I'm getting pretty fed up with all this.

NOVAK: What can you do? That telex should have been sent yesterday but the silly bitch didn't get it off till this morning. Now the prisoner's working on a building site, 30 miles from the camp . . . so how the hell can you take him over if he isn't here?

FIDLER: Normally I wouldn't mind. But I've got a date.

NOVAK: Better forget about it. You won't make it back to Prague today.

FIDLER: (*Laughs bitterly.*) I made a date *here*—only 10 miles this side of Usti. At a mountain inn.

(*After a perfunctory knock the door opens and Major Makovsky, the Camp Commandant, enters.*)

MAKOVSKY: Good afternoon, comrades, here I am at last. Major Makovsky. You could say this whole place comes under me. (*Laughs.*) Only sometimes it gets on top of me.

FIDLER: Fidler, State Security.

NOVAK: Novak, State Security.

MAKOVSKY: Yes, I know, comrades. My deputy reported to me, but it's just a case of bad luck. Nothing to be done. Prisoner Hevrle works at a building site 30 miles from the camp, and this happens to be his shift. When the telex arrived his party had already left.

FIDLER: But surely, Comrade Commandant, it would have been no problem to send a car out and bring the man back so he could be handed over to us!

MAKOVSKY: Depends how you look at it, comrades. You say no problem . . . But prisoner Hevrle is the leader of the work detail. He's in charge of a whole sector. If I snatch him away in the middle of his shift the daily quota's all shot to hell. Believe me, with the material they send you here, it's not so easy to find a guy who can run a whole construction sector. Here, I've specially brought his personal record card with me . . . There, you see . . . Recommended for discharge after serving half his sentence. Let's not kid ourselves, comrades, he's a real worker. And he wasn't brought in for theft of State property or for parasitism or for disturbing the peace. I'll miss him.

NOVAK: (*Laughs maliciously.*) I don't think you'll miss him for very long. We'll take him away for interrogation and then he'll have another sentence slapped on him.

MAKOVSKY: (*Measuring his words.*) *That* is no longer my business. I'm responsible for the plan, I am interested in people who can work. Even if they're prisoners. The paradox is, the ones I need most because they're good guys are sent home after half their term just because they're good guys.

NOVAK: Never mind, you'll be lucky with Hevrle. He'll be yours for quite a few years yet. (*Laughs maliciously.*)

MAKOVSKY: (*After a pause.*) Have you had anything to eat, comrades?

FIDLER: (*Sarcastically.*) Somehow in this setting one loses one's appetite.

MAKOVSKY: I'll have some coffee sent in for you, and in about an hour, when the shift comes back, we'll settle the whole thing. You'll excuse me until then. You understand, I'm not here for my health. (*Footsteps, the door being opened and shut.*)

NOVAK: (*After a pause.*) A little tame, don't you think, our dear Commandant? He could do with a dose of pepper up his ass.

FIDLER: (*Casually.*) Waste of time. They come under ᵗʰᵉ Justice Ministry.

(*Crossfade from stirring march music from the camp loudspeaker to music from a car radio, just before the car pulls up.*)

2.

OUTSIDE THE MOUNTAIN INN

A Zhiguli-1600 car brakes to a halt with a flourish. The light music from the car radio is immediately drowned by a woman's voice.

SONYA: Well, this is it. For the duration of the weekend my dear family can go to hell. Including my beloved husband.

JANE: (*Making herself heard over the music.*) What's that, Sonya?

SONYA: (*Turns the radio down.*) That my dear husband comrade colonel can go to hell. As for the kid, she's with her grandmother.

JANE: Fantastic. You say the rooms are reserved?

SONYA: Yes. Fidler fixed it.

JANE: Who?

SONYA: Fidler of course!

JANE: Victor? So *that* was the surprise? You're still playing around with him?

SONYA: What do you think? What I like about him is, he takes risks. There's a kick in it, my dear Jane—having an affair with a subordinate, and all the time my commander-in-chief husband could squash him for it like a cockroach.

JANE: And the other one? What kind of man is he?

SONYA: Oh, quite presentable. But married unfortunately. So, once again, no wedding bells for you.

JANE: (*Peeved.*) As if I were dying to get hitched to some guy . . . Look, can you see what I see? Garlands and Chinese lanterns! Is there a party on or something?

SONYA: (*Contentedly.*) So much the better. Music, dancing, love, wine . . .

JANE: What time will they be here?

SONYA: Just after seven, he said. Promised to be on the dot.

JANE: Time for a dip then!
SONYA: Sure. There's a swimming pool just behind the place.
JANE: Fantastic!

(*Crossfade: The car door is slammed shut. Footsteps on the gravel. The music from the car radio, audible through the open window, gradually fades out.*)

3.

OFFICE OF THE LABOR CAMP COMMANDANT

Fidler and Novak are still waiting. Background noise following the return of the party from the building site: trampling feet, shouted commands, reports, now and again laughter.

FIDLER: (*Nervously.*) You know, that guy's trying to make fools of us! The bus with our man has been back for at least half an hour and we're still sitting here like bumps on a log.
NOVAK: Tell me, Victor, what's the other one like?
FIDLER: Not bad at all. Dark hair, first-class boobs. Looks like we'll have to put this commandant in his place!
NOVAK: (*Refuses to be diverted.*) I wouldn't mind at all . . . So long as my old woman doesn't hear about it. (*A knock at the door.*)
FIDLER: Finally. Come in!
KUBELKA: (*Cautiously opening the door.*) Comrade Commandant, sir, prisoner Kubelka reporting for cleaning duty!
FIDLER: (*Furiously.*) What do you want?
KUBELKA: Mop the floor.
FIDLER: (*Sarcastically.*) You can tear it up for all I care. I'm not your commandant.
KUBELKA: (*With exaggerated politeness.*) Won't take a minute. I'll just show it the wet rag. (*He wrings out his floor cloth, fusses about with his bucket.*)
NOVAK: (*Continuing the conversation.*) And she's a friend of Sonya's?
FIDLER: (*Lowering his voice.*) Yes. Some girl typist from the Public Procurator's office.
NOVAK: Listen, Victor, does she know that we'll show up two strong?
FIDLLER: Naturally I told Sonya what a puritan you are, but I also promised her that I'll convert you.
NOVAK: I'm no puritan! I just don't want my old woman to get wind . . .
FIDLER: Don't worry, those two aren't going to shout it from the rooftops. It would be a lot worse for Sonya. (*Laughs meaningly.*)
NOVAK: You know I think it's phenomenal, the way you have the nerve to chase the old man's wife.
FIDLER: Except that it's the other way round. She's chasing me, as you can

see.

KUBELKA: (*Wringing out his floor cloth.*) Comrade Commandant, could you please step over to where I've done already? I still have to swab under the table . . .

NOVAK: This isn't your commandant.

KUBELKA: (*Slyly.*) But how should I address him? As a prisoner, I'm not allowed by regulations to address him any other way.

FIDLER: (*Irritably.*) Well, get on with it, finish your damned job and go and address someone else! By the way, what did you do to get here?

KUBELKA: (*Cheekily.*) Oh, I addressed some old woman as "miss". . .

FIDLER: I don't think that's all that funny. (*Sound of the door. The Camp Commandant enters. Footsteps.*)

MAKOVSKY: Well then, comrades, the prisoner Hevrle is with us once more. A few formalities and you can move off. (*Barks at Kubelka.*) Kubelka, what the devil are you doing here?

KUBELKA: I'm mopping the floor, Comrade Commandant, sir. I've been detailed for office cleaning.

MAKOVSKY: Get the hell out of here, man! How did you get in in the first place?

KUBELKA: (*Quick-wittedly.*) From this morning's service roster.

MAKOVSKY: (*Almost pacified.*) Well, you can carry on in the evening. Dismiss! (*Kubelka disappears with the speed of lightning.*)

FIDLER: Well, where is he?

MAKOVSKY: As soon as the shift change-over is finished and a report's been made he'll have his bath and I'll hand him over to you.

NOVAK: (*Attempting a joke.*) We'd be happy to accept him unwashed. Main thing, we finally get away. We're in a hurry.

MAKOVSKY: Would you like another coffee? Or something for the road?

FIDLER: We've already had three coffees. (*Flicks his lighter.*) Damn it, have I really smoked twenty cigarettes in two hours? That was a full pack.

MAKOVSKY: (*Seemingly out of context.*) I'll finish that fellow! Excuse me for just one moment . . .

(*Crossfade: hurried footsteps, a door being slammed, a police whistle.*)

4.

WASH ROOM

Thirty men washing. Joking and the sound of water.

KUBELKA: (*Shouting in a whisper.*) You, Butts! Come into the last shower with me. I know something.

HEVRLE: (*With affectation.*) Can't you see, my dear fellow, that I can't hear anything especially with the water running? Besides, my ears are full of soap.

KUBELKA: Stop clowning, Hevrle! This is serious.

HEVRLE: Now what interesting tale have you got to offer, you king of pickpockets? (*Turns the water off.*)

KUBELKA: You'll be surprised. Over there, in the camp office, there are two Security guys who want to pick you up and take you back for interrogation.

HEVRLE: Oh shit! Come along to the shower! (*Hurried footsteps on wet tiles.*)

KUBELKA: (*On the way, hurriedly.*) I saw them and heard them through the window while I was sweeping in the courtyard . . . They've been waiting for two hours. So, out of sheer curiosity, what do I do but march straight in, pretending I want to clean the office, and would you believe it—they swallowed it hook, line and sinker. Let me tell you, Butts, let me tell you it smells of arrest! Better stock up with butts!

HEVRLE: Greater love hath no man.

KUBELKA: Oh yes, one other thing. They're in a hell of a hurry because they have a date with two broads afterwards. Somewhere near here . . . Oh yes, and one of them is the wife of their superior officer—just in case it comes in useful. And one other thing. One of them's called Victor—if that means anything to you. He's got a real ugly mug, makes you itch to push it in. And the other is a—well, looks like a nice enough guy, a bit on the stupid side.

HEVRLE: (*Laughing.*) The good one and the wicked one. Seen it all before. The usual pair of comics.

KUBELKA: They're certainly in a hurry, so you'd better keep your foot on the brake pedal a bit, Butts, and get them really steamed up.

HEVRLE: Many thanks, Kubelka. And now I need your help, or else I won't be able to manage. Listen carefully—my most important things are in the sick-bay, locked up in the poison cupboard. The young doctor who's in here because of that road accident knows all about it. Get the guys to smuggle them out somehow, but not till after three months or so, just in case I don't come back. Next, I have a little cash in my civilian shoes. Glued under the insole. But if they won't let me change clothes, somebody will have to lend me a little and slip it into the pack of cigarettes in my locker. But into an unopened pack because they're sure to frisk me. Oh yes, and my knife is hidden in the pipe on the left behind my bunk. You can keep that. It's got a nail-file and scissors. (*The door is snatched open.*)

A PRISONER: (*Hoarsely.*) Kubelka, the old man is storming through all the huts, screaming he's going to kill you. Got to go—cheers! (*The door is slammed shut again.*)

KUBELKA: That's all I needed.

HEVRLE: D'you know why he wants to kill you?

KUBELKA: I do. I emptied a packet of cigarettes for one of those two in the office, and I lifted some 30 crowns or so from a jacket hanging over the back of a chair.

HEVRLE: Idiot.

KUBELKA: I can't help it. It's stronger than I am. But they won't find anything. I've hidden it in the Commandant's map case. I'll take it back next chance I get. (*The rushing sound of the water is drowned by the camp loudspeaker.*)

VOICE: Attention, attention, here is an announcement: Gang leader prisoner Hevrle, Edward, 1931, to report immediately, with his day-work sheet, to the office of the Commandant of the Correction Center! I repeat, Hevrle with work sheet immediately to the Commandant!

HEVRLE: This is it. Wish me luck.

(*Crossfade: A lively polka comes from the camp loudspeaker.*)

5.

OFFICE OF THE LABOR CAMP COMMANDANT

Vigorous knocking at the door.

HEVRLE: (*Clicking his heels with military precision.*) Comrade Commandant, sir, prisoner Hevrle reporting present as ordered!

MAKOVSKY: (*Officially.*) You have your work sheet with you? You're being collected by an escort.

HEVRLE: The work sheets are always processed after supper, Comrade Commandant. I had no idea—

FIDLER: (*Angrily.*) We have no time.

HEVRLE: Permission, Comrade Commandant, to make an observation?

MAKOVSKY: Granted.

HEVRLE: I must first of all make a report on an accident at work. Skorkovsky has, saving your presence, sir, cut his ass open on a rusty piece of tin.

MAKOVSKY: Why didn't you tell me before, man?

HEVRLE: I had to take him to the sick bay as soon as we got back.

FIDLER: (*Nervously.*) We have no time.

HEVRLE: (*Cheekily to Fidler.*) *I* didn't cut his ass open, Comrade Investigation Officer, but I have to write out the report—unless, of course, the comrade Commandant decides to do without it.

FIDLER: (*Solemnly.*) In the name of the Republic—

MAKOVSKY: Hevrle, will you please finish this business right here in the office . . .

HEVRLE: Skorkovsky has to sign it.

FIDLER: (*Solemnly.*) In the name of the Republic—

MAKOVSKY: (*Desperately.*) Hold it, Comrade Lieutenant. I'm not allowed to hand him over without his work record. I have my regulations. A special case due to an accident at work is a special case due to an accident at work. There's nothing anyone can do about it. {*To Hevrle.*} How bad is the injury?

HEVRLE: Tolerable, I'd say, on the whole. What's worse is that the civilian foreman is responsible because he sent him down the shaft to cement in the rungs on a simple flat seat. But safety regulations demand that a scaffolding be set up for such work. So I've got to make a report or else I'll be in hot water myself. Besides, Skorkovsky is the only skilled bricklayer in the whole construction gang, Comrade Commandant, which means that, saving your presence, we are even deeper in the shit. Because even *if* you can find a replacement for tomorrow I would at least have to give the new man a rough explanation of what the job's all—

FIDLER: In the name of the—

HEVRLE: (*Continuing unperturbed.*)—about on that building site. Otherwise you might just as well bury your quarterly plan now—not to mention the fact that we are lagging behind already. And that, Comrade Commandant, means that the supervisory staff won't get their bonuses—including, if you will permit me, yourself, Comrade Commandant—and the prisoners will immediately lose their extra rations, and all their other privileges as well, and this will mean—

FIDLER: (*At last shouts him down.*) In the name of the Republic—are you the sentenced prisoner Hevrle, Edward, born January 6, 1931?

HEVRLE: (*Yelling back.*) Yes sir, Hevrle, Edward, January 6, 1931!

FIDLER: In the name of the Republic—you are under arrest in accordance with Article . . .

(*Crossfade from Tchaikovsky's piano concerto in B Flat Minor to a contemporary hit tune, setting the atmosphere for the dance at the mountain inn.*)

6.

DANCE AT THE MOUNTAIN INN

Garden restaurant with provincial dance band trying to copy international stars. Poor sound system. The MC welcomes the guests in a booming voice and introduces the musicians.

M.C.: Dada Nemechek's band welcomes you most cordially and thanks you for turning out in such large numbers. (*Their signature tune is played.*) Our soloists—Jerry Dub, saxophone; George Kridlo, trumpet; and at the drums Frank Kurka. (*Applause, ebbing away as the dialogue begins.*)

JANE: Sonya, don't turn now. Not until I tell you. Then look towards the bar. There are two types propping it up and goggling at us all the time.

SONYA: I know. I saw them in the mirror.

JANE: They are the ones with the Renault 30. I noticed them by the pool.

SONYA: Look like currency fiddlers or pimps.

JANE: So long as they aren't local police narks!

SONYA: I'd laugh my head off imagining how Fidler would make it hot for them. I watched him at it in Karlovy Vary once, when one of the cops there was getting a little too big for his britches. He let him go on for a quarter hour, then he simply produced his warrant card and said: "Very well, we'll take a statement at your station. But let me first point out to you that you have seriously infringed service regulations in at least ten different ways." You should have seen that local bumpkin all of a sudden pull in his tail!

(The signature tune wells up again.)

M.C.: At the piano Jaromir Kyncl . . . Overall musical direction Dada Nemechek! *(Flourish, applause.)*

(The following dialogue takes place at the bar.)

VINCE: *(Stammers now and then.)* Have a look, F-Frankie, those t-two girls over there aren't b-bad.

FRANK: *(With a man-of-the-world air.)* My dear Vincent, the way I see it those two are here on their own. Two little dollies out for thrills.

VINCE: N-naturally! And afterwards they'll d-denounce us for b-being drunk in charge, like those two g-girls from the Army Directorate whom we p-picked up in the g-game park last year.

FRANK: Don't be morbid! If I suspected every skirt of being a police mark—

VINCE: You'd be about r-right.

FRANK: Now you zero in on the little dark one and I'll pick up the red-head.

VINCE: T-take it easy! I need a little refreshment first to stop me s-s-stammering. P-properly oiled I talk like a b-book.

FRANK: Then get on with it! Else you'll stammer till someone else beats us to it and we are left out in the cold.

(Crossfade: Band starts up a new number.)

7.

SQUARE OF THE LABOR CAMP

Car with engine running. "Retreat"—the evening drill period of the prisoners. From a

*distance come bellowed words of command, such as: "Hut 7 C, at the double, quick
march!"—"Pick them up, you flat-footed bums!" "You look like a damn pack of god-
dam schoolgirls!" and the like.*

MALEK: Let's have your hands, Hevrle!

HEVRLE: (*Mutinously.*) I have to travel in bracelets?

MALEK: (*Softly.*) Regulations. Otherwise I'd be in trouble.

HEVRLE: (*Likewise softly.*) One moment. Let me have a word with Fidler first.
He bullied me for eight months during my detention—maybe he'll forget
about these bracelets—(*laughs*)—for old times' sake . . . (*Loudly.*) Comrade
Lieutenant, forgive me for interrupting, but is it really necessary for me to
wear handcuffs during transport? You know perfectly well there's nothing
further from my mind than resisting the authorities. Well then, with a little
goodwill surely one might let me keep my right hand free so I can scratch
myself a little. Or light a cigarette. Seeing as how I'm not a criminal? I'm
inside under Article 98, subversion of the Republic, isn't that so, and
everybody inside on that charge is an angel.

FIDLER: (*Irritably.*) I'm not going to discuss escort regulations with you,
Hevrle.

HEVRLE: (*Continues irresistibly.*) Comrade Commandant, sir, couldn't you put
in a good word for me? After all, I've enjoyed every possible privilege for
model behavior and good work performance, complete freedom of movement on camp territory, and even civilian footwear. During my two years
here, have I behaved like a gangster—somebody who deserves to be put in
chains now?

MAKOVSKY: Comrade Lieutenant, Hevrle is indeed in the category of
"prisoner enjoying freedom of movement."

FIDLER: (*Grumpily.*) Very well, Comrade Major. Once we are in the car I'll
have them taken off again. But let's get out of here finally! Did you hear
that? Now he's demanding civilian footwear!

MAKOVSKY: He's entitled to that—what can I do? After all, you're not ar-
resting him as a free citizen. We are a kind of authority. (*Laughs.*) Well,
we're nearly ready. All he has to do now is collect his ration discontinuation
slip from catering.

FIDLER: (*Furiously.*) This is the—

MAKOVSKY: I can't help it. If I hand him over to you *without* discontinuation,
his four dumplings are left over *here*, while on the other hand he won't get
anything to eat in detention. (*Laughs.*) I couldn't square that with my conscience.

FIDLER: (*Loudly.*) Malek, leave his right hand free or else we'll have to lug his
carton!

HEVRLE: (*Exaggeratedly.*) I'm most obliged, Comrade Investigating Officer.
You're an understanding person. Unfortunately I haven't received my

dried goods ration yet—but today is Friday, so with a little luck they'll give it to me out of turn—otherwise I'd have to go hungry all night, and unless I'm checked in first thing tomorrow morning—and don't forget tomorrow's Saturday—I would have died from starvation by Sunday, Comrade Investigating Officer, and you might have to—

FIDLER: (*With a sneer.*) Don't worry, Hevrle. You'll survive—don't you think?

HEVRLE: (*In a similar tone.*) I'm covered—I've reported it to you.

NOVAK: (*Explodes.*) Hevrle, stop acting the good soldier Švejk—we'll soon put an end to your clowning around!

(*Crossfade: from "The Radetzky March" to the mountain inn, where things are getting livelier all the time.*)

8.

GARDEN RESTAURANT OF THE MOUNTAIN INN

The festivities are in full swing.

M.C.: (*In a booming voice.*) Once again we invite you to the dance floor to let yourselves be carried away by the rhythm of popular favorites. First we have that evergreen number from the repertoire of our top performers —"Come let me guide you through Paradise." (*The music starts. Frank and Vince pounce on their chosen partners.*)

FRANK: (*To Sonya.*) May I have this dance?

SONYA: (*Laughing.*) You took your time! You may.

VINCE: (*To Jane.*) May I have the pleasure?

JANE: A pleasure . . .

VINCE: You were saying?

JANE: My pleasure.

VINCE: I m-mean: would you like to dance?

JANE: My pleasure! (*Rises.*)

VINCE: T-t-thank you.

JANE: My pleasure.

VINCE: D-don't mention it.

(*The music is getting noisier. The sound of feet shuffling on the dance floor.*)

FRANK: (*Dancing.*) You can call me Frank. Or Frankie. Whichever you like.

SONYA: What makes you think I want to call you *anything*?

FRANK: Well, in case you do.

SONYA: And what did they call you at home? Frankie, I bet. But Francis is quite a pretty name . . . (*Adding maliciously.*) Except that nobody's called that nowadays.

FRANK: (*Lying.*) My granddad was French and they called him François. I was supposed to be named after him, but the registrar turned me into a plain Francis. You know what it was like in the fifties . . .

SONYA: Me? No idea.

FRANK: O.K. . . . How about you joining us at our table? Or the other way round. (*The music is getting louder. Shuffling of feet.*)

VINCE: Hot, isn't it?

JANE: Not at all, chilly if anything.

VINCE: T-that's what I t-think . . . That b-band's really s-swinging, isn't it?

JANE: I've heard better.

VINCE: Sh-sure. God knows where they found them.

(*Crossfade: The dance music is drowned in the monotonous roar of a car engine, accompanied by the slobbering of the police dog Kazan.*)

9.

INSIDE THE OFFICIAL CAR, A ZHIGULI 2001

The engine is running smoothly. The Alsatian Kazan nuzzles against the prisoner Hevrle, uttering friendly sounds.

HEVRLE: (*Breaking the silence.*) What a nice friendly dog . . . What's his name?

MALEK: (*Involuntarily.*) Kazan.

HEVRLE: There you are, Kazan . . . Good thing you're wearing a muzzle, otherwise you'd be licking me lovingly from head to toe.

FIDLER: Hevrle, stop this nonsense. Hold your tongue and don't play with the dog.

HEVRLE: Me, play with the dog? Why don't you take a look, Comrade Investigating Officer? Who started it, then? He wants to play . . . As I'm saying, he's friendly.

MALEK: (*Scoffing.*) Friendly . . . One word from me and you wouldn't know where you are!

HEVRLE: No, I can't believe that—what an idea.

NOVAK: Hevrle, shut your trap! Spare us the wise-cracks!

HEVRLE: (*Undaunted.*) How can I be quiet with 100 pounds of dog on my lap? He wants to play with me so I've got to try to communicate with him somehow. If he comes snuggling up to me the least I can do is say "Good doggie, good little . . ."

FIDLER: I'm warning you for the last time, no arguments! (*Laughs maliciously.*) But you can say "Good doggie, good little doggie" till hell freezes over.

HEVRLE: (*Loudly.*) Yessir. Good Kazan, little . . . What an obedient . . .

Shake hands, doggie . . . But of course . . . He can tell a fellow who's fond of dogs . . .

NOVAK: (*Lowers his voice.*) Leave him alone, Victor, and come closer. I want to ask you something.

(*Kazan grunts with pleasure. The engine is running smoothly. Fidler and Novak are whispering so that Hevrle won't hear what they are saying.*)

FIDLER: (*Lowering his voice.*) What's up?

NOVAK: (*Softly.*) What time did you tell those girls we'd be there?

FIDLER: Shortly after seven. But it's nearly nine now.

NOVAK: Can we phone them there?

FIDLER: You're joking. Where would I find a telephone in the middle of the forest?

NOVAK: You're right there.

FIDLER: We'll be in Usti by ten thirty, at this speed. (*Loudly.*) Couldn't you step on it a bit, Malek?

MALEK: (*Harshly.*) Maximum regulations speed for transport of escorted prisoners is fifty em-pee-aitch.

NOVAK: (*Lowering his voice.*) Damn it, he's right.

FIDLER: (*Continuing in a whisper.*) By the time he's signed in it'll be eleven. The prison's at the far end of the town. Take us an hour to get back provided we find a taxi straight away . . . (*Lowers his voice further.*) And from *here* it's no more than a stone's throw, through the forest—no more than nine miles from the main road.

NOVAK: You could just drop me, and I'd wait. After all, I'm not really concerned with this transport.

FIDLER: (*In a whisper.*) Put your ear closer . . . Any other driver and I'd do it like a shot. One pack of cigarettes and he'd keep quiet forever. But *this one* would use it the first chance he got. I know him, he'd either blackmail us or file a complaint. He knows how to operate.

NOVAK: How could he know where we are going or why?

FIDLER: Any detour from our route would be enough.

HEVRLE: (*From the back seat.*) Forgive me for interrupting, Comrade Investigating Officer, but it seems to me that the doggie needs a break. His nose is getting dry and that's an infallible sign that he's got to go for a walk. As a matter of fact, I do too—while we're at it.

FIDLER: Damn it, man, you've got a nerve!

HEVRLE: (*Enjoying himself.*) Comrade Investigating Officer, sir, as a prisoner I'm State property, as it were, and if I allow my bladder to burst they could prosecute me for damaging State property. For that you can get up to three years, according to article whatever-it-is, section 1, and that's something I'd rather not risk.

FIDLER: Oh for Christ's sake, Malek, stop the car or I'll lose my temper . . .
(*To Hevrle.*) But I won't give you the pleasure, Hevrle, of making me hit
you!

HEVRLE: I'm delighted to hear it, Comrade Investigating Officer.

(*The car brakes, the engine stops. The door is opened. The dog barks joyously.*)

10.

IN THE OPEN

*The summer evening is darkening. Chirping of crickets and the soft rustle of an evening
breeze.*

MALEK: (*Outside the car.*) Get out, Hevrle, and let's have your hands. And no
nonsense. . . . An escorted prisoner is an escorted prisoner. I don't want to
have to get rough.

HEVRLE: May I light a cigarette?

MALEK: By all means if you've got one.

HEVRLE: I've got a cigarette but I haven't got a light. (*The dog is sniffing all
round the car, barking occasionally.*)

MALEK: Kazan, to heel! Here are some matches. (*Kazan begins to growl.*)

HEVRLE: Thank you.

MALEK: (*Softly.*) Come round behind the car, I want to ask you something.
(*Footsteps on sand.*)

HEVRLE: (*Behind the car.*) What is it?

MALEK: (*Peaceably.*) Look, I'm only a corporal, as you can see, and I am merely doing my duty. But take my advice—don't provoke those two. They'll
make mincemeat out of you.

HEVRLE: (*Stoically.*) What will be will be.

MALEK: You're a funny sort of prisoner. (*Softly.*) What have they picked you
up for this time?

HEVRLE: That's what I'd like to know. They probably want to keep me inside
longer than my original sentence.

MALEK: You haven't done anything wrong while you've been serving it?

HEVRLE: No.

MALEK: Well, you're in the shit then.

HEVRLE: Looks like it.

MALEK: (*Amicably.*) Go on, smoke it to the end. They'll just have to be patient
. . . Kazan!

(*A soft whistle, sound of dog's paws. Muted conversation inside the car.*)

FIDLER: (*In the car.*) What d'you think—shall we risk it?

NOVAK: I don't know. Even though I'm notorious for my bad luck, I don't really see how anything could go wrong. We stop nearby, you write a little note for me, and I'll take it along. I've met Sonya.

FIDLER: (*With a man-of-the-world air.*) Sure. Hell has no fury like a woman scorned. (*Sarcastically.*) Especially the wife of one's superior officer. Mustn't shirk your duty there, work as hard as you can . . . The call of duty, ha ha ha.

NOVAK: What about the driver? Will he keep his mouth shut?

FIDLER: Not really so important. I'll squeeze him a bit. There are ways. You know the first principle of the perfect cop: know something about everybody. Buckle your holster on, pretend you're relieving him in guarding the prisoner, and send Malek over to me. An official matter . . . (*Sound of the car door. Muted talk outside, then Malek gets in.*)

MALEK: What's up?

FIDLER: Listen, Malek, I've got to make a detour. Twenty minutes or so, turning left, up into the mountains.

MALEK: Official business?

FIDLER: (*Giggling.*) Fifty-fifty.

MALEK: Oh. Well, if you'll sign my log.

FIDLER: I'm not keen on that.

MALEK: Surely, Comrade Lieutenant, sir, you cannot expect me to do unofficial trips with an escorted prisoner on board. Got to think of my own skin! Might find myself up in court for that!

FIDLER: (*Cozying up to him.*) I'd be in it too, wouldn't I?

MALEK: But *you'd* get out again. You come under another department. Seriously, I can't do it without your signature in the log.

FIDLER: (*Now matter-of-factly.*) Very well, then I'll say something else to you, Malek, so we don't waste any more time. I've got a tiny little report in my desk drawer, something about theft of gas coupons. About 2,000 litres . . . In other words—major theft of socialist common property. Here's my proposition. I keep the report buried in my desk and you drive me wherever I choose and keep it to yourself. Well? Is it a deal?

MALEK: (*After a long silence.*) O.K. . . . . It's a deal. (*The car door is slammed shut.*)

11.

OUTSIDE AND INSIDE THE CAR

During re-embarkation and subsequent journey.

MALEK: (*Furiously.*) Here, Kazan!

HEVRLE: Marvellous air . . . Well, come along, doggie, let's continue our

journey . . . This is the life, isn't it, Kazan, being driven around like a
Cabinet Minister, hardly have to put our feet on the ground.

NOVAK: Come on, Hevrle, on the double and no commentary! Once you get
going you don't know when to stop.

HEVRLE: It's been proved that chatty people live longer. Their circulation
functions more efficiently.

NOVAK: (*Now in a good mood.*) On the double! You're allowed to recite poetry
during the trip. We don't want you to complain that we've ruined your circulation.

(*The engine is started, the car moves off. The engine is humming. The men have fallen
silent.*)

FIDLER: (*After a pause, in a voice of command.*) After that transformer there, turn
left and uphill!

(*Crossfade: Percussion solo.*)

12.

DANCE AT THE MOUNTAIN INN

The band has just had a break. The sound of confused voices and the clatter of glasses.

VINCE: (*Cheerfully.*) You see? The moment I'm oiled I stop stammering.

JANE: It's true! Listen to him, Sonya, he's talking like Cicero.

VINCE: Who's he?

JANE: Oh, some loudmouth.

FRANK: Let's drink to that and then we'll order something hard. Vodka with
pepper or something like that. Drink makes life worth living!

VINCE: The cops won't look at it that way. Last spring they took away my
driving license for twelve months. And I got six months probation for
drunk driving.

SONYA: If you're silly enough to let it come to a trial . . .

FRANK: What else could he have done?

SONYA: (*Knowingly.*) There are ways of avoiding . . . By personal contacts for
example.

FRANK: Let's drink to that. Bottoms up!

SONYA: To what, if I may ask?

JANE: (*Laughs.*) To personal contacts, he means.

FRANK: Precisely.

VINCE: D'you know the one about the policeman who stops a drunken driver,
and the man gets out, has to heave, and the law gets covered in vomit from

head to toe. "You pig!" he yells at him. And the drunk says: "Me a pig? Just look at yourself!" Ha ha ha ha! (*The others utter a forced laugh.*)

SONYA: And what are your plans today? You driving back home or will you spend the night here?

FRANK: We have a holiday chalet quite close. Only three miles along the road. No risk, at this time of night. After that it's all forest tracks.

SONYA: How can you be sure? For all you know the place may be swarming with cops tonight! (*The band strikes up a smoochy tune.*)

VINCE: How about another twirl, Janey? I love smoochy tunes.

JANE: (*Gets to her feet and exclaims.*) God, am I drunk!

VINCE: Never mind. Hang on to me.

(*Crossfade: Dance music, out of tune.*)

13.

ACCIDENT IN THE FOREST

The engine is being raced and screams. It is clear that the driver has the jitters.

FIDLER: Where are you going, Malek? I told you: Turn left by the transformer.

MALEK: That was a transformer? Looked like a wayside shrine.

FIDLER: Stop the car! Right now! (*The car stops.*) Listen to me. You're changing places with me. You can play with the dog and I'll take the wheel.

HEVRLE: If it's at all possible, Comrade Investigating Officer, I'd much rather wait here by the roadside. I won't run away, cross my heart!

FIDLER: (*Sarcastically.*) You don't say. (*Slamming of doors. They change places.*)

FIDLER: I mustn't deprive you of the pleasure of a nocturnal drive through the forest. Just take nice deep breaths and fill your lungs with oxygen. You may need it.

(*The car is started up again and reversed. After that the engine is raced again.*)

MALEK: (*Anxiously.*) Comrade Lieutenant, when you're changing up into third the synchro always acts up a bit. Better double clutch.

FIDLER: Malek, Malek, how can you drive around in a car like this?

(*The engine revs are getting higher all the time, the tires can be heard screeching in the bends. So can Fidler's complacent chuckling.*)

MALEK: Everything wrong with it has been reported. The car was due for a check-up three months ago.

FIDLER: (*Laughs.*) Three months, four months, what the hell. This old wreck is still good for 90 miles an hour. (*Screech of tires.*) Once learned never forgotten. What'd you think, Ferdie?

NOVAK: I'd rather not comment.

HEVRLE: (*Declaiming.*)
There was an old girl on a stretcher
in an ambulance sent out to fetch her.
the ambulance crashed
and the stretcher was smashed—
and a surgeon will now have to patch her . . .

NOVAK: Shut your trap, Hevrle!

HEVRLE: Already silent, sir.

(*The dog begins to whine. Fidler changes up and down. He is driving like a lunatic.*)

MALEK: (*Just about manages to shout.*) Look out, a deer!

(*Noise of brakes, squealing of wheels, a crash. Glass splintering. A second crash. Then a long oppressive silence after the impact.*)

(*Abrupt change of scene without crossfade.*)

14.

DANCE AT THE MOUNTAIN INN

Utter confusion, the roar of drunken voices joining into the chorus of a silly song.

EVERYBODY:
Take your hand off my knee, there's nothing but bone there,
Nothing but bone there,
Nothing but bone there.
Move it up to my thigh, it's a meatier zone there,
A meatier zone there,
A meatier zone there.

VINCE: (*Bawling drunkenly without stammering.*) To each his own! (*Jane and Sonya shriek with laughter. The band is playing something between a foxtrot and a polka.*)

FRANK: (*Shouting.*) Hip, hip—

SONYA, VINCE, JANE: (*Answering in a roar.*) Hurray! Hurray! Hurray!

FRANK: And when we've yelled ourselves hoarse we'll all drive to the chalet.
A pal just bought me the latest Travolta disc from Vienna. Super!

(*The music breaks off in the middle of a bar so that the silence after the car accident is immediately restored.*)

15.

IN THE FOREST AFTER THE ACCIDENT

Outside and inside the car, whose doors are open. Forest noises. The panting and whining of the dog Kazan is the first sign of any life.

HEVRLE: (*Savagely.*) It seems to me, Comrade Investigating Officer, that your investigation is over. I've certainly broken my leg and at least two of my ribs have had it.

FIDLER: (*Hysterically.*) Ferdie, are you alive?

NOVAK: Yes. Only knocked my head bloody.

FIDLER: Where's Malek?

NOVAK: Thrown out of the car.

MALEK: (*Indistinctly from outside.*) Bruised my behind and bitten through my tongue.

FIDLER: Thank God.

HEVRLE: In my opinion, God can do very well without your thanks. But my leg is really broken.

FIDLER: Hevrle, please don't tempt providence. Get out and I'll have a look at it.

HEVRLE: Get out? With *this* leg? That's a bit of a problem.

FIDLER: Malek, where's the first aid box?

MALEK: (*Indistinctly.*) Should be in the trunk.

FIDLER: Bring it here, damn you! Here, take this flashlight.

MALEK: (*Indistinctly.*) I feel like I'm cut in half . . . Kazan, heel! Stop it, you filthy mutt!

NOVAK: What's he doing?

MALEK: Lapping up the deer's blood.

HEVRLE: Hope he enjoys it.

FIDLER: Hevrle, if you're faking that broken leg, you're really going to get it.

HEVRLE: And so are you!

FIDLER Ferdie, give us a hand, we'll put him on the grass.

MALEK: First of all I'm going to take the battery out. The car's over sideways in the ditch, and if the acid spills out we won't have any light.

NOVAK: Just have a look at my forehead, Victor, will you?

FIDLER: It's only a scratch . . . Come on, Hevrle, get out.

HEVRLE: (*Moaning.*) Ow, ow, ow . . .

FIDLER: Come on, come on . . . A guy like you!

HEVRLE: I didn't know you cared! Seriously though, boss, my leg has had it.

FIDLER: Just what we needed.

HEVRLE: Just what *you* needed.

NOVAK: For Christ's sake, Hevrle, hang on to me! You're like a sack of lead.

HEVRLE: I could think of someone a lot prettier to hang on to. But if it gets you out of trouble I don't want to add to your problems.

MALEK: (*Lamenting in front of the car.*) Look at that mess! The radiator's pushed right in! How am I going to explain that?

FIDLER: To hell with the radiator, Malek. For the last time, get that first aid box! Come on, Hevrle, be a good boy and sit on this tree stump where the headlights are on you and let me have a look at that leg.

HEVRLE: It's really swollen . . . I told you at the beginning—let me travel in civilian clothes. Now you have to cut my shoe open . . . Ow! Give me that knife, I'll do it myself.

FIDLER: Never lose your sense of humor, do you?

HEVRLE: Why should I? Is this *my* screw-up? It is not. I'm going to have a nice rest in the sick bay and enjoy the thought of your superior tromping on the three of you. Ha ha ha!

NOVAK: (*Without thinking.*) What do you mean—the *three* of us? I certainly didn't know— (*Pulls himself up.*)

FIDLER: Does it hurt?

HEVRLE: It hurts like hell.

MALEK: We'll never get that heap out of the ditch without a tractor.

FIDLER: It's got to come out of the ditch without a tractor, if it kills us. Otherwise we'll be in the shit up to our necks. And don't you two start thinking you're not involved in this!

HEVRLE: (*Moodily.*) Beg pardon, sir, but have you forgotten *me*? Looking at my leg it certainly concerns *me* first—I mean from a dialectical point of view.

FIDLER: Hevrle, be good enough to keep out of this. This is not *your* business—it's *mine*.

HEVRLE: (*As if suddenly transformed.*) Really, really . . . D'you think I'm a complete idiot? This is *my* business now, here on this tree stump, with you two still shaking in your boots!

NOVAK: (*Horrified.*) How dare you?

HEVRLE: You keep quiet!

FIDLER: (*Intervenes diplomatically in view of the precarious situation.*) And what exactly d'you mean by "your business," Hevrle?

HEVRLE: Comrade Lieutenant, after all those years . . . let's not kid each other. You know very well the trouble you've got yourself into and you know that I know it. And to make perfectly sure we don't misunderstand each other—will you come a little closer, I've got something private to tell you . . .

(*Fidler walks over to him.*)

HEVRLE: (*Lowering his voice.*) I'd just want to tell you that I know *why* you've made this detour, and who you intended to meet.

FIDLER: (*Taken aback.*) How could you know that?

HEVRLE: (*Whispering.*) A guy's got ears, he's got brains, he's got his sources.

FIDLER: (*Softly.*) You're an absolute swine, Hevrle.

HEVRLE: In front of you I'm not even ashamed of it.

MALEK: (*Cutting in loudly.*) Comrade Lieutenant, we'll never manage it with just the three of us. We've got to have a tractor—or maybe there's a jeep around somewhere.

FIDLER: Are you crazy, Malek? Either we do it ourselves or we've had it. If anyone finds out about this he could finish us.

HEVRLE: (*Resignedly.*) He that soweth the wind shall reap the whirlwind.

NOVAK: (*Wearily.*) Prisoner Hevrle, I order you to be quiet.

FIDLER: (*Softly.*) Cut it out, Ferdie. Don't make a fool of yourself. Can't you see he's enjoying it?

MALEK: (*Still harping on the same theme.*) Or else we might try the jack, Comrade Lieutenant. (*Yells at the dog.*) Kazan, stop it, you greedy pig!

FIDLER: (*Coming to a decision.*) We'll try that. And don't forget: a thing worth doing is worth doing well, as my grandfather used to say.

HEVRLE: You had a grandfather? You surprise me. I always thought people like you multiplied by a show of hands.

(*Much groaning and puffing, crossfading into music.*)

16.

DANCE AT THE MOUNTAIN INN

The party is livelier than ever. Drunken voices bawling, and some loose talk.

DRUNKS:
    We won't give them Prague, our town
    We'd sooner pull it down,
    We'd sooner pull it down,
    Pull it down!
    Not one afraid,
    All undismayed,
    Heads upright,
    Into the fight . . .

FRANK: It's nearly eleven. Shall we split? The band's had it up to their ears and the waiter's running round in circles with one single beer because he's forgotten who ordered it.

VINCE: At our neighbor's place there's a birthday party going on, with some types with guitars. How about it?

JANE: And you seriously want to drive there? Suppose the cops pick you up?

VINCE: (*Stammering again.*) You're j-joking, the c-cops here? By this t-time they're all drunk.

SONYA: (*Maliciously.*) Unless, of course, a few sober ones from some other district are roaming around.

VINCE: I'll organize some stuff to t-take along. White or red?

SONYA: Better get white *and* red.

FRANK: D'you know the one about Cohen trying to borrow 200 crowns from Silberstein?

JANE: No I don't.

FRANK: As I'm saying, Cohen is trying to borrow 200 crowns, and Silberstein says to him: "Listen to me, Cohen. Yesterday I caught you with my wife in my own bed. The day before yesterday you seduced my only daughter. Today you're trying to borrow 200 crowns. I warn you, Cohen, one of these days you'll go too far!"

(*Sonya and Jane burst out laughing. Crossfade: their laughter dies down in the silence of the forest.*)

17.

AT THE SCENE OF THE ACCIDENT IN THE FOREST

Puffing and grunting by the three men trying to maneuvre the car out of the ditch.

MALEK: (*Commanding.*) Hey-hupp! (*Heavy breathing.*)

NOVAK: Shit.

MALEK: I'll start her up and put her into reverse and then I'll help you push again. Maybe it'll grab hold.

(*The engine is started, screams, the wheels spin and skid. The men groan and curse.*)

FIDLER: That's no good.

HEVRLE: (*From a little distance.*) Needless to say, gentlemen, I'd love to help you, I'm a kind-hearted sort of guy, but with the best will in the world with this leg, it's impossible.

NOVAK: (*Under his breath.*) Any minute now and I'll crown him.

FIDLER: Don't do that. Knowing him, that's exactly what he's waiting for.

MALEK: So what do we do? We've been screwing around for nearly an hour now. Kazan, heel! Kazan . . . Maybe I'd better tie him up. There are all kinds of scents here in the forest. He's behaving like a lunatic.

HEVRLE: (*From a litle distance.*) He's behaving quite normally. He is in his natural environment. When he's sitting quietly under an office desk he's behaving like a lunatic. Same with humans. Come here, doggie . . . Kazan, chuck, chuck, chuck . . . That's a good dog . . .

FIDLER: Hevrle, spare us your pearls of wisdom!

HEVRLE: (*Undeterred.*) Bear in mind, boss, that my leg's getting bigger all the time. And I'm hungry enough to start eating these trees. I slaved all day like a cart horse. Besides, as a prisoner I am under the protection of the Czechoslovak Socialist Republic . . . (*A few seconds' silence.*) Well? What d'you want to do with me now? What's next?

NOVAK: (*Menacingly.*) I could think of an answer.

HEVRLE: Me too. In South America you'd just shoot me down and say I was trying to escape. But here? Where should I escape to when this whole country is surrounded by barbed wire like a cow pasture? The whole place is one big cage, and the three of you are inside just as much as I am. You've got no other choice but to accept my conditions.

FIDLER: (*With sudden resolution.*) Anything seems preferable to a court martial. All right, and what's your opinion?

HEVRLE: First of all, the way I see it, you've got to get the car out of the ditch and, from where I'm sitting, that looks to me like child's play. If you'd paid more attention at school during your physics lessons you'd know that force equals mass multiplied by acceleration. We'll come back to that later. And even though I don't know why you are taking me back into detention again, Comrade Lieutenant, I'm pretty sure that you're trying to pin some new charge on me, and that means you've got all your papers together. Fix it any way you like—but you'll retract that charge. *How* you do it is your business. After all, you weren't born yesterday.

FIDLER: (*Viciously.*) Carry on, Mr. Hevrle! I only hope your philosophizings don't misfire!

HEVRLE: Have no fear. I've worked it all out. The moment I get your car out of the ditch for you you're going to take me to a regular hospital.

FIDLER: I'm not allowed to do that. You're a prisoner.

HEVRLE: Of course you're allowed to! If there's a risk to life you are allowed to. I know the regulations.

FIDLER: A fractured leg is no risk to life. No one's going to buy that one.

HEVRLE: Keep your shirt on. I'll give you a little help if you play it my way.

FIDLER: I'm not retarded! The hospital will make a report instantly, within two hours a commission will have arrived from Prague, and you will land us in it before we've even *washed* the car!

HEVRLE: Why should I? Tell me that. After all, I want something from you and you need something from me. A perfectly normal deal.

FIDLER: (*Comes closer, softly.*) Hevrle, surely you realize that as soon as I've had two days' breathing space I'll turn off your oxygen, and you won't have anything against me at all, because tomorrow morning you've got to make a false statement unless you want to push us in, as you say. Needless to say, that statement will be on my desk within twenty minutes. And once your leg has healed we'll take your case up where we left off.

HEVRLE: Yes, Comrade Investigating Officer, I realize all that, but I wasn't born yesterday either. Because I'm going to suffer from shock, Mr. Fidler. And I'll go on doing so until you officially inform me and my lawyer that the charges have been withdrawn. Naturally I'll help the shock along a little with a stone against my skull—I can spare a little blood. And you will get to work quickly. As soon as I have your notification in my hand I'll recover from my shock and make whatever statement about the accident you want. That's a fair offer, isn't it?

FIDLER: (*After a pause.*) Ahem. Do you think I'm omnipotent? How can I withdraw the charges?

HEVRLE: Mr. Fidler, do I really have to tell you how charges are dropped? The same way they're made. You've got false witnesses, haven't you? They simply change their statement. They don't mind what they swear to.

FIDLER: God Almighty! Don't provoke me!

HEVRLE: You're in the shit and you've got to get out—that's clear. You can even work on your superior—through his wife. She'll be jittery too, afraid her double life will be discovered . . . She'll eat out of your hand!

FIDLER: (*Sadly.*) What a policeman you'd make, Hevrle! You'd be a real hyena!

HEVRLE: Possibly . . . But I'm not a policeman. My stomach wouldn't be up to it. All right then, if you don't get all this done by let's say Tuesday, then I'll have to come out of my shock and make a statement that'll give your old man a little pleasure in this world. Then you'll see some action.

FIDLER: That's enough! There's a limit to everything. (*Loudly, so the others can hear him.*) You go running on but the car's still in the ditch. All right—let's hear your bright idea. Then we'll think again.

HEVRLE: (*Softly.*) Is it a deal?

FIDLER: (*Softly.*) It's a deal.

HEVRLE: A cigarette. (*A match is struck.*) All right then. See that young beech tree on the far side of the road? If three strong men bend the stem over as far as it'll go, and if the other end of the tow-rope is fastened to the bumper, all of a sudden, then you'll be six guys, and not just three. And if you put your shoulders to the wheel at the same time, then that tree will pull your heap out of the ditch like a noodle out of a clear soup.

NOVAK: (*Starts to organize.*) Malek, have we got a tow-rope?

MALEK: Of course.

HEVRLE: If that's not enough, you can cut up a blanket and do the same with the birch tree next to it.

MALEK: (*Admiringly.*) Not bad, Hevrle. I take my hat off to you.

HEVRLE: Where would you get one? Hats went out with the bourgeoisie.

(*Crossfade: Swing music.*)

18.

CAR PARK OUTSIDE MOUNTAIN INN

Footsteps of four persons on the gravel. From the distance the sounds of the dance nearing its end.

VINCE: (*Reassuringly.*) There's not much highway. Only about f-four miles, and then it's all t-tracks.

JANE: You're stammering again, Vince darling. You afraid? Gosh, my head's swimming.

FRANK: (*In a wheedling voice.*) You need some brandy or some vodka. Something hard.

SONYA: (*Suggestively.*) I wouldn't mind something hard inside me.

VINCE: P-please, ladies, the c-carriage awaits. All aboard!

(*Sound of car door and the squeak of seats. Vince switches on the quadrophonic cassette player. Elvis practically bursts his vocal chords.*)

SONYA: Would you believe it—such equipment! How come a country boy like you owns stuff like this?

VINCE: B-before they eased me out of my job I was in Hamburg every m-month, working on a barge on the Elbe. Where else would I get the m-money f-for this car?

JANE: Oh, you're a real globe trotter!

VINCE: You can s-say that again. P-practically at home in the w-west.

FRANK: (*Aping him.*) And p-practically up the ass when at home.

(*The engine is started. The car drives off slowly.*)

19.

AT THE SCENE OF THE ACCIDENT IN THE FOREST

Three men grunting and panting with effort.

MALEK: (*Giving the commands.*) Now we go, hey-hupp! and again, hey-hupp! And a little more—hey-hupp! (*Heaves a deep sigh.*) Well, we're over the worst of it.

HEVRLE: (*Triumphantly.*) Well, did it work or didn't it?

MALEK: (*Satisfied.*) Not half as bad as I thought. Minor damage to the bumper. Lucky the ground was soft.

HEVRLE: And now may I please have a medium-sized stone with some nice sharp edges?

NOVAK: (*Attempting a joke.*) Maybe *I* should perform the operation to save you the effort . . .

HEVRLE: Better not. You might get a little too enthusiastic and I'd be a thing of the past.

MALEK: The way it looks—we'll all get about two years.

HEVRLE: With a little extra for me for self-inflicted injury.

MALEK: Quiet! I can hear a car. Quiet . . . Yes, something's coming. (*Distant sound of a car engine.*)

MALEK: Over there! Headlights up there at the bend!

FIDLER: Damn. We can't let them see us like this. Quick, get behind the trees! Come on, Ferdie, give me a hand with him!

HEVRLE: Careful with my leg! If you hurt me I'll scream!

FIDLER: Shut up now! (*Calling.*) Malek, you're in uniform. Put on your cap and stand by the car. If they're civilians, tell them to go to the devil. If it's the local police, then . . .

(*His voice is drowned by the roar of the engine and the quadrophonic music of Vince's car.*)

20.

MONTAGE SEQUENCE

In the car of the two couples, then at the accident spot, then again in the car of the two couples.

FRANK: (*In high spirit.*) D'you know the one about little Pete asking the teacher: "Miss, have you got a bosom?" And the teacher replies didactically: "Of course I have a bosom. Every woman has a bosom." So little Pete looks up at her and asks: "Why don't you wear it then?" (*Laughs.*) That's a good one, isn't it?

JANE: Fabulous. But when I'm drunk I can't remember a thing.

VINCE: (*Suddenly.*) Shit. There's a car standing at the bend there, and a cop next to it. What now?

FRANK: Drive on. (*Hysterically.*) Drive on! Come on, man, step on it! By the time they turn round we're gone!

VINCE: Impossible—I'd have to run him over. The car's across the road, there's hardly room to get past.

FRANK: Drive right past without stopping!

VINCE: But there's hardly room to get past.

SONYA: (*Suddenly quite sober.*) Turn off the music and don't do anything of the sort. If he stops us, leave everything to me. I'll get out of the car. And you'll see—we'll drive on as if nothing had happened.

VINCE: (*In despair.*) I've got to drive very slow anyway, or else stop altogether.

I've got no choice.

(*The tape is switched off. Silence in the car. Noise of the wheels in the sand. The car rolls to a stop, the window is wound down.*)

MALEK: (*A moment later.*) Drive on, comrades, drive on. There's nothing to see here.
SONYA: Has anything happened, Comrade Corporal? D'you need help?
MALEK: Everything O.K., comrade. Forestry duty. Regional operation.
SONYA: Good luck then, comrade.
MALEK: (*Unintentionally.*) We'll need it.

(*Cut. The car accelerates fiercely. A moment later Fidler's voice is heard whispering excitedly from the undergrowth.*)

FIDLER: Ferdie, take his number! It was them! Write it down or memorize it—ULP 10-67-15. Memorize it, it's important! ULP 10-67-15!
HEVRLE: I'll remember it, Comrade Lieutenant—I guarantee it. You can count on it. I've got a memory like an elephant.

(*Cut. In the car of the two couples.*)

VINCE: That's what I call luck. I feel like I've started living again. I'll switch the music back on, shall I? (*The music blazes out again.*)
JANE: Luck? Ha ha ha . . .
SONYA: Know how—that's all.
FRANK: What was that card you shoved under that guy's nose?
SONYA: Never mind that, love. I'm here in a private capacity and I'm looking forward to that little orgy in your chalet.
VINCE: (*Cheerfully.*) D'you m-mean you are one of—
SONYA: So what?
VINCE: I'm l-laughing myself s-silly? (*Laughs like a lunatic.*) So what, we only l-live once. And it's m-much too short.

(*Someone turns the music up so loud that not another word can be made out.*)

21.

AT THE SCENE OF THE ACCIDENT IN THE FOREST

Forest sounds, the dog is running about.

MALEK: (*Whistles, then.*) All clear. They're gone.

FIDLER: (*To himself.*) That, sweetheart, is going to cost you dearly. Ferdie, get them to find who owns that car—tonight. I'm having that guy picked up tomorrow morning. He won't know what hit him when he gets pulled out of bed.

NOVAK: What for?

FIDLER: What for? My dear boy, you have a lot to learn. Remember: types who own cars like that are like wax in your hand. They always have something to hide. He'll sing all right—including such details as the mole on her right buttock—(*with a sneer*)—a detail not unknown to me. He'll be in such a panic about his driving license, he'll sign anything I ask him to. And we'll have that girl in the palm of our hands. She'll really go to bat for us!

HEVRLE: There you see, Comrade Lieutenant, how fortunately one thing leads to another.

FIDLER: You're lucky Hevrle. That young lady is sure to put in a good word for you—(*to Novak*)—when I show her all the evidence against her.

HEVRLE: (*Factually.*) How about getting me back on that tree stump. So I don't catch a cold.

(*Fidler and Novak get hold of Hevrle and start panting again.*)

NOVAK: This guy weighs a ton!

FIDLER: You certainly look well fed. At least you can't complain that you starved while doing time.

HEVRLE: I wouldn't dream of complaining, Comrade Lieutenant. I love those carefully planned calories.

NOVAK: (*Breathing heavily.*) Why don't we put him straight in the car—what do you say?

HEVRLE: Why don't you lock up the whole nation—that would solve the food problem. No more lines outside the shops, no more bribes, everybody getting his ration in his tin bowl, and off to work they go. (*Maliciously.*) But unfortunately that's not possible, right, Comrade Lieutenant? Put them all in jail and the nation wouldn't multiply. And why? Because sex is forbidden there . . . Ow, ow, careful with my leg!

FIDLER: Well, I'm not worried about you any more, after your demonstration today. You'd talk a virgin pregnant!

HEVRLE: There's a saying: "If a man gives thee stones, give thou him bread." But I think the bread would have to be six months old at least and pretty hard. Or else with a brick baked into it.

FIDLER: All right. But remember: if you get me into trouble you're finished for good!

HEVRLE: (*Jocularly.*) Beg to report, sir, I'll make a note of it. And now may I please have a stone axe or some such similar instrument for bashing heads in?

FIDLER: Will this one do?

NOVAK: I can't bear to watch. (*The sound of a screech owl.*)

MALEK: A screech owl! That's all we needed.

HEVRLE: Why? If the screech owl call at night—happiness is within sight. (*A dull blow.*) Ow!—If I've knocked a hole in my brainbox from sheer enthusiasm and my brain starts running out, you can do with me what you like. (*A second dull blow.*) Ow! That should be enough.

NOVAK: Man, you're a tough one!

HEVRLE: The roads to freedom are manifold and mostly rocky . . . Damn it, that head hurts like hell! But "Greater love hath no man . . ." That's not by me—I read it somewhere.

FIDLER: Malek, the first aid box! I'll bandage him up quickly, and we'll get to the hospital.

MALEK: (*Whistles at the dog.*) Kazan, here! (*Whistles again.*)

(*Musical crossfade: Solveig's song by Grieg.*)

22.

IN THE CAR OF THE TWO COUPLES

The engine is purring, the music is playing.

FRANK: (*Casually.*) What kind was he? Traffic police?

SONYA: (*Pensively.*) No . . .

VINCE: The m-main thing is he didn't t-take our n-number.

JANE: Even if he has—what can happen to you? They can't breathalize you now.

VINCE: I k-know that b-bunch. They'll ask q-questions at the r-restaurant.

SONYA: If things are the way I suspect they are *they* will certainly *not* ask questions at the restaurant. (*Laughs maliciously.*)

JANE: (*Understands her.*) I only hope he won't make you pay for it . . .

SONYA: (*Sulkily.*) He should have been punctual and turned up when he said.

FRANK: Who?

SONYA: Oh, just an admirer.

(*Musical crossfade into the other car.*)

23.

IN THE OFFICIAL CAR

The engine is purring.

HEVRLE: (*Irritably.*) My head feels like a football after a hard game. (*Silence. After a while.*) If at least you were human . . . (*Silence.*)

MALEK: (*After a pause.*) Would you like a drink? There's some tea in the thermos.

HEVRLE: With rum?

NOVAK: (*Attempts a joke.*) Giving alcohol to prisoners serving their sentence is forbidden.

HEVRLE: Oh, forbidden. What a pleasure to be reminded of the good old days!

MALEK: (*Automatically.*) What do you mean?

HEVRLE: Well . . . In those far-off days the rule was that anything that wasn't forbidden was permitted. Nowadays it's anything that's not permitted is forbidden, ha ha.

MALEK: (*Naively.*) That's the same thing, isn't it?

HEVRLE: That's where you're wrong. The same thing, my foot! That is the key to the whole mess you've made here.

FIDLER: (*Calmly.*) Stop it, Hevrle. I know you've got a headache but that doesn't mean we have to listen to your provocative talk.

HEVRLE: But you do! You know damn well you do! Surely you don't think I staged all this just to make life easier for you two? What an idea, Comrade Lieutenant! You can't be that stupid. I've got to get some things off my chest. A prisoner's spiritual life requires him to create the necessary conditions to do that. (*Malek bursts out laughing.*)

NOVAK: I don't know what there's to laugh about.

HEVRLE: Seeing it's you you'll never know. A classless society positively swarming with classes—isn't that a scream? Find out from the Comrade Lieutenant here how the charges against me were knocked together, the charges for which I was put *inside* for three years. You'll die laughing.

FIDLER: (*Cynically.*) You were sentenced in accordance with valid Czechoslovak law.

HEVRLE: That's very reassuring, as you can see. But that's not what I'm talking about. You know better than anyone what it was like.

FIDLER: You just thought you could run your head against the wall.

HEVRLE: I'm delighted to hear that. Because I've just done it. I can still feel it.

MALEK: (*Laughs undisguisedly; after a while.*) Forgive me, Comrade Lieutenant, but I can't control myself. Somehow I'm still a normal person.

HEVRLE: Why shouldn't you laugh. It's all a big joke. I remember reading somewhere that there are regimes with female characteristics and regimes with male characteristics, but I don't think the author developed his idea to the end. For what *you've* staged here is typically infantile. And children, as everyone knows, are cruel and irresponsible.

FIDLER: Go right on—if it makes you feel better.

HEVRLE: You can count on that. You've chopped up a collective state into fifteen million individuals—poor, greedy, frightened individuals. Congratulations! Marx must be turning in his grave like a turbine at the Kaplan power station. Three thousand revolutions per minute!

NOVAK: (*Slow to understand.*) What do you mean?

HEVRLE: Just what I'm saying. Each one on his own rusty track. But what I don't know is why you imagine they must all unite in the communist future—when every school kid knows that parallel lines meet at infinity—if ever. (*Malek now laughs undisguisedly.*) I know every creature acts solely and exclusively in its own interests. But to have created conditions under which acting in one's own interest runs counter to one's own interest—that is a truly admirable idiocy, and that—I can't help it—you have succeeded in achieving.

FIDLER: Who's "you"?

HEVRLE: (*Taken aback.*) I beg your pardon. *We* have succeeded—is what I wanted to say. I accept my share of the responsibility.

FIDLER: Well, I'm deeply touched you're not putting the entire blame on two lousy policemen and one driver! (*Begins to whistle to himself.*)

MALEK: (*Factually.*) We're nearly at the hospital. Shall I drive straight in?

FIDLER: If the barrier is up, just whiz through, understood? . . . (*Turning backwards.*) Mr. Hevrle, wake up, you're going to faint!

(*Silence. Only the engine is still running at full revs.*)

MALEK: Yes. The barrier's up and the porter is snoring. Like everywhere else.

FIDLER: Drive on, Malek. Straight to Casualty.

NOVAK: (*Lowering his voice.*) I'd feel happier taking him straight to Autopsy . . . (*Screech of tires.*)

FIDLER: (*Turning backwards.*) Nevertheless, Hevrle, you're wrong.

HEVRLE: (*Softly.*) No, I'm right. Because it doesn't prevail? Truth doesn't prevail. If it did, I wouldn't want it. (*Brakes. Car door.*)

FIDLER: Novak! Come along with me, we'll sign him in. (*Footsteps of two men, then door bell.*)

VOICE: (*Croaking from the speaker equipment.*) Casualty reception.

FIDLER: Police. Delivering an injured prisoner, unconscious. (*Alarm bell, ringing.*)

NOVAK: (*After a little while.*) If he doesn't keep his mouth shut we're finished.

FIDLER: (*With sovereign assurance.*) Don't worry. He'll keep his mouth shut. Word of honor still seems something to him. Because he's stupid.

(*The door is flung open. The ringing of the bell gets louder. Footsteps of the hospital staff quickly approaching the car.*)

END

Games

Ivan Klíma

translated by Jan Drabek

Touchstone Theatre

GAMES
[Touchstone Theatre, Vancouver, Canada]
Directed by Jon Cooper

CHARACTERS:

Petr, a physicist. Twenty-five years old.
Irena, Petr's older sister.
Filip, a lawyer and Irena's husband. In his forties.
Kamil Sova, a sociologist. About Petr's age and his friend.
Jakub, an athlete. Twenty-seven years old. Nephew of Filip.
Deml, an architect, about fifty years old.
Eva, his girlfriend. A singer, she is about twenty-five years old.
Bauer, about fifty.

*The action takes place in a roomy living room from which there are steps leading up. The
room is furnished in the baroque style. There are armchairs, table, a bureau and a stand-up
wardrobe closet. There are pictures on the walls, old maps and antique weapons. Several
big wooden beams form the ceiling.*

*Because each scene constitutes at the same time a separate play, its name should become part
of the staging. It could be projected in some way; ballet could be used, or it could simply be
announced.*

ACT ONE

FIRST GAME

The Cooking Game

IRENA: (*Onstage, keeps bringing to the table bowls filled with salad. She straightens them out into a neat row. There is a pleased expression on her face, then suddenly she frowns and runs off. She returns with a cutting board, an onion and a long knife. The doorbell rings and she goes to open the door. Half way there she puts down the cutting board on an armchair and opens the door.*)

SOVA: Good evening. I don't know if you recognize me.

IRENA: Of course I do, Kamil. Petr talks about you often. He calls you red Hippo.

SOVA: That is what they used to call me, but that was a long time ago. I never quite understood why hippopotamus, and today I don't even know why a red one. (*He laughs.*) I am delighted that you thought of asking me. But at the same time I should warn you: I was never very good at games.

IRENA: That doesn't matter. Did you know that the other day I finally got hold of a copy of your book? I hear it has been taken out of all libraries. Why? It has such beautiful and encouraging thoughts in it. Filip—my husband— was so enthusiastic about it. I even memorized some things from your book: (*She recites with pathos.*) "The freest heads rest on that body whose hands are fettered." (*She remembers.*) Although that wasn't exactly the most encouraging thought. Please excuse Filip for being so late. He has to work on some report on the penal system and there is so much work with it.

SOVA: (*He is about to sit down in the armchair where Irena has left the cutting board with the onion.*)

IRENA: (*Taking away the cutting board at the very last moment.*) I'm sorry. I'm a bit nervous. You see, I've never had an evening like this. But I thought it would be so nice if people got together and instead of talking about politics and violence, they'd just play. You know—forget that we are grownups and that we have to cope with this terrible world. Like right here—it's been barely a month. In the park next to the castle someone murdered a young student. A girl. The body was never found, they say that the garbage men took it away. (*She refers to newspapers.*)

SOVA: These games are really an excellent idea, Irena. Do you think that I could help you? Lately, cooking has become something of a hobby for me.

IRENA: They have a brand new truck. It's orange and there is an opening in the back with these rotating blades. And they say that's what they took her away in. Everyone knows it but what can you do! Someone has to take away the ashes and the garbage generally. Do you really like to cook, Kamil?

SOVA: Yes. I decided to go into cooking because of some basic philosophical principles. One should not be dependent on anyone when it comes to something as essential as the preparation of food. Not that I didn't encounter certain difficulties at first. Once I almost poisoned myself because I read the list of ingredients incorrectly and instead of one quarter of a decagram of baking soda, I mixed in with the dough fourteen decagrams. But now even the Naples salad isn't any problem.

IRENA: Oh, a salad from Naples! I knew I would hear about something unusually interesting from you! Later I would like to ask you for the recipe. Perhaps I could give you my own recipe for a pumpkin salad in return. I don't know if you feel it too, but there is something so becalming in cutting up an onion or a pumpkin into small pieces. At that moment I forget everything unpleasant that has ever happened to me. Maybe you don't even know that my second husband has . . . (*She stops.*) I have something like one hundred and eleven salad recipes. There is an escargot salad and a banana salad. There is the Bosnia salad, the sharp one with cucumbers, a cheese salad with crabmeat, the fennel salad and the salad from Hana. There is the Miami salad, the Greek salad, the Austrian one and the Japanese melon salad.

SOVA: I'll try to write mine down for you, but first of all one should know the basic ingredients. They include cooked macaroni, paprika pods, capers, garlic and onions. Then the spices: pepper, vinegar, salt.

IRENA: And your proportions?

SOVA: My proportions? Oh, yes. This is what I like about the whole process the most. The finding of relative proportions for a given situation. Each situation demands a whole new set of proportions. I made this discovery quite recently. When I was young I was of the opinion that the optimal proportions of a given situation are absolute. I even thought that *I* knew them. I found that optimal proportions cannot be established once and for all. It is impossible for example to arrive at the optimal proportions of the aroma and bitterness of tea just as it is impossible to establish the optimal proportions of liberty and responsibility for each citizen. Only such things as the size of a military uniform or of a banner can be established with any degree of certainty.

IRENA: (*Suddenly cries out.*) My goodness, I've promised you a recipe for the pumpkin salad and the guests will be here any moment. Do you have a piece of paper?

SOVA: (*Looks through his pockets, then comes up with a thick notebook.*)

IRENA: I'm a little nervous, dictating a recipe for someone like you. You see, Filip is not at all interested in cooking. All right? The pumpkin must first be skinned and the soft insides cleaned out. (*She notices that Sova isn't writing it down but is searching for something through his pockets.*) I'm sorry, what I am telling is probably not necessary but . . . (*There is the sound of an arriving car, then the doorbell.*)

SOVA: No, no, on the contrary. Your introduction about the cleaning of the pumpkin is quite useful.

DEML: (*Offstage.*) I hope that we haven't missed the beginning. A wonderful idea, Irenka—the Games!

IRENA: (*To Sova.*) This is Mr. Deml. He is an architect and designer. (*She looks at Eva, puzzled.*)

DEML: This is Eva.

EVA: (*Puts down the guitar which she has brought in with her and with a flirtatious walk comes nearer to Sova.*) Don't we know each other from somewhere?

DEML: (*Quickly.*) And this is Jenik Bauer.

SOVA: (*A bit embarrassed.*) I'm not sure. From the university? But that would have been more than three years ago. I no longer lecture there.

EVA: Yes, yes, I used to sing there. Don't you play the drums?

SOVA: Unfortunately no. As a boy I started to play the piano, but then there wasn't time any more—politics, meetings, one meeting after the other. Those were different times.

EVA: Somehow I keep seeing you drumming.

BAUER: (*Stops in front of a big canvas.*) Quite nice, although I am not an expert on the modern ones. (*He notices a gun on the wall.*) Hey look—a real Colt .45. The Hartford model, I'd say, from the early fifties. (*He tries to take it off the wall.*)

IRENA: Watch out, it's loaded!

BAUER: Oh.

IRENA: It really irritates my husband, but my brother wants it like that. He's a bit of an eccentric, I guess. (*Points to the weapons.*) They are all loaded. He says that they won't go off by themselves, but that it's so lovely the way they constantly lead us into temptation.

BAUER: Yes, yes, of course. It's already quite valuable. Mother of pearl handles.

DEML: Jenik helps me find the right materials for the interiors. I don't get a chance to do that kind of work any more.

EVA: (*To Irena.*) Honsey bunsey is really terrifically busy. He is getting divorced. At the same time he's also building the biggest tunnel under the sun.

DEML: (*Irritated.*) A bridge. How many times have I told you that it is a bridge and not a tunnel . . . Darling.

EVA: Well, there isn't really that much difference, is there?

DEML: (*To the others.*) We are trying to be broad-minded and solve finally the traffic situation. You all know that just around here there are no less than a hundred thousand houses and cottages which are being used only a few weeks each year. At the same time that this is happening we are also going through a housing crisis. And do you know why? Because of inadequate transportation. People simply would not be able to get to work from their houses and cottages. Just recently I spoke about it with the minister. The average trip to work would be seventy-eight minutes. That's really a sad fact.

IRENA: (*To Eva.*) He has always been such a man of action.

DEML: Not any more. (*He looks at Eva.*) I'd really like to say to hell with everything and concentrate on my own personal things. (*Full of importance.*) But can one do that? Look at the young people, can one not sympathize? (*To Sova.*) Did you know, dear friend, that thirty-six percent of all marital breakdowns are due to the housing crisis? And there are no statistics about couples who never got married on account of it. One just can't remain indifferent to it all. (*To Eva.*) That's the way I am: I feel other's troubles as if they were my own.

BAUER: (*Approaches another picture.*) And this little horsie, if he was a bit more bluish, I would say was by my master Chagall. When he was showing me his studio I stopped in front of a picture much like this and I said: Sir, I am no expert when it comes to modern art but this one I would take at any price. And he smiled and said: You say you are no expert, Jean? Three hours ago Henry Ford from Detroit offered me three hundred thousand. And then he told me: It can be yours if you do something for me. He drew on a piece of paper . . . (*he searches through his pockets, finds a piece of paper and thrusts it at Sova*) . . . this house. Actually, as you see, it's a small castle, that's what it is, complete with a glass roof for his studio. And here he sketched in some trees on the shore and he says: Build a villa like this for me, Jean. (*He takes an open-faced sandwich.*)

DEML: (*Coughs meaningfully.*)

IRENA: (*To Sova.*) You certainly must be an interesting man to sit down to dinner with. Most men behave like barbarians at the table. And did you know that Filip refuses to eat meat? (*With evident satisfaction.*) But he is also a teetotaler!

BAUER: Of course, it's nothing compared to the castle of our prince. When I was locked up in the fifties, on the ᐳbunk next to me was Prince Schwarzenberg. You know, the one from the Krumlov branch of the family — (*Sound of a car arriving outside.*)

FILIP: (*Enters with Jakub.*) Darling! (*He kisses Irena.*) I'm sorry we're late. (*To Sova.*) I don't think we've met.

IRENA: That's Kamil, Filip.

FILIP: Oh, is it? (*He shakes Sova's hand.*) Your name is mentioned around here quite frequently. Irena reads your books. I have also read that forbidden volume. Interesting. The problem of freedom, isn't it? (*Recites.*) "The freest minds rest in heads with hands" . . . well, if you'll permit me, this is my nephew, Jakub. He knows all about games and about fair play. He is an athlete.

JAKUB: (*Who until now had been staring at Eva, bows to Bauer and hands to Irena the mask of a savage.*) Hi, Irena! I got this for you at Tananarive.

SOVA: Are you interested in African studies?

FILIP: No, no! He started to study . . . What was it you started to study actually?

JAKUB: Nothing. (*Still staring at Eva.*) You know I didn't study anything, Uncle Filip.

FILIP: Oh yes, yes. He had to give up his studies because he got . . . he got into hot water. Yes, he was swimming in it.

JAKUB: I was on the rowing team, Uncle Filip. (*To Eva.*) Uncle Filip doesn't know too much about sports. But I always say that it's the only way nowadays that a man is really able to show something and to be really satisfied with what he has done. (*He takes courage and comes even closer to Eva.*) I have seen you on television lots of times. Last time when you sang that song about Columbus, that was great.

EVA: You look pretty familiar yourself. I think I must have seen you in a newsreel or something. Didn't you win some swimming meet just a while ago?

JAKUB: But I'm on the rowing team.

EVA: Yeah, well that's what I mean. Do you row a canoe or kayak?

JAKUB: A skiff.

EVA: Sure, then it was you. Why don't you call me Eva?

JAKUB: Thank you, I feel real honored. I have been a fan of yours for a long time . . . People talk about us athletes like sport was pretty easy. And actually it's been scientifically proven that an olympic skiffer has to use three times more energy to cover two kilometers than Einstein needed to discover that theory of his.

IRENA: (*To Sova, quietly.*) When Filip was starting out he went through quite a lot. Since that time he can't stand any killing—not even of animals!

FILIP: Let's not talk about that. There is absolutely no connection.

IRENA: (*Nervously.*) I think I hear my brother.

PETR: (*Enters, looks around, nods to Sova, then bows.*) I greet you my dear friends, even though I see faces among you with which I am not at all familiar. I apologize to all potential enemies.

DEML: (*Points to Bauer and Eva.*) These are my . . .

PETR: No, no—please no introductions. We'll become acquainted through action, because my dear sister has decided to organize an evening of parlor games. She fervently believes that through them we shall be able to return into the age of innocence. But why are you all so quiet? Why aren't you gushing with thoughts, stories and remarkable statements? (*To Deml.*) What about your imposing figures? Shouldn't you be mentioning that the Moscow subway carries 5 million passengers a day and that not far from Warsaw they have put up a television tower which is 634 meters high? Isn't it all a wonderful testimony to the human mind that it is constantly rising to loftier challenges, and that, as a result we should be able to get through this evening without any worries. Why aren't you all pleased?

BAUER: I would like to propose a game. A game that you (*to Filip*), as a public prosecutor—sir—might possibly find quite interesting.

SOVA: (*Talking about Irena.*) But perhaps first we should play a game suggested by one of the ladies.

IRENA: (*Somewhat worried.*) You think I should suggest a game? Well—I've thought of one, except that it's a game we used to play as little girls, maybe it isn't quite suitable. Here—those ten salad dishes. You tie a handkerchief over your eyes and try to figure out what the ingredients are. The blindfold . . .

FILIP: You didn't really have to choose this particular game!

IRENA: (*Desperate.*) I'm sorry . . . I forgot . . . You see, I thought that—the eyes are covered up only so it's harder to guess the ingredients, so that only people's smell and taste can be used.

BAUER: It's truly an outstanding game, my lady, and it reminds me of a funny story. You see there are these two Jews on a train and one of them, named Abeles, has this cutting board on his knees and he is cutting up a cucumber.

IRENA: (*Taking a napkin off the table.*) If we could get started. Who wants to be first?

EVA: I will.

FILIP: (*To the others.*) I don't like it when people are blindfolded. It's barbaric.

EVA: It's all right. I don't mind. (*She takes the napkin from Irena.*)

BAUER: (*To Petr, who is the only one that is still listening.*) And when he finishes cutting up the cucumber he throws it out the window. Then he cuts up the potatoes and again—right out the window. Cohen, that's the other Jew, is wondering what Abeles is doing: he says, May I ask what it is you're doing? I am making a potato salad, Mr. Cohen. Ah yes, a potato salad. And may I ask why you are throwing the ingredients out the window? And what do you expect me to do with them Mr. Cohen, when I hate potato salad. (*He laughs.*)

PETR: (*Gazes at Bauer without any change in expression.*)

BAUER: Please forgive me, professor, if I tire you.

PETR: Not at all! It's an excellent story, go on. That's the trouble with such stories. They don't go on. The universe has such an advantage here—it goes on and on, even though Einstein claims that the world is finite. Of course that's only true if the average density of a weighable mass in outer space doesn't equal zero. But that particular eventuality shouldn't disturb you. (*He suddenly points to Eva.*) Or does it? Does it disturb you?

EVA: (*Confused.*) No . . . no, it doesn't.

PETR: Then why are you so silent? You who are so young and pretty.

EVA: (*Quickly covering her eyes with the napkin.*) Let me have the dish. (*She takes the dish from Irena, smells it.*) Onions.

IRENA: Perfect.

EVA: I used to eat salads until I hated the very sight of them. While doing one-night stands. Of course: pepper!

IRENA: Very good. You really are good.

BAUER: (*While this is going on he walks to a wall and takes down a gun, examining it.*)

FILIP: (*Notices it.*) Put back that gun. Immediately.

EVA: Vinegar. And I would say a bit of ginger, too.

FILIP: And please take off the napkin. (*He walks over to Eva and tears the napkin from her eyes. Hysterically.*) I just can't stand this fooling around with the eyes covered and with guns and everything. . . .

JAKUB: Why don't you think of another game if it bothers you so much?

BAUER: Yes, precisely. I should like to suggest . . .

EVA: We used to play charades every night after the performance. I don't know if you know it.

IRENA: Yes, that would be nice. (*To Sova.*) But I didn't finish dictating that recipe to you.

SOVA: I don't want to bother you with it.

IRENA: It's no bother. I can write it down for you.

EVA: We'll split up into two groups. (*She indicates to people where they should stand, putting Filip beside her, along with Sova and Irena.*)

IRENA: (*As she writes she also recites it in sotto voce.*) Let's see: The skinned pumpkin's seeds are cleaned out and cut into small pieces. In the meantime we roast red pepper in oil . . .

SECOND GAME

The Game of Charades

Filip, Irena, Sova and Eva have left the stage. The others remain, obviously having a good time.

DEML: (*Nervously.*) Well, where are they? (*Looks at his watch.*) They have been talking for ten minutes.

JAKUB: Waiting is part of every game. You just have to be patient. Sometimes when you're competing you stand around for hours. And the whole thing is over in two minutes.

DEML: Unfortunately I'm not a racer. I have to work for a living.

JAKUB: (*Has a piece of paper in his hand.*) Ready!

SOVA: (*From the other room.*) Ready for what?

JAKUB: Send in someone from your team.

FILIP: (*Enters, looking jovial.*) I must admit that I haven't been paying much attention. I'm not quite sure that I am too clear as to the rules.

JAKUB: Here's the sentence. (*Reads from the paper.*) Liberty has been violated by laws.

FILIP: So what?

BAUER: You see, sir, you must act it out.

FILIP: I am supposed to act out this phrase? Why?

JAKUB: So that other people could guess what you mean.

FILIP: Let me see it. (*He takes the paper from Jakub's hands and reads softly.*) Liberty has been . . . For God's sake how does one act out liberty?

JAKUB: That's up to you to figure out, Uncle Filip.

DEML: (*Impatiently.*) Maybe you could be the Statue of Liberty.

BAUER: No helping!

FILIP: (*Allows the idea has some merit.*) O.K. . . . . But how does one act out "has been?"

JAKUB: You don't act out just "has been" but "has been violated."

FILIP: Well . . . all right. (*Suddenly realizes.*) But how can I act out "has been violated?" Besides, I don't agree with the content.

JAKUB: But Uncle Filip, we've already said that it can be anything. It doesn't even have to make sense.

FILIP: Fine. Except that this phrase is not without sense. It's without truth. It's designed to throw doubt on the very meaning of law and justice.

PETR: No phrase can possibly throw doubt on the meaning of law unless you have thrown some doubt on it yourself.

FILIP: Is that supposed to be some sort of insinuation? About myself? I have never . . . I don't like it. I, who have done so much to make the law serve truth and liberty . . . (*He is taking off his jacket, takes out his shirt so that it hangs over his trousers, rolls up his sleeves, ties a handkerchief around his forehead. He fastens a pencil, pen and a fork to his forehead by the handkerchief.*)

JAKUB: Ready.

FILIP: It is our law that protects our material securities, and without these material securities what good is liberty?

JAKUB: Ready.

IRENA: (*Enters with Sova and Eva. They sit down next to each other while Filip remains motionless in the Statue of Liberty pose.*) So, do something! Act it out! (*To Eva.*) You have to help us out a bit. We aren't too good at this thing yet.

FILIP:(*Remaining motionless.*)

EVA: He is probably already acting. You have to act it out a bit more, you have to loosen up a bit.

IRENA: Are you acting already?

FILIP: (*Nods in agreement.*)

IRENA: And what are you acting out?

EVA: You can't ask like that. You have to ask: are you acting out, say, an ostrich?

IRENA: Is it an ostrich?

EVA: Is it a thing?

FILIP: (*Shrugs his shoulders.*)

IRENA: He has no idea if it's a thing. What could it possibly be when even he doesn't have an idea what it is?

SOVA: It's by no means certain that he doesn't know. Perhaps we are merely asking the wrong way.

IRENA: He's probably supposed to be a famous person. Are you a famous person? (*She asks several times in rapid succession while Filip shakes his head.*) Are you a vagrant? A hobo? A bum? (*Proudly.*) I know! A moron, retarded. crazy? (*She hesitates.*) An exhibitionist?

SOVA: Wait a minute, his hand is up. He's trying to show something.

FILIP: (*Agreeing.*)

SOVA: Are you a Nazi?

IRENA: So what are you? (*Suddenly she thinks of something.*) An Indian—a savage!

FILIP: (*Thinks of something else. He drags a chair to the chandelier, unscrews a lightbulb, keeps throwing it from one hand to the other until it cools off. Then he grabs it with his right hand and returns to his original position.*)

EVA: He took the lightbulb! Excellent. Are you a light man? Cameraman? A photographer? Or maybe Edison?

IRENA: Maybe it's the play—*The Lantern.* Are you a watersprite?

SOVA: What is it that you are trying to represent? Is that which you hold in your hand truly supposed to be a lightbulb? (*Begins to lecture.*) You see, what I find so fascinating about this game is that nothing represents itself. All, as I see it, is a symbol for some other substance. So we must inquire again and again.

IRENA: Does your hand hurt? Are we still getting warm? I'm so excited!

SOVA: I think we should approach the whole thing a bit more systematically. We should narrow the field by the process of elimination. Are you supposed to represent something concrete?

FILIP: (*Shakes his head.*)

SOVA: Something abstract?

FILIP: (*At first shrugs his shoulders, then nods, full of uncertainty.*)

SOVA: Then it's something symbolic?

FILIP: (*Agrees.*)

SOVA: Then, more precisely—you symbolize something that is abstract!

IRENA: (*Full of admiration for Sova.*) You ask such excellent questions.

SOVA: You're very kind, but I'm really only applying principles of first order logic. (*He begins to explain painstakingly.*) Carroll, for example, presents only three types of statements: some fresh cakes are tasty, no fresh cakes are tasty and all fresh cakes are tasty. Do you follow the logic?

IRENA: Yes, of course, although I would say that fresh cakes are always . . . excuse me for saying it, but they . . . they give me gas.

FILIP: (*Smashes his fist against the table.*)

EVA: Don't get so mad! Try and act out something. Why are you just standing there like a statue?

FILIP: (*Agrees with obvious enthusiasm.*)

IRENA: (*Astonished.*) Are you supposed to be a statue, darling?

SOVA: Oh yes, of course: He's the Statue of Liberty. (*The three clap.*)

FILIP: (*Agrees, full of relief.*)

IRENA: Really? (*To Sova.*) How did you manage to figure it out so fast?

SOVA: Oh, so it's liberty. (*To Irena.*) Notice how absolutely devilishly thought out is that word. (*Begins explaining again.*) There is nothing more difficult to define and therefore to act out than liberty. You have to remember that today's man, if he is to be called human at all, must accept his knowledge —starting with language but also stereotypes and values as they are handed down to him by someone else. He has to accept his life's goals automatically. So where does one find the proper border. . . .

FILIP: (*Smashes his fist against the table.*)

SOVA: Yes . . . sorry. What are we playing now?

FILIP: (*Shows three fingers.*)

IRENA: Are you showing three?

FILIP: (*Agreeing.*)

IRENA: Three what? That there are three of us? Three brothers?

SOVA: (*Helping her.*) A triad?

IRENA: Three wise men?

EVA: A trio? A tricolor?

IRENA: The three witches?

SOVA: The Holy Trinity?

EVA: The three good fairies? The three wishes?

SOVA: A tryptich?

IRENA: A trident?

EVA: A threesome?

SOVA: Three sources and three parts . . .

FILIP: (*Screaming.*) I'll murder you. I'm acting out the third word.

EVA: Don't get so mad, it's only a game.

SOVA: We have to be more systematic. Which part of speech are you acting out—a verb?

FILIP: (*Nods, but doesn't begin acting it out. He hesitates.*)

SOVA: Liberty is doing something?

FILIP: (*Through gestures shows that it's the other way around.*)

SOVA: Something is being done to liberty?

FILIP: (*Agrees.*)

IRENA: (*To Sova, full of admiration.*) You're so clever, I'm glad that I can play with you.

FILIP: (*Goes to the light switch and turns off several lights. He is acting out a girl. Innocent walk. All laugh. Suddenly he sees someone, freezes in terror, is attacked, defends himself, seems to fall on the ground, biting, scratching. Finally he remains lying on the floor.*)

SOVA: What does it mean—some sort of enlightenment or divine light?

IRENA: It's more like running amok. Or were you brawling with someone?

FILIP: (*Gets up, agreeing with qualifications.*)

IRENA: Were you knocked down, upset?

SOVA: Trampled under?

IRENA: Put down? Wounded?

SOVA: Out flanked? Defenestrated?

IRENA: Killed?

SOVA: Interrogated?

FILIP: (*He comes to a decision. From the table he takes a knife, puts it behind his belt. He approaches Eva and forces her to get up and cross the room the way he has done it before. Then he makes an ominous howling sound and hides behind an armchair.*)

DEML: (*Jumps up but Bauer stops him.*)

FILIP: (*As Eva passes him he attacks her.*)

EVA: (*Inadvertently cries out.*)

FILIP: (*Knocks her down into an armchair.*)

DEML: (*Tears himself away from Bauer, grabs Filip by the shoulder and pulls him away from Eva.*) You . . . you rapist, this isn't a game anymore.

FILIP: (*Attempts to present calm superiority.*) What is all this? Will you tell me how I was to act it out?

DEML: Why didn't you use your wife?

FILIP: Because I would throw them on the wrong track.

EVA: (*Recovering.*) It wasn't so badly acted out.

DEML: Acted out? I have nothing against acting but that was just plain crude.

FILIP: (*Tired of it all.*) I didn't think up the phrase.

PETR: At the Roman games they used to carry the Christians around in pots full of boiling oil.

IRENA: But those weren't really games.

PETR: Oh, quite to the contrary my dear sister. If you define a game as something that is human activity with accepted rules but with a goal only in itself — an activity which has the feeling of being an escape from everyday life—then you realize it was a game like any other.

DEML: Not necessarily for those inside the pots.

PETR: They of course represented only a small minority.

DEML: (*To Petr.*) You are a cynic and I refuse to play with you any more. I don't find any amusement or escape in insolence.

EVA: Yes you do. I saw you laugh when Filip was acting out liberty.

DEML: I was laughing about something else.

JAKUB: Let's play another game.

PETR: Sure. We need a change, even if we don't know what for. There is a certain amount of relief in change itself, although it may be a change to the worse. Who said that? (*Points to Sova.*) He doesn't know. How then can he hope to change the world to the better?

SOVA: (*Shocked.*) I haven't wanted to do that for a long time now. Let the world stay the way it is.

JAKUB: We used to play this game—don't be afraid, it's got a bit of a scary name—called "The Murderer." Let me try to explain the rules: The referee gives out slips of paper and only two have something written on them. One has "the detective" on it and the other "the murderer." So everyone knows which part to play. Then the referee turns out the light and everyone tries to hide from the murderer. The murderer in the meantime is looking for his victim, finds her (*he searches through the room with eyes whom to use as an example, then approaches Eva*), and puts his hands on her throat. (*Shows it.*)

EVA: (*Cries out.*)

JAKUB: That's it. The victim cries out and falls to the ground. From that moment on, of course, she can't speak. The detective immediately turns on the lights and orders everyone to stop. He begins to investigate. Everyone must tell him the truth—what he's heard and what he saw in the darkness. Only the murderer is allowed to lie.

DEML: I'm definitely against playing this game.

FILIP: What if the detective gets murdered?

DEML: (*He is categorical now.*) I absolutely refuse to play this game. How do you guarantee that in the darkness the murderer will be able to find the throat? And that he will concentrate on murdering? I know why everyone wants to play this game—the idea is to turn out the lights, isn't it?

JAKUB: It's so hard to play games with you. (*To Filip.*) The detective doesn't have to cry out and the murderer knows right away that he'll have to find another victim. (*He tears out a few pages from his notebook and starts writing.*)

SOVA: Actually it isn't such a bad game. Suddenly there is darkness and we all know that death is stalking one of us.

FILIP: (*To Sova.*) The idea of death seems to attract you, doesn't it? (*Being categorical.*) I don't like it when people play around with death. It isn't here for our amusement. And it certainly isn't a suitable subject for a game.

IRENA: (*To Sova.*) You see, when Filip was still young . . .

FILIP: Shut up!

JAKUB: But the idea of the game is not to kill. It's to investigate.

BAUER: I should like to suggest a game which would certainly be more entertaining.

DEML: (*Although all have already forgotten him.*) Very well, I'd be willing to play. But I'd like to be the murderer.

JAKUB: But that's . . . You see, the whole idea of the game is to discover the identity of the murderer.

DEML: It's a stupid game. (*Gives the impression of one who has been insulted. Looks at his piece and makes a weighty pronouncement.*) There is nothing written on my paper!

JAKUB: (*Astonished.*) But that means . . . I just finished explaining it . . . that you are neither the detective nor the murderer. Only they have papers with something on them.

DEML: (*Categorically.*) It's a stupid game! You can play it without me.

SOVA: Dear friend, it is clearly understood that there may be games which are not entirely to our liking, but in being able to get over our distaste for them there is a certain self-cleansing process. . . .

JAKUB: So everyone has read his paper? Can I turn off the lights? (*Turns them off.*)

(*There is darkness, steps, chaotic running around. Someone is struck, he falls. A scream. Another scream. A bang. A series of hysterical screams, a door squeaks, someone falls down.*)

FILIP: (*Nervously.*) Why doesn't someone turn on the lights?

SOVA: Someone pushed me away, I can't find the switch.

(*Finally the light comes on. Eva and Jakub are lying on the floor. Petr is in an armchair reading. Bauer is crouched on top of the buffet. Deml is jumping up and down on one foot, the other is bare. Evidently he is looking for his shoe.*)

SOVA: (*Unsure.*) Stop everyone! I am the detective. But . . . I thought there would be only one victim.

FILIP: (*Lying on the floor.*) I don't want to spoil the game, but where is Irena?

SOVA: Yes, she isn't here!

PETR: (*Without lifting his eyes from his paper.*) She has quite likely really been murdered. I have often thought that according to the laws of polarization she must attract every degenerate and repulsive individual for miles around.

FILIP: (*Hurt.*) Now just a moment!

SOVA: Very well, let's start. (*To Petr.*) What were you doing at the exact moment that we heard the scream?

PETR: Which one?

SOVA: (*Unsure.*) The first.

PETR: (*Referring to his newspaper.*) Catching up on current events.

FILIP: (*Jumping up.*) She couldn't have just disappeared. We have to find her.

DEML: Someone tried to get in here. (*Points to his pocket.*) I hit him with my shoe but it fell out of my hand.

IRENA: (*Two stifled cries.*)

FILIP: (*Hysterically.*) Someone is choking her! Choking! Do something. (*Running around the room.*)

PETR: (*Walks over to the buffet and opens it.*)

IRENA: (*Almost falls out of it, sobbing.*) Someone, someone grabbed me here. (*Points to her throat.*) That's how it probably happened to that poor girl the one the garbagemen took away. I was terrified, so I opened the door here (*points to the closet*) and I climbed in but someone closed it again and there inside there was something strange and warm. And it smelled so . . .

DEML: Here it is! (*Grabs his shoe from the closet.*) I said it was a stupid game!

IRENA: I'm sorry. I don't think we should play these crude, barbarous games. We're nice people. (*To Jakub.*) Please get up!

FILIP: I also demand categorically that we choose another game. Let's stop all this choking and violence and putting blindfolds over people's eyes.

SOVA: But despite it all, the games should somehow follow each other logically. I am of the opinion that what is most prominently missing from our lives is some sense of a proper sequence. This starting anew again and again—that is the cause of our rootlessness, of our uncertainty and finally even our tendency toward violence.

BAUER: (*On top of the closet, raising his hand.*) I know a terrific game!

SOVA: And do you know what is the result of our lack of sequence, our tendency toward violence and our subconscious death wish? Revolution. I can say it, I know. I too once tried to change history by violent means. Death seemed so attractive that I actually dreamt about it. I imagined how I was being led to the place of execution, I saw the sharply pressed uniforms of the execution squad. And hearing the flutter of the banners in the wind I cried out: Long live liberty and the glory of the revolution! You can't imagine the feeling of self fulfillment that comes from such thoughts.

BAUER: (*On top of the closet.*) I would like to suggest a game that ties in perfectly. It's called Execution.

FILIP: What?

BAUER: Execution. It doesn't need much. One person plays the executioner, one the executioner's henchman and the third one plays the condemned.

FILIP: You've gone completely out of your mind.

JAKUB: Let him finish.

BAUER: We will also choose the judge and the priest. You put up a gallows and the executioner starts doing his job. And you keep playing and playing until someone can't take it anymore and cries out to stop. Then the one who cried stop becomes the condemned.

IRENA: It sounds . . . horrible.

FILIP: I don't see how you could possibly suggest that we play something like that in this house—in the house of a judge. Especially after what I just said.

EVA: But we'd only be playing a game.

FILIP: I'll never allow something like that to be played in this house. There will be no executions here.

BAUER: Oh, excuse me, Mr. Prosecutor, if I have been the cause of distress.

FILIP: (*Shouting.*) And don't call me Mr. Prosecutor. I was only the judge in the midst of some very difficult times.

PETR: People most often show their true selves in difficult times.

FILIP: What do you mean? Is that suposed to be another insinuation?

PETR: Just as they show themselves in games. Games resemble difficult times because they constantly demand new decisions. So who will suggest a new game? An innocent one, if possible. Without blindolds, without evoking the past, and without turning off the lights.

DEML: All right, I know one.

THIRD GAME

The Hostage Game

Eva, Irena, and Filip are seated in armchairs. The armchairs can be arranged behind each other as if in an airplane. Petr is taking out of the closet an old Austro-Hungarian helmet and sabre. Deml is seated at the table and he is smoking.

IRENA: (*Visibly excited, she stands up and sits down again.*) What's the weather like outside? Doesn't it seem as if the wind is picking up a bit?

EVA: I don't know. It's dark outside. Are you nervous?

IRENA: I can't help it. I have lived through so much I'm terrified of the silence just before the door opens. My father, when they came for him, we were still quite small . . . and my first husband . . . I'm sorry, I realize this is all something entirely different.

JAKUB: (*Enters. He should be wearing something that would at least vaguely suggest a pilot's uniform.*) Ladies and gentlemen, I have to announce that we must make a forced landing. I hope that even though the aircraft is in the hands of armed terrorists you'll remain calm.)

BAUER: (*Enters with Sova, holding a hunting rifle in his hands.*) Unfortunately that is exactly the situation. My apologies, ladies and gentlemen.

JAKUB: (*Walks over to the table and starts eating the sandwiches.*)

SOVA: (*He can have a colorful sash or a tricolor across his chest.*) We are not terrorists. We are members of a shock group. . . .

FILIP: (*To Bauer.*) Where did you get that rifle?

BAUER: (*Shrugs his shoulders.*)

FILIP: Put it down. Immediately. It's loaded. (*Screaming.*) Haven't you heard what I just said?

BAUER: (*Not making a move.*) You see, sir, they gave . . .

DEML: Let him have it. It's only a game. Besides it's pretty effective. They wouldn't have much of a chance without a weapon, would they?

FILIP: They have the same chance with weapons as they have without them. Because I assume that they do not plan to use them.

EVA: It's so much more realistic with the gun.

FILIP: I do not intend to play games in front of the muzzle of a loaded rifle.

PETR: (*Mixing in.*) But you have played that so many times!

FILIP: What is that supposed to mean?

PETR: Or maybe it wasn't a game, was it? All those condemned peasants and supposed spies who went to the gallows because you duly delivered a verdict demanded by the times.

FILIP: I . . . I . . . that's insolent. I don't intend to play!

IRENA: Petr, how could you . . . here before everyone. And he suffered so much because of it.

FILIP: (*Forcing himself to be calm.*) And it wasn't my game. You know that very well. Unfortunately there are times in life when we have to play along with something we don't like or with which we even disagree. (*To Bauer.*) But not here and now.

IRENA: So put down the rifle. My husband doesn't like it.

SOVA: (*Makes a decision.*) Only after you agree to our demands.

DEML: Yes, that's right. (*To Irena.*) And your job is to convince the aggressors that they should give up their demands. Or at least that they modify them. Keep them busy until the police arrive.

IRENA: (*To Sova.*) And what are your demands?

SOVA: One hundred million.

IRENA: A hundred million? But we don't have it. I don't understand. When I think that they could really want that much . . .

SOVA: You don't have to pay it. You are only the hostages.

IRENA: Who does?

SOVA: The airline company. The government. United Nations. We'll find someone.

IRENA: And if no one pays?

SOVA: You'll be blown up. A few useless people more or less, what does it matter? Do you know how many people die of hunger every day?

IRENA: But you can't be serious. We didn't do anything.

BAUER: That's life, lady.

IRENA: But I have children. In two days they'll be back from their holidays. I have to be here.

SOVA: Millions of children don't get a chance to go away for their holidays.

IRENA: You shouldn't say that. It's too cruel.

EVA: (*Who suddenly becomes interested and barges in.*) How much time do we have?

SOVA: (*Looks at his watch.*) Your captain is just sending out our conditions. We gave him sixty minutes.

EVA: You are quite obviously a decisive man.

SOVA: I only serve the cause.

EVA: (*Gets up and moves toward him.*) No, you are a real man. I've always wanted to meet a real man.

DEML: (*Coughs.*)

SOVA: Don't come any nearer.

BAUER: (*Aims the gun at her.*)

IRENA: My God! You'd better sit down.

JAKUB: (*Gets up from the table, his mouth still full.*) I have sent out your conditions.

SOVA: The reply?

JAKUB: What could they possibly say?

EVA: How much time is left?

SOVA: (*Looks at his watch.*) Fifty two minutes.

EVA: And then?

SOVA: It's over.

EVA: With me too?

SOVA: I don't make exceptions.

EVA: What will you get by killing me?

SOVA: Me? Nothing.

EVA: So why don't you make exceptions?

SOVA: It's our cause. They'll pay next time when they realize we don't make exceptions. We need money. To buy weapons, print books, influence public opinion of the world.

IRENA: Do you write books?

SOVA: I have written one.

IRENA: That's fascinating. I'm glad that I met you. What was it about?

SOVA: About truth. About law and justice and who are their enemies.

IRENA: You think it would be justice to kill us?

SOVA: Your death would help the cause of justice.

IRENA: But that's horrible. Filip—I think he really believes it. (*Shocked.*) But it would be murder. Man doesn't have the right to take the life of his neighbor.

FILIP: (*Reaches a decision.*) Listen, listen to me. I'm a lawyer. You can call me . . . (*he can't think of a name*) . . . Filip. What should I call you?

SOVA: My name isn't important.

FILIP: Look, you have selected us to sacrifice us for a truly noble cause, although even that could be disputed. You have selected us at random. Are you so sure that the right people are being sacrificed? You want to say that it doesn't matter which people are sacrificed, but that isn't quite true. For example, me: I am working on an extensive study concerning correctional institutions. I am trying to prove that the entire penal system is outdated. That we are punishing the very people we should be attempting to cure. The result of my work could be an extensive reform that will make life less difficult for many poor and suffering people. I see that you have deep sympathy for such people. Why do damage to your cause by killing me?

SOVA: The world can no longer be helped by reforms. Quite the opposite is true. You and your type of people prolong the agony of a society which must die anyway.

FILIP: I thought that because of your cause which is, so to say, right on the borderline, you could have a bit of understanding for my own efforts.

SOVA: I know all about people like you: you aren't concerned about the prisoners. You only want to get rid of some guilt.

FILIP: What do you mean by that?

SOVA: Some people think they can get rid of guilt. They can't. Guilt is part of us.

BAUER: (*Butts in.*) Absolutely. My prince would add that the worst madmen are reformed sinners. Also the most dangerous.

FILIP: What exactly do you want? People like you always start up the merry-go-round of violence which then no one is able to stop. What do you expect? Eventually they're bound to catch up with you and put you on trial!

SOVA: No! We'll put *them* on trial!

FILIP: And what if the police catches you before then?

SOVA: They won't get me alive.

IRENA: Aren't you afraid of death?

SOVA: If I die in the battle for a better world then I am not afraid.

FILIP: You . . . you're a fanatic!

SOVA: No. I only know that truth is on my side.

PETR: (*Walks to Deml and salutes.*) We have just received a message that one of our aircraft, flight 289 from Colombo . . .

DEML: Hijacked?

PETR: They demand a hundred million. In Western dollars, naturally.

DEML: Madmen! They don't know where to stop anymore.

PETR: They gave us an hour to think it over.

DEML: They'll extend the time limit. As usual.

PETR: I am not sure. Their leader is an unusually stubborn fanatic. (*Confidentially.*) I happen to know him. He is a former schoolmate.

DEML: If we pay the ransom we will only encourage them.

PETR: But there are people aboard.

DEML: (*Foxily.*) But he's aboard too. If he decides to go the limit he knows what'll happen.

PETR: He also knows that he's replaceable. They are absolutely interchangeable—they're like flies and lately they have really started to multiply.

DEML: So what do you suggest?

PETR: Pay them!

DEML: You know what they'll do with the money? They'll buy guns and arm more insurgents with them. Soon not only flying but walking as well will be out of the question. They'll start taking us as hostages first on the street and then in our own beds.

PETR: What about the people on board. Everyone will say we sent them to their deaths.

DEML: We can't be concerned only with those who are aboard. We must be concerned also with the others. With the whole world. So that we would not be handing the world into the hands of such adventurers. We cannot finance criminals. It's only logical. Everyone will understand.

PETR: Not the ones who are aboard. They will definitely never understand.

DEML: Naturally we'll do our best to save them. And if we're not successful, then it really doesn't matter if they understand our motives or not.

IRENA: (*Can't help speaking out.*) But that's cruel! We can't think like that.

DEML: (*Stops in his tracks.*) No, of course, you're right. (*To Petr.*) I am sure you'll think of something to get them out of it. (*In a low voice.*) There'll be quite a reward in it for you.

PETR: Yes, of course. As usual, the responsibility is laid on the shoulders of the police. You'll see your mistake but it will be too late.

EVA: Do you like to do that—killing people?

SOVA: It's not a matter of liking or not liking it. It is my mission.

FILIP: Who entrusted you with it?

SOVA: My conscience.

FILIP: He's a fanatic. They're the worst. They can't be paid off or frightened off. I have seen people like that. When they blind-folded them they used to shout . . . (*He stops in mid-sentence.*)

IRENA: (*Quickly.*) And you've never thought, you've never thought that your wife or some girl you like could also, like this . . . like us?

SOVA: I don't have one.

IRENA: What don't you have?

SOVA: A wife or a girl.

EVA: You don't have a girl? So why don't you find one?

SOVA: That's not for me.

EVA: (*Gets up and unbuttons her blouse.*) And what about me? Don't you like me?

DEML: (*Coughs and makes signs.*)

SOVA: Don't come near!

EVA: Aren't you even interested in finding out who I am?

SOVA: I know who you are. You are a hostage.

EVA: Do you know that I'm a singer?

IRENA: You're not going to sing for him? Now?

EVA: At least it will take our mind off things.

IRENA: Now I'll really feel like one of the condemned. I read somewhere that they used to do that in one of the American states. That before they led him into that room with the chair they sang to him. . . .

EVA: Would you mind if I sang to you?

SOVA: We don't have time.

EVA: But now you have time.

SOVA: It's senseless. There is no real sense to listening to stuff like that.

EVA: We could travel the world together. Have you ever been to Monte Carlo or Miami? You'd really see something!

SOVA: I am not interested. This world of yours is already in its final agony anyway. Thirty minutes left!

FILIP: Enough! Enough of such talk! Where are the police?

PETR: (*Reaches them, waving a white handkerchief.*)

BAUER: Stop!

SOVA: I warn you that if you attempt anything we will blow up the plane and the hostages before the time is up.

PETR: Why should we attempt anything?

SOVA: Because you are the police. At a certain stage of social organization the police takes on a power which . . . (*Stops himself.*) The police always defends the interests of property and the ruling class. Those who are not rebellious—they pay the police.

PETR: You are absolutely wrong. The police have long ago developed their own interests.

SOVA: The interests of the police don't interest me.

PETR: I see. (*Quietly.*) But our interests could be yours as well.

SOVA: Fortunately your interests and ours are absolutely opposite.

PETR: Are they? Every revolution has always begun by doing battle with the police, but has ended up by handing power over to the hands of its own police.

SOVA: And you deduce from this I should hand the power over to you?

PETR: Not at all. I am not that naive, but neither are you. What can you really do against us? You know very well that there is no other force that could be victorious in this world. Against your little bomb we can put up megatons of explosives. And I don't think I even need to go into our much finer instruments which are far more effective.

SOVA: There exist situations where even you are completely helpless. (*The game is becoming increasingly realistic—he is playing himself now.*) These are situations where you come face to face with real determination.

PETR: You are wrong. We can be helpless when it comes to individual acts, but I thought that you were interested in much more. (*Confidentially.*) With us you'll be able to control history. You'll be omniscient and omnipresent. You will hear of everything that happens. And you will be invisible at the same time. You will install, place and replace at your will. You will think up what didn't happen and deny that which has. You will peruse, poison and prejudge. Isn't all that much more enticing than to walk about with a little bomb?

SOVA: Your offer doesn't interest me. It is interesting only as a symptom of power in its final agony.

PETR: You are making a mistake.

SOVA: You are making the mistake. You have only twenty-five minutes left.

IRENA: Can nothing move you? God, how cruel some people are.

FILIP: (*To Bauer.*) They'll shoot you down like dogs. Aren't you afraid?

BAUER: They will? But only after we have shot you. And you are much more afraid!

FILIP: (*Forgetting all about the game.*) How do you figure that—that I'm more afraid?

BAUER: I'm used to things. I've seen a few things already.

FILIP: You don't think that I have?

BAUER: Maybe, from another perspective.

FILIP: And I've had just about enough of your constant insinuations. Also of this entire comedy. As if there wasn't enough excitement in this world. (*He tries to leave.*)

BAUER: Not a step further! (*He raises his rifle and fires into the air.*)

FILIP: (*Grabs his chest and collapses into a chair.*)

IRENA: Filip, my God! Kamil, how far are you going to carry this?

BAUER: (*With mild astonishment.*) It was really loaded. Don't get excited lady, it's just buckshot. (*Talking about Filip.*) He was getting on this high horse again. If it were the other way around, he'd be doing all the shooting and we all know at whom.(*He hangs the gun on his shoulder.*)

FILIP: That's too much! In my house and with our gun!

PETR: (*Laughs.*)

IRENA: (*To Filip.*) Calm down. At least he's got it back on his shoulder.

FILIP: (*To Petr.*) What are you laughing about? What's so funny? Why don't you disarm him and take him away if you think it's so funny?

PETR: (*Steps closer to Bauer.*) I see that you have your principles. But let me ask a question: What will you get out of the hundred million?

BAUER: I am not discussing anything with you. (*Quietly.*) He might hear me.

FILIP: He's still talking to him! He's talking to the man who just discharged a gun in my house!

PETR: (*To Bauer.*) Did you hear what I said before?

BAUER: (*Carefully.*) I hear when I want to and then again, I don't hear when I don't want to.

PETR: That's good. How did you get into this group? You aren't that young and you've seen a few things.

SOVA: (*Shuffles around, a bit embarrassed.*) I'm sorry, madame, life is like that. But you have only twenty minutes left.

FILIP: I am beginning to believe that. In twenty minutes he'll shoot us all down like partridges. Just for the fun of it—so they can test it all out.

PETR: (*To Bauer.*) Revolutions, assassinations and dreams about redemption and changing the world—that's for less matured spirits, not you. Do you know how old St. Juste was when they chopped off his head and threw it into the lime pit? Twenty-seven. And Marx was a bit younger when he wrote the manifesto according to which some people have been trying to organize the Toulon? What about Christ when he decided to save mankind? They were all kids, without the maturity and objectivity. But you? (*Quietly.*) Hundred thousand in cash and the job of my deputy. With good prospects for a career.

SOVA: (*To Bauer.*) Stop talking to him! You're a disgrace—chatting with policemen!

PETR: Very well. I'm leaving. Very much disappointed by your stubborness. (*To the others.*) All policemen are powerless when faced with terror that they have not organized themselves. (*Moves aside.*)

SOVA: Fifteen minutes left!

EVA: Won't you give us more time?

SOVA: No! I never compromise.

EVA: (*Approaches him.*) Not even with me?

SOVA: Don't come any nearer!

EVA: I wanted you to kiss me. For once I want to be kissed by a real man!

SOVA: Women bring betrayal with them.

EVA: (*Turning to Jakub.*) And you captain?

JAKUB: (*Looks up from the table, his mouth full.*) Unfortunately I'm powerless.

EVA: Not even you want to kiss me?

JAKUB: Oh, that? Sure, gladly. (*He walks toward her, swallows, kisses her.*)

DEML: (*Jumps up.*) That's not part of the game!

EVA: Of course it is. What should I be doing during the last fifteen minutes of my life?

IRENA: I don't know. (*To Filip.*) I'd still like to say something. We must explain to them . . . (*To Sova.*) Please tell me what you want? What do you want to get out of all this?

EVA: (*Disengaging herself from Jakub and his embrace.*)

SOVA: (*To Irena and Eva.*) There is no time for that any more.

IRENA: What if we believe in similar things? I've always wanted to live in a society where people weren't selfish, where they voluntarily gave up all useless things and where they searched for a meaning of it all in something much higher. People could understand each other so easily. Tell me, maybe you have a mission for me.

SOVA: Your mission has been established. You are a hostage.

IRENA: (*Almost crying.*) Maybe we could be more helpful to you alive than dead. You can't kill us without finding out what we want and what we believe.

SOVA: An ocean lies betwen you and me and our particular whirlpools cannot ever meet. (*To Jakub.*) No news?

JAKUB: Nothing.

SOVA: I'm sorry. There are only three minutes left now.

IRENA: It's horrible. Maybe he doesn't hear me? He can't feel sorry for anyone. He can't even understand when he doesn't hear us.

SOVA: Two minutes. Do you want to pray? (*To Eva.*) To sing?

IRENA: Don't you feel any compassion? Regret? We've all come to this world the same way and the same fate awaits us . . . we have so much in common. How can you even talk about justice when you can't feel that?

SOVA: Justice is not the same thing for you as it is for us.

BAUER: How much time remaining?

SOVA: One minute.

BAUER: And we're supposed to blow ourselves up with them?

SOVA: We can't leave this area. There is at least a battalion of sharp-shooters outside.

BAUER: Oh. (*He approaches Sova from behind and hits him on the back of his head with the stock of his rifle.*)

SOVA: (*Staggers, then falls.*)

IRENA: My God! You . . . you're with us? (*Comes to about the situation.*) Did you really hit him?

BAUER: Only partially, lady.

FILIP: (*To Sova.*) That's what happens (*Gloating.*) when you mix up games with real life.

IRENA: Come on, Filip, you have to admit that Kamil is an excellent actor. (*To Petr.*) You egged him on like that. It was only a game, you shouldn't do that!

SOVA: (*Getting up.*) Don't wo . . . (*Magnanimously.*) Don't worry, nothing happened. It's all part of the game. (*Tries to go aside.*)

BAUER: Nobody move please. I have been promised a reward and have not received it yet.

DEML: (*Walks over to Bauer.*) What are you talking about, Jan? The game is over. The hijackers have been overpowered, they didn't get what they wanted. We have won. Along with the police, actually. So put away the gun.

BAUER: Why? Aren't we playing any more? Have you been fooling with me?

PETR: He has a point. To betray someone and not be rewarded for it? And in the end to allow himself to be disarmed too? That is supposed to satisfy him? His appetite can't be satiated when he has just pushed himself through an unsuspected success? I admit that I'm not happy either. I'm supposed to have won. But the police can never really win because their game is never really over. Therefore, I declare the game is not over.

FILIP: (*To Irena.*) They've all gone mad.

DEML: You can't do that. That would be against the rules. The game is over.

PETR: I should like to announce that the police have succeeded not only in ruining the plans of the hijackers but in its tireless efforts has also uncovered some serious circumstances concerning one that is present here.

DEML: I repeat: It's against the rules.

PETR: (*To Bauer.*) Naturally he's rebellious. He knows that he's the criminal I am talking about.(*To Deml.*) We make the rules now! Haven't you understood whose hands (*He raises his palms.*) now firmly grasp your fate? From the moment you gave up the right to your own defense and surrendered it along with your weapons into the hands of strangers, you have given up your right to make the rules! Now we will appoint the court. The evidence we will present will shake you. (*To Bauer.*) At the moment no one is to leave this house. You are responsible for that. I appoint you deputy, in other words, my representative. Of course you know that deputies are the ones who are most generously rewarded. Although there are times when they too are given over to the executioner. When they betray the trust.

IRENA: I don't understand anything any more. This is not the way I thought it would be.

EVA: (*To Sova.*) I just wanted to tell you that you are an excellent actor. You played it beautifully. You really are a born talent.

SOVA: You think so? But I didn't really have to act. I just reminisced.

ACT TWO

FOURTH GAME

The Game of the Court

The scene is the same as during the previous ones. Bauer is patrolling between the table and buffet, then around the table too, with a gun. Petr, wearing a black robe, is writing in a file. He finishes, closes it, and speaks as he stands.

DEML: I protest. Make him put away the gun. He is threatening me.

EVA: But a little while ago you said to let him carry it

DEML: That was an entirely different situation.

PETR: Some of us will be on the defense team, others on the prosecution one. In the end the judge—that's me—will deliver a verdict.

DEML:That was an entirely different game. They were conspirators.

PETR: You see, the guard must have a weapon. A verdict of not guilty will constitute a victory for the defense, guilty for the prosecution.

DEML: I am not going to play this game.

PETR: (*Manages to quiet him through a gesture.*) Now we will choose our parts. We already know who is the accused.

DEML: What—me? Why is it supposed to be me?

PETR: Because you have committed a crime. (*Points to his files.*)

DEML: I am not going to be the accused. Get one of the hijackers, at least there will be some connection.

PETR: A moment ago I explained to you that hijackers seldom make it to trial. (*To the others.*) Can't you all see! Who lost his nerve the moment even the slightest violence took place: Who was terrified at the very suggestion that we should turn out the lights for the next game? What sort of a nocturnal horror did he recall at that moment? And who had his doubts that the murderer would be able to find the throat? Weren't we hearing the voice of a horrifying experience?

EVA: It all sounds very interesting.

DEML: Darling!

PETR: So we have already decided who will play the judge and the guard. What we need is the prosecutor, the lawyer for the defense and witnesses.

DEML: (*To Eva.*) They talk about me as if I were some sort of criminal and you don't mind.

EVA: Oh, now come on, honsey bunsey, you really don't know how to play the game. You take everything much too seriously.

BAUER: If I'm supposed to be the guard, I should have a gun. The prince, just before he died, used to say that it's much better to be running around naked with a gun than to sit in the cooler with a fur coat on.

IRENA: He died there?

BAUER: Unfortunately, my dear lady. Along with lots of others.

PETR: (*To Filip.*) You will be the prosecutor!

FILIP: What? You still insist on treating me as if I were some sort of a prosecutor? (*Violently.*) You've all united against me, I can see that now. You are trying to provoke me, put me back somewhere I haven't been for a long, long time. But I am calm about it; it takes more than this to upset me. If you want to blindfold, choke and bomb each other, have trials and I don't know what else, that's your business. Go on, play! After all, you are the guests here!

PETR: Fine. Who is going to be the prosecutor, then? (*To Eva.*) You?

EVA: Me? And what am I supposed to be prosecuting him for?

PETR: It's all in here. (*Hands her the files.*) You just have to read it, that's the best way to resemble a real prosecutor. (To Irena.) You will be the lawyer for the defense.

IRENA: I don't know if I could do it. I get so terribly excited.

EVA: It's really here. You got it ready beforehand.

PETR: (*To Jakub.*) You will be a witness for the prosecution.

SOVA: I think it would be better to draw lots for our parts.

PETR: Why? I am giving everyone the part he is most suited for. That's the best way. A moment ago you were such an excellent revolutionary. But now of course you think you're on the other side. So try the defense witness. And you for the prosecution. And now I would like the accused to take his place. (*He shows where.*) The witnesses should probably leave the room, but it's fine if they just stand a bit aside. (*Motions them to chairs.*) Thank you.

DEML: You really want to play this game? I . . . . I don't exactly know what I should be doing. I haven't had anything to do with any murder.

JAKUB: Who said anything about a murder?

DEML: (*Insulted.*) What's that remark supposed to mean? Are you saying I know something that the others don't?

FILIP: Don't expect me to play along in this game. Except perhaps (*He's jovial.*) as the court attendant. (*Amused.*) I used to be rather quite envious of them. Of their independence. Also of the charwomen. No one would dare to order them around.

PETR: Fine. You are the court attendant then. You certainly have excellent qualifications for the job. And now we begin with the case against Josef Deml.

DEML: I . . . I . . . (*About to protest.*)

EVA: Come on, don't be a spoil sport, honsey bunsey. It's only a game.

DEML: Well, all right. (*To Eva.*) But just because you want it.

FILIP: This way please. (*He leads him to a chair.*)

IRENA: (*Quietly to Eva.*) My God, it reminds me of . . . Are you as nervous as I am?

EVA: No, I am used to being on stage.

PETR: If the lady prosecutor would please.

EVA: (*Going through the papers. She reads.*) On July 20th of this year—exactly 29 days ago—Pavla Mala, student, 19 years old, went to visit her schoolmates staying at a cottage near St. Jan. She stayed there until almost midnight, then left because she wanted to reach her home before morning. When she left she was wearing a light blue cotton dress and a kerchief over her head since it was starting to rain. But she never arrived back home. I accuse Josef Deml, who is present here, of enticing, on July 21st, the missing woman into his car and of taking her to a place called the Castle Park, then murdering her there. Further, that with the help of the crew of a refuse truck CC 27 27, he arranged to have the body taken away and cremated.

DEML: (*Looks over the others who are listening intently but he is a bit embarrassed.*) You can't be serious. Such a thing!

EVA: Then there are some newspaper clippings here.

PETR: Those come later. You have heard the charge. Do you plead guilty?

DEML: (*Catching hold of himself.*) Such vileness. Something so base! Shame!

IRENA: But the girl really . . . (*Points to the window.*) . . . here in the park . . .

FILIP: (*To Deml.*) You mustn't be so touchy. Just say no. (*To Irena.*) And you are supposed to defend him, not . . . (*Petr uses his gavel.*) Sorry.

DEML: I am not playing this game and I demand an apology from him.

PETR: This is not the way to convince anybody. If you are not guilty, it will be proven.

DEML: If I am not guilty . . . Do you actually doubt it?

PETR: We must assume that everyone is innocent. Until they are proven otherwise.

DEML: What are you trying to say? I didn't have anything to do with it. (*To Eva.*) And you read out loud such a God-awful thing. You know that I have lots of work to do at home. I came only because you wanted me to. Because you like to be amused.

EVA: But I am amused, don't worry about that, honsey bunsey.

PETR: Very well, let's begin with the testimony of the accused. (*To Deml.*) What were you doing 28 days ago between 4 and 5 a.m.?

DEML: What a question! Do you have any idea what you did a month ago? What day of the week was it?

PETR: Same as today. You know it very well!

DEML: So what could I be doing? I know: I was sleeping. (*Attempts to joke.*) It may seem strange to you but I am usually sound asleep at that time.

EVA: No, honsey bunsey. (*Stops suddenly.*) I mean, accused, will you please try and remember!

DEML: Remember what?

EVA: Four weeks ago today!

DEML: It's actually nobody's business what I did. No game can give anybody the right to interfere with my privacy. And that's my final word.

EVA: Go on and say it!

DEML: No.

EVA: Weren't we returning from a trip to the country that night?

DEML: If I was returning from somewhere or not is my business.

PETR: I caution you, accused.

EVA: It was past midnight and we picked up a hitchhiker—a girl

DEML: And so what even if I did pick her up? It was dark and it was raining. She was standing by the road and no more than two cars could have passed there every hour.

EVA: And when you let me off you said you would take her home.

DEML: I did take her home.

PETR: Where? Do you remember where you took her?

DEML: That's nobody's business!

FILIP: (*Excited.*) You can't answer like that. Think of something to say. People think up all sorts of stories in real court. If you go on like that, you'll really be under suspicion.

PETR: (*Uses his gavel.*)

FILIP: (*Stops talking, bows to him.*)

DEML: I don't feel like thinking up stories. (*Looks at his watch.*) It's almost midnight.

PETR: Very well, then, where did you take her?

DEML: I don't remember anymore.

FILIP: (*Unable to control himself.*) That won't help you! (*Stops.*) If that's the way you want it!

PETR: It's all very interesting. Do you at least remember what she looked like?

DEML: (*Angry.*) I don't need any help. I just gave her a ride.

PETR: Will you answer the court's question, accused!

DEML: To hell with your court. I won't answer anything more!

IRENA: (*Quietly to Deml.*) Maybe you should . . . It would perhaps be better if you did. Otherwise it might look like you are really trying to hide something.

PETR: Could you describe the student?

DEML: (*Yelling.*) I don't know if she was a student. I never said that she was a student. I didn't know her.

EVA: Oh yes, she was. Do you remember, honsey bunsey? You asked her where she was going in such a hurry in the middle of the night and she said she had her first lecture at seven in the morning.

DEML: She said that? I don't remember.

EVA: And you talked about what she was studying and she said that she was going to take some test in chromatics or something.

DEML: I really don't remember. I (*losing his nerve*) I forbid you to talk such nonsense about our trip—which was private.

PETR: How was she dressed? What did she look like? Was she big? Small? Light-haired?

DEML: I don't remember. She was wearing a handkerchief. Or maybe she wasn't. I didn't look at her head.

EVA: She was blonde.

PETR: What color was her handkerchief?

DEML: I don't know.

EVA: Blue. Just like her dress.

IRENA: All that doesn't prove a thing. There are plenty of blue dresses around.

PETR: And then it didn't rain anymore?

DEML: When?

PETR: When you were taking the girl back home.

DEML: I didn't take any girl home.

PETR: Oh you didn't? You didn't know she even existed? You have never seen her?

EVA: (*Surprised.*) That's interesting. And here is an article from the paper about the murder. (*She reads from the files Petr gave her.*) Bloody footprints, a piece of blue silk material and several long light strands of hair have been found at the spot. Analysis showed that they came from a female about twenty years old.

IRENA: What article is that? (*Astonished.*) I have never seen it.

PETR: Very well. Did you or didn't you take her home?

DEML: I have had enough. I am not playing any more. (*To Eva.*) Let's go home.

BAUER: (*Raising his hand.*) Could I make a comment?

PETR: No, you are the guard.

BAUER: That's too bad, because I could tell you a few things about this man's character. He has been married three times and now . . .

IRENA: (*To Petr.*) All that doesn't prove that my client is connected, excuse me, I'm a bit excited, that his actions were in any way connected with the criminal act. He simply gave a ride in his car to a girl in a blue dress.

PETR: Did you drive her home or not?

DEML: (*With relief to Irena.*) Of course I gave the girl a ride. (*Points to Eva.*) She knows all about it. She was in the car and talked with her. She can testify that it's all nonsense.

EVA: No, I can't. You know that I got out first.

DEML: So what? She got out right after you. I took her to her street and she got out there.

EVA: So you admit that you drove off with her. Why didn't you say so?

DEML: I didn't drive off with anyone. It's all a dirty lie.

PETR: Will the accused stop or be charged with being in contempt of court!

DEML: Don't call me the accused! I remember you when you used to run around the garden in your birthday suit.

PETR: Will the accused please stop getting so excited.

SOVA: (*Jumps up from his place.*) I know exactly how he feels! There are acts and rituals which should not be demeaned by an undignified comedy. Why do you bring a real, tragic happening into it?

PETR: (*To Bauer.*) Escort him out of the court please!

BAUER: (*Arranges his rifle.*) Let's go.

SOVA: You play games about the law, but you're presenting us with lawlessness. I demand that this game be ended.

BAUER: Come on, let's go. (*Quietly.*) Maybe it's not a game at all. Maybe he really did do it. I know him better than you do.

SOVA: And you're not ashamed, talking like this about a friend?

BAUER: What do you mean—a friend? I am the guard and he is the accused. A little while ago you threatened to blow them all up.

SOVA: Let's end this game.

BAUER: What are you so afraid of? That your turn will come too?

SOVA: How dare you say that?

BAUER: Nobody has a completely clear conscience. My prince used to say that the innocent differ from the guilty only in that their turn hasn't come yet. But when one day there'll be enough interrogators to go around . . .

SOVA: Shut up! You're really crude, you know! And a while ago you really hurt me.

IRENA: Kamil, please don't get mad!

SOVA: (*To Bauer.*) Violence goes against my grain and he's the very source of it. (*Returns to his place.*) I am not going to be any further part of this game.

PETR: Fine. Sit down and observe, even though violence didn't always go against your grain. And remember that violence is helped not only by him who commits it, but also by him who submits to it. Now we will hear the testimony of the witnesses. (*Motions to Jakub.*) Bring in the witness for the prosecution, please. You will testify before this court as a witness. You must tell only the truth.

JAKUB: Yes.

PETR: Can you remember what you were doing exactly four weeks ago today, early in the morning?

JAKUB: Yeah, I happen to remember. I got up at three a.m.

PETR: Why so early?

JAKUB: I was going to race. The plane was going at six-thirty. And I have to do my morning exercises.

PETR: Do you exercise every morning?

JAKUB: I have to keep in shape.

EVA: (*Mixing in.*) Can you tell us how?

JAKUB: (*With enthusiasm.*) In two phases. According to Smith-Voronov.

EVA: Could you show us?

JAKUB: Yes, of course. But I'll need—some rope.

PETR: (*To Filip.*) Let him have some rope.

FILIP: (*Goes to hall, returns with rope.*)

JAKUB: (*Throws the rope across the beam at the ceiling, climbs up and does several exercises.*) We had three in our squad who tried the three-phase exercises according to Kaiserschada-Kowalski, but it didn't exactly work out. They tripled the size of their muscles but it was too much for the heart. The last one left us a month ago.

PETR: Go on. What did you do after the exercises?

JAKUB: Then I had breakfast. About four o'clock I went to catch the bus. (*He lets himself back down.*)

PETR: A bus coming from where and going to where?

JAKUB: From where? From here. It stops here, near the park. And we were going to Madagascar!

IRENA: (*Astonished.*) Yes, that's true. (*To the others.*) He slept here and left early in the morning. (*Hastily.*) But that doesn't mean a thing. He sleeps here often and the bus stop is just a little way from the park.

PETR: Did you see anything interesting or unusual while on your way?

JAKUB: Sure. I saw . . . well, actually I heard something first. Something like a cry.

IRENA: But you . . . you never said anything about it.

FILIP: You mustn't get so excited. It's only a game, my dear.

IRENA: Yes, of course. But it all sounds so strange.

JAKUB: I wasn't sure if the cry meant anything, you know. Besides, I was in a hurry.

PETR: Where did it come from?

JAKUB: From where? Well, I'd say from somewhere in the park.

PETR: What kind of cry was it?

JAKUB: What do you mean?

PETR: Was it articulated?

JAKUB: No, it was a man's cry. Well, actually a woman's, but sort of muffled, you know. Like when you're choking somebody and they cry out.

IRENA: You . . . witness! Have you ever choked anyone?

JAKUB: Sure. Like for a joke, you know.

FILIP: This is really too much. These things are not to be made fun of. (*To Irena.*) Why don't you protest?

IRENA: I protest against that answer. It's cynical.

PETR: What could possibly be more cynical than reality when somebody is actually being choked? Go on. What did you do then?

JAKUB: I hurried to catch the bus. I couldn't miss it, they would take off without me. And I was almost at the park when I see this garbage truck. On this walk between the trees like, you know? So I thought that was pretty funny—I mean what's a garbage truck supposed to be doing on a walk in the middle of a park at four-thirty in the morning?

PETR: What did it look like?

JAKUB: What—the truck? Well, it was red, maybe a bit more like orange. Almost new, I'd say, you know? And the number was CC 27 27. I remember that, because I'm twenty-seven right now.

PETR: Did you see anything else?

JAKUB: Well, there was another thing that was strange . . . but I don't know if I should say it because I don't wanna cast any false suspicions, you know?

PETR: Just say it.

JAKUB: So suddenly this guy runs into the park. And he's all covered with dirt, breathing hard and maybe there was even some blood on him, I'd say. And then my bus came.

PETR: Did he board the bus?

JAKUB: He? No—I did. He got into the truck. It was pulling out of the park and just before it did they opened the door and he got on.

PETR: Do you think you would recognize the man?

JAKUB: Yeah, sure. He really stood out, being like he was, so short and fat. (*Looks at Deml.*) He's sitting right here. It was him!

IRENA: (*Blurting out.*) But this is terrible!

DEML: (*Getting up.*) O.K., enough's enough! You're gonna take all that back, you bastard! Right now! He has never laid eyes on me before tonight. It's all a big lie!

PETR: Will the accused be silent!

DEML: (*Stepping closer to Jakub.*) I am going home now, but before I leave I want to hear you say it was all a lie. I want to hear an apology!

JAKUB: Who are you pushing around? (*Pushes Deml so that he literally flies off.*)

DEML: (*Fighting his way back to Jakub.*) You'll take it all back and apologize!

PETR: (*Using his gavel.*)

JAKUB: What lies? I am a witness for the prosecution!

EVA: Come on, honsey bunsey, don't get so excited. It's only a game.

IRENA: People mustn't lie. Not even in a game and especially not when he is a witness.

DEML: So you won't apologize? I'll show you, you punk! (*He tries to strike Jakub, but Jakub grabs his arm and twists it.*)

BAUER: (*To Petr.*) Should I step in?

PETR: I don't think we have a choice, faithful jailer!

BAUER: (*Throws his rifle across his shoulder, then grabs one of the pieces of rope which Filip took out of the closet and throws himself on Deml.*)

SOVA: That's enough! (*Tries to restrain Bauer.*) Gentlemen, you mustn't do that. Don't forget that we came here as friends.

BAUER: (*Pushes him away.*)

IRENA: My God, please don't. (*A melee, ferocious screams, an upset chair.*)

EVA: (*Restraining Irena.*) Leave them alone, they finally loosened up a bit. Do you think I played my part O.K.? There was almost nothing in those files from your brother and I really don't like to improvise the spoken word.

FIFTH GAME

The Game of Kindred Souls

The melee has ended. Deml and Sova are tied together, also to the armchairs on which they are seated.

DEML: I demand . . . this is unheard of. (*To Filip.*) First you invite us here, then you start accusing us of things, you insult us and finally you tie us up.

PETR: (*Using his gavel.*) The court is adjourned for fifteen minutes. (*Gets up.*) I trust that by then peace and order will be restored. The verdict should be handed down in a dignified atmosphere. (*Exits.*)

IRENA: Petr, you can't leave now. You have to untie them. (*To Filip.*) We can't leave them like that.

FILIP: I didn't think up those games and I almost got shot when I expressed my doubts about them, remember? (*To Deml.*) I didn't tie you up. And you brought that felon here, not me.

IRENA: Filip, how can you call somebody that?

DEML: If I am not untied immediately, I will start yelling for help. I refuse to be dealt with as if I were some sort of a criminal.

JAKUB: And what if you are one? We've heard some pretty strange things about you.

DEML: *You* are the criminal! I am gonna take care of you, you scum. Don't think I haven't noticed how you've been after her all evening. (*He manages to move with his chair and to kick Jakub in the shin.*)

JAKUB: (*Cries out in pain, turns around, picks up Deml, chair and all, and holds him in the air.*)

IRENA: For God's sake be reasonable, we can't have such violence.

BAUER: What's a bit of violence among friends, ladies and gentlemen, eh? The prince used to tell how he was taken by the Turkish janissaries . . .

FILIP: Don't get so excited about it. You didn't start it. They did—with the loaded gun.

BAUER: Except he was lucky, he knew seventeen languages. Once, when reveille was at three in the morning the block chief caught him still in bed. And when he started screaming his head off, the prince says, kusimama durefu kunamchokesha mzee. And that sure shut him up.

SOVA: (*To Bauer.*) Let me ask you a question. Don't you find it a bit awkward that we met here as friends to play games and you suddenly start dealing with us as if we were real criminals?

BAUER: So why are you still acting like criminals? In real life a scoundrel plays innocent and in a game an innocent guy plays a scoundrel. It's all the same people. (*To Sova.*) Except you're not able to see the proper connections.

SOVA: You don't have to lecture me about connections . . . you . . . you . . .

EVA: Let it go. I don't know why we couldn't stay here a little longer. We could play some other games or just try and loosen up a bit.

IRENA: But first we have to loosen them up, don't we?

SOVA: I am not saying that the situation in which we find ourselves is entirely outside the framework of the game. I even find it somewhat inspirational. I confess that quite frequently I imagine that I am being brought before my interrogator with my hands tied. And actually I feel a certain satisfaction over the fact that I am the one who is fettered. But these (*he raises his tied hands*) may not be the worst fetters. Power and false belief put us into much tighter ones.

IRENA: Of course, Kamil, but I don't think that violence should be part of any game. And there has been so much of it here tonight.

EVA: Why don't you suggest another game? (*To Filip.*)

IRENA: I don't think that under the circumstances we should be starting another game.

EVA: Why not? Even all this is only a game. You can't imagine all the things one can do as part of a game. You don't think I've ever been tied up? And the things they did with me!

DEML: (*Thumps the floor.*)

FILIP: (*To Eva.*) All right then, I'll try to lead you away from the edge of the crevasse. I know a very simple game. (*To Irena.*) Everyone goes into different corners of the room and there they try to concentrate on the one person in the group that he feels nearest to. Then everyone starts writing down things that enter his mind. It can happen that sometimes two people can come up with words so similar that it's incredible. Real kindred souls. But I am not sure after all this you won't find my game a bit too tame.

JAKUB: I'll play. Give me some paper.

EVA: We'll be playing this game, honsey bunsey, you want to play with us?

DEML: (*Thumps floor.*)

IRENA: (*Pulls up her chair to Sova.*) You can't imagine how sorry I am Kamil. I was so much looking forward to this evening, and I hoped you'd like it. Such terrible knots. You see, I may be cursed. As soon as I come across someone whom I love or respect, he meets with some sort of misfortune. My first husband—we had been married barely a year—they called him to a patient. He'd had a drink or two, it was a sort of weakness of his. It was icy, we didn't say good-bye, nothing. My second husband, he . . . (*stops*) I am sorry. That has really nothing to do with all this, does it?

SOVA: Don't apologize Irena. I assure you, this whole evening is all an unusually interesting and stimulating experience. I don't think you are able to perceive it, but just now the world is beginning to change before my very eyes. As if just now I was beginning to see it's proper dimensions. He represents (*speaking about Bauer*) power. Dull, merciless, deaf. Like death itself. It's the final negation of all our efforts. Absolute degradation. The swollen confidence of emptiness. Or let's take you. Eternally striving for harmony that can never be fulfilled—therefore tragedy. And me? I feel a friend of so, so many people, suddenly united with them (*raises his hands*) by this. Perhaps they are unaware. Perhaps they don't suspect that they too are fettered.

JAKUB: How about starting, eh?

IRENA: We can't play if they can't. (*To Bauer.*) It doesn't make sense now that we're playing a new game.

BAUER: I have my orders. I'd really like to know what the verdict is.

JAKUB: I'll be thinking of you while we are playing.

EVA: But you have to go off somewhere.

JAKUB: I could go off and sit in the corner maybe.

EVA: (*Pushing Jakub out in the opposite direction, away from the patrolling Bauer.*) We'll call you when it's time to read out the slips. (*As soon as Jakub leaves, she quickly straightens herself out, opens a button of her blouse. Then she walks under the steps.*) Petr!

PETR: (*Enters.*)

EVA: Don't you want to play kindred souls with us?

PETR: You think I could find a kindred soul here?

BAUER: (*Also walks to the steps. Hopeful.*) And the verdict?

PETR: The verdict? Oh yes. You are really insistent. But it seems to me that this is not the right time for the verdict.

BAUER: What do we do then? (*Motions with his head to the two bound men.*)

PETR: We arm ourselves with patience. There are verdicts for which one has to wait for years. Maybe centuries. And I am not even mentioning those verdicts which are never announced. They just hover over us.

JAKUB: Ready.

FILIP: Ready.

EVA: Ready.

BAUER: Ready.

JAKUB: Who should start?

EVA: You can. (*She stands facing Petr and is actually speaking to him.*)

JAKUB: (*Yelling from the other room.*) I have man written down.

EVA: I have woman.

JAKUB: Fate.

EVA: Destiny.

BAUER: It's my turn now. I couldn't think of anything else: Beer.

FILIP: Winter. Frost. Footsteps.

JAKUB: Moon over some water.

EVA: Stars.

JAKUB: Airplane.

EVA: Miami.

BAUER: I have hide-out written down here.

FILIP: Courtyard, cobblestones. Footsteps. But I've already said that.

BAUER: Verdict. Judgment.

FILIP: Document.

JAKUB: A beautiful woman.

EVA: A maiden.

JAKUB: Gee, that's a coincidence. I have love.

EVA: Waiting. The telephone.

BAUER: Ball and chain.

FILIP: Scaffold. A rope. I know it's not right but I couldn't concentrate. Can one concentrate here? It's insane. All my life I've been unnable to concentrate. Constantly someone is talking and keeps hearing someone he doesn't want to hear at all.

JAKUB: Night. Kiss.

EVA: Evening. Tomorrow.

JAKUB: I don't have anything else down. (*To Eva.*) Doesn't matter. It's clear that we're kindred souls, if you know what I mean. Come on with me, there's a great couch in the other room. Come on, I'm waiting.

EVA: (*To Petr.*) Should I?

PETR: Why shouldn't you?

IRENA: Finished, Kamil! (*Throwing down the cut fetters.*)

PETR: (*To Sova.*) Congratulations. It must have been a great feeling to have on one's shoulders the freest head around here.

BAUER: (*Comes to and grabs his gun.*)

IRENA: And you too. (*She is untying the sweater which has been wound around Deml's mouth!)*

JAKUB: Come on, come on!

DEML: (*Screaming.*) I have heard everything. You bastards. I want to see you all hang.

IRENA: Please don't fight! We want to part as good friends.

DEML: (*To Eva.*) You drunken whore! I hate you!

EVA: Let's go.

BAUER: (*To Eva.*) Stop! No one is to go anywhere.

PETR: (*Disgusted.*) May I remind you that the games during which you were the guard or even my deputy are over. So kindly put the shot gun away.

BAUER: That's just it: they're over. So you don't give orders around here anymore.

IRENA: For God's sake, stop it! (*Hysterically.*) I am afraid!

BAUER: (*Bows.*) And that, ladies and gentlemen, means that the proper time for my game has come!

SIXTH GAME

The Execution Game

DEML: (*To Bauer.*) You think that I will play another game with you? That I will ever speak to you again?

EVA: I want to play his game.

FILIP: (*To Bauer.*) May I ask what sort of game it is?

BAUER: (*Putting his gun aside.*) I have already explained it. It's the Execution Game. We used to play it as little boys. The condemned is chosen by lot, but the executioner is a volunteer. So—who's volunteering?

IRENA: Why an execution? Please don't. There has been too much unpleasantness already.

PETR: Just follow him, dear sister, he has just invited you to visit the domain of his youth.

FILIP: I suspected it—I knew you'd come up with something like this. (*Violently.*) And you really think that you will find your executioner in this house?

BAUER: (*While he is making a noose from the rope still hanging from the beam.*) It's an excellent game to wind it all up with. Because, quite unlike most of your games, if you'll allow me to say so madam, this one simply has to have a definite end. Either when someone says stop or when no one says it.

IRENA: But that's a terrible thought.

FILIP: I am warning you for the last time. All of you!

DEML All right. I'll be the one.

FILIP: What do you mean?

DEML: I'll be the executioner.

EVA: You, honsey bunsey?

DEML: Don't talk to me, you . . . whore!

JAKUB: Doesn't it seem strange that when one of us was a terrorist, we put another on trial and now it'a a third guy we're supposed to be hanging?

BAUER: Why? It's a different game.

PETR: (*To Jakub.*) If you can't accept this sort of logic you won't make it through life. Besides—so far as the trial-is concerned we haven't had a verdict yet.

JAKUB: So we're supposed to be hanging an innocent man. But why?

PETR: Because that is the fate of all the innocent ones. Fortunately there are fewer and fewer of them around.

JAKUB: I don't know. Now, I don't know. It doesn't seem right.

BAUER: (*Tests the strength of the noose, then takes stool off table.*)

SOVA: I should like to express my own opinion. I cannot hide the fact that I am worried about the effect this game could have on our basest instincts. On the other hand . . . (*He walks excitedly back and forth.*) Even as a boy I wanted to talk with a condemned man the night before his execution. I read a few books about it but they didn't satisfy me. The authors usually didn't take the trouble to visit the prisoner's cell or, if they did, they weren't asking the right questions. So I ask: Does one alter his sense of time and values at the moment he feels the noose on his neck? Does he hate, does he forgive, does he love or does quite the opposite take place: does he lose all affinity with the world? (*To Jakub.*) And you say that he is innocent too. That is really the epitome of human fate!

BAUER: (*Taking a box of matches from his pocket.*) All right, let's choose the one who is condemned!

EVA: (*Pulling the first match. To Deml.*) You'd hang me too?

DEML: Oh gladly!

BAUER: (*Offers a match to Petr, Jakub and then Irena.*)

IRENA: My match is broken. (*In horror.*) Does that mean. . . ?

BAUER: Unfortunately, my dear lady. Unfortunately!

IRENA: But I, that's a horrible thought that you would . . . (*Looking at the noose.*)

EVA: Don't worry, someone won't be able to take it and they'll yell to stop.

IRENA: But what would you . . . what do you want to do with me?

SOVA: I should like to volunteer!

FILIP: What? As the condemned?

IRENA: No, I can't ask you to do that, Kamil! It wouldn't be right. Actually, we shouldn't play this game at all.

SOVA: (*Taking off his coat.*) There is a certain amount of logic in this game—for me. (*Opens his shirt collar.*) I am ready.

BAUER: Not so fast. (*Talking about Deml.*) He has to have a henchman and then someone has to read out the verdict. And someone has to be the priest too.

IRENA: No, enough! I say enough!

BAUER: You can't say that, madame: we haven't even started yet. (*To Filip.*) You could read out the verdict.

FILIP: I have told you already: I am not going to play this game.

BAUER: But we only want you to read the verdict. You have by far the best delivery. (*To Irena.*) And you will be the priest.

IRENA: But I—I don't know if my faith is strong enough.

EVA: It doesn't have to be. I don't believe everything that I sing either.

BAUER: (*To Jakub.*) And you'll be the henchman.

JAKUB: Me?

BAUER: You know judo. We have all seen you.

JAKUB: But that was in self-defense.

BAUER: So what?

DEML: Can we start then?

FILIP: I'll have to have a drink, the way I used to—(*Pours himself a glass and drinks it to the bottom.*)

IRENA: But Filip, you promised to stop, to never again . . .

JAKUB: The executioner's henchman? No!

EVA: (*Takes the mask.*) It all seemed sort of stilted at first, but now we are beginning to loosen up a bit. (*Offers a glass to Sova.*) Would you like to have one last drink?

SOVA: No, definitely not. I want to take in with all my senses what my precise feelings are.

EVA: What good will that do you now? (*Takes a drink and puts on her mask.*)

DEML: (*Winds some black material around his body.*) O.K., let's start. (*To Sova.*) Here, stand on this stool.

SOVA: I am innocent.

BAUER: Just a moment, not so fast. First of all we have to read the verdict. (*To Filip.*) O.K., do your job!

FILIP: (*Empties the glass which Eva handed him.*)

IRENA: Filip, you know that you're not used to it! (*To Petr.*) Petr, darling, do something. We mustn't play this game!

FILIP: There are so many things one is not used to. For example, I am not used to talking about myself. But now I am going to deliver a speech about myself anyway.

BAUER: You are not supposed to be delivering a speech but rendering a verdict.

EVA: (*About Filip.*) Oh let him speak. You should be glad that he has loosened up a bit.

FILIP: I will now address you concerning myself, and concerning law and justice.

IRENA: Filip, please!

FILIP: Ladies and gentlemen, what is the law? As a student I had been particularly impressed by an ancient saying: In ius est ars boni et aequi. Law is the art of truth and justice. That is why I had this particular quotation made out of brass letters and I hung it over my desk. Then when I was twenty-five I started at the district court.

IRENA: Filip!

FILIP: Quiet! My predecessor was just finishing his last year there. He was an older man, the product of Austrian schools, experience under six different regimes; he told excellent jokes, knew the entire Napoleonic Code and frequently used to say to me: my boy, the law is nothing more than a legalized form of lawlessness because ever since its inception it has been serving power and not justice. Allow me, who for twenty years tried the guilty as well as the innocent ones to corroborate that: he was absolutely right.

BAUER: This isn't to the point. We're wasting time.

FILIP: (*With a gesture silences him.*) And allow me, ladies and gentlemen, to tell you that the innocent have always received more severe punishment than the truly guilty. Because, first of all: for him who is truly innocent, any sort of punishment is unduly harsh. Secondly, innocence tried in a court of law is usually punished much more harshly than a criminal act. Thirdly, to try the truly innocent irrationality must be invoked and it is never embarrassed by the severity of the punishment. Ladies and gentlemen, don't hold it against me that I am a bit drunk. I admit that I have always known that whenever I put on my black robe I become an actor who can do nothing but improvise. I could also instead of saying 'in the name of the law here is the verdict,' I could just as easily say (*to Bauer*) Kusimama kurefu kunamchokesha mzee, or (*to Eva*) to sing. (*Sings.*) Oh let me fly fly fly over stony water, oh let me walk 'round miles of rolling sea . . .

EVA: Boy did he ever loosen up. Great, Filip!

FILIP: It would all be the same to me. I am not, I did not make the laws. I myself live in fear. And I, my friends, have been thinking about that all my life and about all those people—there are so many of them, they don't even fit into my head. My venerable colleagues always muttering the same empty phrases, sent them to prison and off into exile, to the galleys, into gas chambers, to the gallows and under the axe, into camps and into ditches where their bones rot. (*Sings.*) Oh let me fly fly fly over stony water, let me walk 'round miles of rolling sea, o let me run run run around the great infernal land . . .

EVA: He is fabulous!

FILIP: I tell you that the bones are rotting there and when I shut my eyes I see them all being pulled together into a skeleton and that gets clothed by flesh and the flesh gets clothed by rags and a long line forms, a long, endless line that takes up the whole land and it starts moving toward me, it starts marching against me and I see that my only chance is to put them all on trial again, and to try them and to once again condemn them, the innocent ones, because they are the ones who call most passionately for justice, which doesn't exist.

BAUER: And now to the point.

FILIP: I had to make that speech to explain that it is not in my power to change the verdict which will be handed down although I know it will condemn an innocent man.

SOVA: What you have said constitutes the most contemptible servility I have ever heard.

IRENA: No, Kamil, you're not being fair. Filip is just being honest. He suffers because of every injustice and he truly wishes he could live in a better world. Just like I do.

BAUER: To the point!

FILIP: Justice is unattainable and I quite understand that from a certain point of view those who are innocent are much more dangerous than the others. Because they, through their very existence, indicate the imperfect nature of all our activity. (*To Bauer.*) You want me to try him. He has been tried and has condemned himself.

BAUER: I don't know if that's quite enough.

FILIP: Kusimama kurefu kunamchokesha mzee. Kupotea njia ndiko kumua njia. Is that any better?

BAUER: Does that mean the noose?

FILIP: Basically.

BAUER: Does it also mean that the verdict cannot be appealed?

FILIP: That would have to be decided by a higher authority. Basically that's him. (*Points at Deml.*)

DEML: Me?

FILIP: You are the executioner; do your duty. And now I leave you, ladies and gentlemen. (*Sits in the chair he has been standing on.*)

EVA: That was great, Filip. I had no idea you could sing like that!

FILIP: We often sang when the trial was over. What else could we do?

DEML: Maybe we could put him up on the stool now.

SOVA: (*Undoing his shirt.*) I am innocent!

BAUER: We still need a priest.

IRENA: I can't! I'm too nervous! Petr!

PETR: (*Keeps reading.*)

EVA: Come on. (*Pushes Irena toward Sova.*)

IRENA: I don't know . . . (*To Sova.*) My son—no, that's no good. Kamil, I wanted you to know that I believe that someday people will create a society like the one I spoke about—where people will feel very close to each other. Do you believe that too?

SOVA: No. Once I believed it, same as you. But now with certainty I know. My life has been one big mistake.

IRENA: But it's terrible what you are saying, Kamil. You have to believe. Now you have to. Otherwise why would we live?

SOVA: It doesn't matter. It doesn't matter why you live.

IRENA: But you mustn't talk like that. You mustn't be bitter. You have to find peace within yourself. I don't know if you believe in God, but think about it. Think about something good. Or imagine some scene from your childhood.

SOVA: (*Closes his eyes.*) Yes, thank you.

IRENA: Are you thinking about him? Do you see him?

SOVA: I see banners. A great number of banners. You can leave now.

IRENA: (*Turns around, sobbing.*) Enough! I'm so upset.

SOVA: No, go on. I am ready.

DEML: (*To Eva.*) Tie him up.

SOVA: That . . . that isn't necessary.

EVA: (*Ties his hands behind him.*)

SOVA: I am innocent!

EVA: Here, get up on this stool.

SOVA: (*Stepping up on the stool.*) My dear friends, where are you? Why do you leave me alone in the executioner's hands? Don't abandon me!

IRENA: (*Walks underneath the steps.*) Do you hear him? He is calling you!

PETR: (*Looks up from his book.*) He is an excellent actor! He's finally found his dream role.

IRENA: But he is calling *you.*

PETR: Unfortunately a friend doesn't play a part in this. You will just have to comfort him yourself.

IRENA: (*Runs to Sova.*) Kamil, they aren't here. They can't hear you but if they could they would certainly save you. But I am here, Kamil. You must believe! In people—in a better world. In goodness that will surely be victorious in the end. Peace, peace be on your soul, Kamil.

DEML: (*Takes the noose in his hands.*) Somebody should perform rites of some sort. (*To Filip.*) What's supposed to be said at a time like this?

FILIP: Another one added to the long line. I already see him clothing himself. And he too will move against me.

DEML: He is also entitled to one last wish.

SOVA: No need. My only wish is to leave this world as soon as possible. I see it clearly now. I see you. Don't you see yourselves? Your whole lives?

IRENA: Peace, peace be on your soul, Kamil. You mustn't talk like this, you must have faith.

SOVA: (*With horror.*) I see you!

DEML: As you wish. (*Puts the noose around his head.*)

IRENA: I can't stand it. (*Goes over to Jakub.*) Could I have a drink with you?

JAKUB: With me? You know I don't drink!

IRENA: (*Takes Eva by the elbow and leads her aside.*) Excuse me, could I have a drink with you?

EVA: Of course.

JAKUB: Let's cut it out. These games are senseless.

SOVA: Banners! Banners! There are more of them than people. More of them than there are words. (*Laughs.*) They'll choke us. They'll choke us all to death.

JAKUB: I . . . listen, I'll show you something you'll never forget.

IRENA: This is so upsetting . . . They act as if they really wanted to kill him. (*Drinks.*) Tell me, do you like to cook?

EVA: Me? No. I usually buy something pre-cooked when I am home. But usually I am on tour anyway.

SOVA: I am innocent!

JAKUB: (*Takes the stool, puts it down next to Sova's, then takes off his sweater.*) I'll show you something you couldn't have possibly seen anywhere.

IRENA: Actually, I don't like to cook that much either—just salads. I have collected 111 recipes.

JAKUB: (*Pulls himself up to the beam, starts his exercise.*) That's a muscle building exercise according to Kaiserschada-Kowalski.

EVA: (*Stays undernath the steps a moment, then puts on her mask again, returning to Deml.*)

JAKUB: (*Out of breath.*) And now I'll add a few basic ones according to Smith-Voronov.

SOVA: Make him get down. It's undignified.

PETR: (*To Bauer.*) You asked me before what my verdict was. I think I have a novel way of expressing it.

IRENA: (*Doesn't even notice that Eva is no longer standing next to her.*) For example the escargot salad, the sharp salad with cucumbers and cheese salad with crabmeat. And the Bosnia salad and the Hana salad, Miami Salad and the Greek one . . . Actually when I am cutting up the cabbage or the pumpkin into little pieces I forget about everything else . . . (*She takes a knife from the table along with some cheese and starts cutting it up.*) What I do though is keep repeating the proportions in my mind so that I don't forget them.

PETR: (*To Bauer.*) The accused Josef Deml and all the others who are present here are found guilty of absolute lack of . . .

BAUER: I'll count to three. (*To Eva and Deml.*) Then both of you jerk the stool away at the same time.

JAKUB: (*Finishes up out of breath.*) This is what I call performance.

SOVA: (*In a big voice.*) I am innocent.

BAUER: One.

PETR: (*Taps Bauer on the shoulder.*) Are you interested in my verdict?

JAKUB: (*Hanging by his arms to the side of Sova, his tongue out, breathing heavily.*) Now I feel satisfied.

PETR: Does anybody at all want to hear my verdict?

BAUER: Two.

SOVA: (*Quietly.*) It's so undignified!

PETR: (*Looks over the others.*) They don't hear me. How wonderfully busy they are!

END